Camden History

Journal of the Camden Historical Society Inc

Vol. 3, No. 1, March 2011.
To
Vol 3, Number 10, September 2015

Editor: Ian Willis

Published by the
Camden Historical Society
40 John Street
Camden NSW 2570

Published by Camden Historical Society Inc.
40 John Street, Camden, NSW 2570
(SAN: 908 3002)

www.camdenhistory.com.au

© 2022 by the Camden Historical Society Inc.

All rights reserved. No part of this publication may be used or reproduced in any manner whatsoever without written permission, except in the case of brief quotations in critical articles and reviews. Contact the Camden Historical Society PO Box 566 Camden NSW 2570 Australia for more information. (secretary@camdenhistory.org.au)

All photographs in the publication are part of the Camden Historical Society's collection or are used with the permission acknowledged in the text.

First published in 2022

1st Edition

ISBN: 978-0-6485894-3-3

Front cover: Lee Abrahams and Noel Lowry (Photo Lee Abrahams) – reproduced from Volume 3 Issue 1.

Back cover: Waistcoat for Madras Cavalry Uniform – reproduced from Volume 3 Issue 10.

Introduction

Camden History is the Journal of the Camden Historical Society. It is published twice yearly and contains a wide range of articles and other local history items about the Camden District.

This book is a reproduction of all issues in Volume 3. It spans the period from March 2011 to September 2015.

Individual issues (except number 7) are reproduced from the original text submitted to the printers and contain the errors and omissions in the actual issues. Unlike the original, colour version of illustrations and photographs are used where available.

Issue 7 is reproduced from a scanned image.

The page numbers are as printed in the original. They do not correspond to the page numbers in this book.

As printed, page numbers start from 1 in March 2011 and should increment across the issues, finishing at 373 in September 2015.

Unfortunately, there are discrepancies with the numbers. Issue 2 was printed with the wrong page numbers, and there are omissions and overlaps at the start and end of the issues.

Following is a table of contents by the author, reproduced from the Society's website. Again, the page numbers refer to the original issue's page numbers. Issue 2 articles are shown with the printed and correct page numbers.

Each issue starts on a right-hand (recto) page.

Contents

Volume 3, Nos 1 – 10
March 2011 – September 2015

A Flood in Camden in 1819. p. 254

Camden News Extract, 1895. p.236
Cobbitty Water Supply (Brochure). p. 260
Cole, Laura, "Sketches from my Notebook" A Portrait of
    Sister Hester Morton, Great War Nurse'. p.88.
Cole, Laura, Tracing the Untraceable- Camden's Great War
    Nurses. p.79.

Downing, Pauline, Dr Robert Melville Crookston, OBE. p.66
(214).

Greene, Sharon, Kirkham to Camelot. p.199

Herbert, Ray, World War One. p.269
Howard, Donald, The Faces In The Street. p.338

Johnson, Janice, Camden in the News. p105.
Johnson, Janice, Tank or Bank? p.220
Johnson, Janice, Margaret Wheeler and Julie Wrigley, 2nd
Madras Cavalry Uniform 361, Assessment of Significance,
    Collection Item No. 1970. p.264
Johnson, Janice, The Gallipoli Evacuation., p.231

Lester, Bob, President's Report 2013-2014. p.275
Lester, Bob, President's Report 2014 - 2015. p.366

Lester, Bob, President's Report 2012-2013. p.212
Love-Lipinkski, Penny, The Junior Red Cross at Camden Public School. p. 11

Macarthur Onslow, Annette, From the Old to New South Wales, the life of Astley John Onslow Thompson, Special Edition. pp.304-331
Macarthur Onslow, Annette, Macquarie Grove to Camden Aerodrome. pp. 148-198
McCall, Peter, An Admiral's Wife In Camden. p.351
Mylrea, Peter, Local Government, Camden Municipality and Nepean Shire. p.118.
Mylrea, Peter, Advertisements in the Camden News 1896-1914. p.42 (190).
Mylrea, Peter, An 1843 Map of Camden. p.61 (209).
Mylrea,, Peter, Development of Law Courts in Cawdor, Picton and Camden. p.139
Mylrea, Peter, European Explorers in the Camden Region. p.90.
Mylrea, Peter, Macarthurs Village of Camden. p. 23.
Mylrea, Peter, The Hassall Family as Land Owners in Cobbitty. p.248
Mylrea, Peter, The Original Village of Cawdor. p. 137
Mylrea, Peter, Water and Sewerage in Camden. p. 7
Mylrea, Peter, Crown Land and the Wild Cattle of the Cowpasture Plains. p.224

Newton, Noreen, The CIFA Story. p.218

Oliver, Jo, A Practical Partnership: library, museum and family history society co-operation at Camden. p.97.

RAAF Central Flying School 1940. p. 286

Rem, Rene, Museum Volunteers. p. 297

Shepherd, Cathey, John Martin Hawkey's Presentation Tea Service. p.282
Stratton, Lee and Brian, Official Opening of Liz Kernohan Drive. p.295

Wheeler, Robert, Elderslie. p.132
Williams, Dawn, The Telephone Exchange – Werombi. p.358
Willis, Ian, Yearning, Longing and the Remaking of Camden's Identity: the myths and reality of a 'country town idyll'. p.107.
Willis, Ian, Lee Abrahams, The District Reporter. p 1
Willis, Ian, Launch of Report Managing The Future of Camden Park. p.271
Willis, Ian, A Conversation with Joyce Thorn of Cobbitty With Cathey Shepherd. p.259
Willis, Ian, Camelot. p.239
Willis, Ian, Community Partnerships: are they all that they are cracked up to be? p.51 (199).
Willis, Ian, Frances Warner. p.74.
Willis, Ian, Joy Riley, Memories of John Street. p.243
Willis, Ian, Book Launch, Author Address, Ministering Angels. p.290
Willis, Ian, Edwina Macarthur Stanham. p.37 (185).
Willis, Ian, John Carlyle Southwell OAM, RFD, ED. p.124
Wrigley, John, My Dearest Ellen. p.273
Wrigley, John, Phillip Haylock, The Very Sociable Policeman. p.256
Wrigley, John, Dick Inglis Death of a Fine Camden Citizen. p.280
Wrigley, John, The Paradox of Beauty from the Great War.

p.299
Wrigley, John, Camden Historical Society, Annual Report, 2011-2012. p.129
Wrigley, Julie, Camden District Red Cross, 1914-1915, Red Cross Book Launch. p.293
Wrigley, Julie, Clarissa Whiteman, First World War Nurse. p.223

Yeats, Christine, Romani convicts and Camden connections. p.333

CAMDEN HISTORY

Journal of the Camden Historical Society

March 2011 Volume 3 Number 1

CAMDEN HISTORY
Journal of the Camden Historical Society Inc.
ISSN 1445-1549
Editor: Dr Ian Willis

Management Committee
President: Cathey Shepherd
Vice Presidents: John Wrigley OAM, Bob Lester
Secretary: Doug Barrett
Assistant Secretary: Julie Wrigley
Treasurer: Ray Herbert
Assistant Treasurer: Len English
Immediate Past President: Dr Ian Willis
General Committee: Dr Karen Farmer   Sharon Greene
                      Roslyn Tildsley   Peter Hayward OAM
                      Janice Johnson   Robert Wheeler

Honorary Auditor: Russell Dawson
Honorary Solicitors: Bowring, Macaulay and Barrett

Society contact:
P.O. Box 566, Camden, NSW 2570. Online <http://www.camdenhistory.org.au>

Meetings
Meetings are held at 7.30 p.m. on the second Wednesday of the month except in January. They are held in the Museum. Visitors are always welcome.

Museum
The Museum is located at 40 John Street, Camden, phone 4655 3400 or 46559210. It is open Thursday to Sunday 11 a.m. to 4 p.m., except at Christmas. Visits by schools and groups are encouraged. Please contact the Museum to make arrangements. Entry is free.

Camden History, Journal of the Camden Historical Society Inc
The Journal is published in March and September each year. The Editor would be pleased to receive articles broadly covering the history of the Camden district. Correspondence can be sent to the Society's postal address. The Society takes no responsibility for the contents of articles published in the Journal.

Donations
Donations made to the Society are tax deductible. The accredited value of objects donated to the Society are eligible for tax deduction.

Front Cover Lee Abrahams and Noel Lowry (Photo Lee Abrahams)

CAMDEN HISTORY
Journal of the Camden Historical Society Inc.

Contents

Lee Abrahams, *The District Reporter*   1
Ian Willis

Water and Sewerage in Camden   7
P J Mylrea

The Junior Red Cross at Camden Public School   11
Penny Love-Lipinski

Macarthurs' Village of Camden   23
P J Mylrea

Lee Abrahams
talks about life as editor/proprietor of the *District Reporter*

Camden Historical Society Meeting
10 February 2011

Ian Willis

Lee Abrahams recently gave an account of her life as the editor/proprietor of *The District Reporter* at the February meeting of the Camden Historical Society. She is a journalist with a Bachelor of Arts and a Master of Journalism.

The District Reporter is a free 16 page weekly newspaper published in Camden each Monday, which started out as a monthly in 1997 in the Austral area. Lee was working for a weekly suburban newspaper at Liverpool at the time, and she and her husband Noel, decided on the 'spur of the moment', that they wanted to have a 'rural newspaper'. They made the masthead blue and green to reflect the rural landscape of sky and grass. According to Lee, 'We try to make it look a relaxed paper'.

Initially Lee and Noel surveyed local residents of Austral and the northern part of the Camden Local Government Area and found that they did not get a suburban newspaper. The timing was fortuitous as another weekly, the Camden Crier, had just closed. They moved into the void left by the *Crier* in Camden and retained the 'Back Then' local history page.

The 'Back Then' page is the most popular section of the newspaper and Lee claims that it is read by 95 per cent of their readership. Lee said, 'It is the first thing people read and a lot of people cut it out'. She expressed her sincere appreciation for the help from the contributors to the page from the historical society, as without them there would be 'no newspaper'. She said that the contributors 'do a great job'. Lee said, 'The back page is important as people in the local area make up the history. Everyday lives make up the town. The stories need to be told and they are interesting'.

Lee stated that she has always had an interest in history, partly from her Egyptian and Greek heritage. She quoted from Robert Heinlein, 'a generation which ignores history has no past and no future'. She maintains that history needs to be told and paves the way. She likens the historical society and the museum to the 'Dr Who Time Lords, who just keep things happening'.

The relationship between *The District Reporter* and the society is beneficial to both organisations. According to Ian Willis, the 'Back Then' page provides

Lee Abrahams and Noel Lowry   (Photo: Lee Abrahams)

a platform for local stories. The history page provides an avenue for the society to publish many stories that would otherwise not be told or be exposed to a wider audience. Willis maintains that 'Local history is an integral 'brick in the wall' of the construction of local community identity and a sense of place'.

The editorial policy of the newspaper, according to Lee, is aimed at telling the local people about their local area, and their stories are certainly part of that agenda. She strongly maintains that Camden is still a country town. Lee said, 'The paper is different from other newspapers.
Her editorial policy has been to run 'good stories' without a negative line and tends to leave out the police and ambulance rounds, although she will run a story is there is a appeal from the local police about community safety or similar issues. 'We tell people about their area. The paper is well received in Camden (and Wollondilly) by everybody and seems to have a lot of clout'.

Lee stated that her aim is 'about informing the community', and tries to do as many Camden and Wollondilly rural stories as possible. Lee overall editorial policy is to 'inform and keep people's interest'. She likes 'expressing the small and the strong, and raise public awareness'. Lee commented, '16 pages is comfortable. We used to have extra pages. The cost beat us. You have to make it work'. Overall Lee maintains that the paper has to 'have balance'.

She claims that she 'does her own thing and it seems to work'. There are hard stories on page one, soft stories on pages two, three and four, with sport in the centre. 'People love photos', says Lee. They try and look at junior sport as much as they can, and 'The Diary' is well read. One female member of the historical society announced from the audience that she always read 'The Diary' first, then the 'Back Then', as if to confirm what Lee already knew.

When she starts to compose the newspaper each week she starts with a 'blank canvas' or a 'blank slate'. The paper is gradually filled during the week as stories come in. Advertising is organised by her husband Noel Lowry, with a 60:40 split of advertising to editorial content. She wryly admits that there have been some lively discussions over this mix. According to Lee, 'The paper slowly builds up' during the week.

When the newspaper is all together it is sent in its final copy form by email to an independent printer at Marrickville and joins the print queue of other community newspaper and general printing jobs. Lee and Noel then set off in their van to collect the bundled papers ready for distribution. In the early days of the newspaper there was a three day turnaround from final copy to the printed version.

Lee gets inundated with spin from the state government and attempts to give media releases a local angle. Typical of all journalists she attempts to leave stories to the last moment. She will have organised photographs and they build with the story, and towards the end of the week they pull it all together.

Whatever else Lee states that 'the newspaper is a business, and has to be conducted like a business'. And as with all small businesses it is all consuming. 'We don't make a lot of money, but we make a living'. 'The paper is currently published from our home office', said Lee, although for many years they had an office in Argyle Street, Camden.

She stated that the newspaper does not have a big team. There are the contributors, including those for the back page 'Back Then' feature, who are unpaid but get a by-line. Michael Rees, a retired police officer, does a quirky column on the council roundup, and according to Lee jumps at the challenge. There is also Joy Maunder who does the accounts.

The *Reporter* has a circulation of 17,000 across a footprint of 37,000 homes in the local area. Of these 14,000 are letterboxed each week, with the remaining 3,000 are bulk drops across 90 outlets, some receiving as few as 10-15 with others up to 400 or more. Noel, Lee's husband and sales manager, reported that on one occasion over 400 were picked up by readers in less than an hour from the front of Sinclair's Newsagency in central Camden. Noel said, 'It depends on the story'. Readers often complain that the paper 'disappears' very quickly each week, with some, according to Doug Barrett, society secretary, coming into the museum specifically for the newspaper. In the early days of the newspaper the family, including Lee's mother, would physically roll 8000 newspaper, and then spend the next three days delivering them 'chucking them out of the car window'. The newspaper has now been online for about a year and there are about 200 downloads a week, according to Noel.

Lee makes the point that the Camden market is highly competitive and there is some tough competition. On the whole the people who work for her competitors are 'lovely people'. 'They have a job to do. We have to compete with each other'.

The District Reporter is a challenging and important role and the newspaper is part of the local community, according to Lee. She said, 'I really enjoy it and it is important to have a community newspaper. To re-enforce that the small size of the whole thing, Lee stated, 'We are media maggots not media moguls'. Janice Johnson, a society member, re-enforced this when she stated that in her role as a library volunteer she clips the local newspapers and between 80-90 per cent of the *Reporter* was clipped each week.

The newspaper business has its own stresses and is an ongoing process. Lee admits that it has had its moments and she is like any other working parent, with her twin 14 year old daughters. She and Noel have had a policy of always being around to drop the girls at school and pick them off in the afternoon. They work the newspaper business around those times. Writing and composing the paper while they are at school and late into the night. There is always a work/life balance, especially when the business is conducted from home. Lee says that she has helped out at the girl's school canteen and she and Noel put in appearances at school events and activities. She admits that her girls say that they never want to 'be around the newspaper business', after always living with it.

Lee said, '*The District Reporter* will be here as long we are around'. Julie Wrigley stated in reply the *Reporter* 'did an amazing job'. Lee replied 'I hope people understand what we do'.

Lee and Noel also publish a trade magazine called *Jewellers Trade*, which has been a successful venture now running for 18 months. The magazine is very 'newsy' and has made inroads into the industry, according to Lee. 'People want to know what is going in the industry'.

On a personal level Lee admitted that the presentation to the society was quite an event for her as it was her first public address. She said that she had always felt self-conscience with her speech impediment. She felt, 'It was time I spoke to members of the community now'. John Wrigley noted that he was glad he had asked Lee to speak and that the society was part of her 'coming out'.

An informative and pleasant presentation was enjoyed by all those assembled present.

Curbing the urban sprawl

Front Page, *The District Reporter* Monday 21 Februay 2011

Water and Sewerage in Camden

Peter Mylrea

The establishment of the supply of gas and of electricity in Camden has been recorded in another paper.[1] The present article deals with the development of water and sewerage services in Camden.

Water

It seems that until the early 1890s Camden relied on wells and water tanks for their water. In drier times the water cart drawing water from the Nepean River was almost a daily routine.[2]

The supply of water to Camden became acute when the Water Board built the water supply canal in 1888. This diverted water from the Cataract River to Prospect Reservoir for supply to Sydney metropolitan districts and reduced the volume of water in the Nepean River at Camden. To overcome this problem it was promised that two weirs would be built on the Nepean to ensure

This photo is of large and small diameter woodstave pipes with iron rings to hold the staves in place. Such pipes were used by the Sydney Water and Sewerage Board and in 1912 the Board purchased 5472 feet of four inch pipes from the Australian Wood Pipe Co. Ltd for use in extension of the water main in Elderslie and Spring Road.[4] (Photo Camden Historical Museum)

water for Camden but these were not built at the time.[3]

There were subsequent political debates which will not be dealt with in this article. The end result was that the Sydney Water Board undertook to supply Camden with water drawn from the water supply canal at Kenny Hill. To cover costs those with properties in streets traversed by reticulation mains would pay one shilling in the pound for the value of house properties and four pence in the pound for land (rental value). The cost of water would be one shilling per thousand gallons as measured by water meters.[5]

At 5 o'clock on 16 November 1899, in front of a large gathering at the corner of Argyle and John Streets, Alderman G.F. Furner, Mayor of Camden, ceremoniously turned on the water supply. Thus the water problem was finally solved and the Camden News could report that '[Camden] had perfect reticulation of water and of high pressure'.[6] However it was not until 1903 that the water service was extended to Elderslie.[7]

"Olding Patent Sanitary Cart" owned by Municipality of Camden probably in the early 1900s. It was used in the collection of night soil from sanitary pans.

Sanitary Service and Sewerage

There was a sanitary service in

An outside lavatory ('dunny') as used in houses until sewerage arrived in 1939. This is a 2010 photo of a toilet in the back yard of a house in upper John Street.

Camden which involved collecting 'night soil' from outside toilets ('dunnies'). When this commenced could not be determined but it was probably only after the Camden Council was established in 1889. The sanitary service was extended to Elderslie in 1923. Anecdotal information obtained from persons who were resident in Camden in the 1930s indicates that probably all houses in Camden had outside lavatories, relied on the sanitary service and that there were probably no household septic systems in Camden at that time. The sanitary service continued to function until the sewerage system became operational in 1939.

The first move to secure sewerage for Camden was made in 1908 by Dr West, a general practitioner and the Government Medical Officer for Camden, but this was not fruitful.[8] In 1935 Dr Crookston, Deputy Mayor, raised the question in Council of sewerage for Camden and this resulted in a report from the Metropolitan Water, Sewerage and Drainage Board in 1936. This gave considerable information on design features and costs. At that time the population of Camden was 1,647 persons and there were 366 tenements.[9]

There followed discussions between the Board and the Council on how to pay for the scheme.[10] It was not till 1938 that these questions were resolved and construction of the sewerage system commenced with its completion in 1939.

From 30 June 1939 householders could apply to the Board for a diagram to show how the property could be connected to the system. Once this was obtained the owner could employ a licensed plumber and drainer to make the connection at the owner's expense.[11] In December 1939 the Mayor could report that about 190 houses and premises had been connected to the sewerage mains and that the total cost of the scheme was £42,681.[12] A more detailed description of the construction is given by W.V. Aird.[13]

A final act in the saga of the sanitary and sewerage in Camden was a complimentary lunch at the 'Camden Inn' given by the council in 1939 to the minister, and the president and officers of the board.[14]

References
[1] Peter Mylrea Camden History 2008 vol. 2 pp. 139-154.
[2] Sidman *The Town of Camden* p. 39.
[3] Camden News 19 September 1895
[4] Camden News 14 November 1912
[5] Sidman p. 41.
[6] Camden News 22 March 1900.
[7] Sidman p. 52.
[8] Sidman p. 56.
[9] Camden News 1 October 1936
[10] There are numerous articles on this matter in the Camden News between October 1936 and July 1939.
[11] Camden News 13 July 1939.
[12] Camden News 7 December 1939.
[13] W.V. Aird *The Water, Sewerage and Drainage of Sydney.* Sydney, 1961, pp. 185-6.
[14] Camden News 7 December 1939

The Junior Red Cross at Camden Public School, 1985-2008

Penny Love-Lipinski

It was an enchanted evening in March 2005 when I had the privilege of accompanying 200 students from Camden Public School to form a guard of honour for their Royal Highnesses Crown Prince Frederick and Crown Princess Mary of Denmark. The event was the Australian Red Cross 90th Anniversary Gala Dinner held at Sydney's Westin Hotel. The children had been invited to the prestigious event to form the guard in recognition for the group's continued involvement and dedication as the longest functioning Junior Red Cross group in New South Wales.

The Camden Junior Red Cross had originally been established at the school in 1918, according to historian Ian Willis, and subsequently wound up in 1922. It was again re-established in 1938 at the school by Mrs J W Macarthur Onslow, a member of the Macarthur family of *Camden Park*. The group has operated continuously at the school since that time, and is regarded as one of the oldest Junior Red Cross groups in Australia.

I became the leader of the Junior Red Cross at the school in 1985. Originally I came to work as a teacher at the school in 1982 along with Mrs Jenny Murphy. I became involved in the Koala Club, which was formed for the Infants classes: Kindergarten, Year One and Year Two. We sold 'little' koala badges, Christmas gift tags, calendars and ANZAC cards. Toffee and cake stalls were everyone's favourite.

Prior to 1985 the Junior Red Cross leader was Mrs Sandra Saunderson. I held the position of leader until the organisation was unfortunately closed by the Red Cross in December 2008.

My personal passion for the Junior Red Cross started as a little girl. I can remember that joining was the best thing about being in Year 3 at Tarrawanna Public School. My sister, being two years older, proudly wore her badge. I became a member of this caring group, where you got to do different things at lunch times. My Junior Red Cross patron, Miss Pam Northey, encouraged me and gave me leadership opportunities. I was honoured to be the president of our Junior Red Cross Circle in 1968. How special it is that our friendship still exists today with her newsy Christmas cards.

The Camden Public Junior Red Cross always had a busy year. In the begin-

Camden Public School Junior Red Cross 2003   Ruby E Storey Shield   Penny Love-Lipinksi (RHS) (Photo P Love-Lipinski)

ning of each school year, all primary school students were invited to join. As the leader, I recall that it was always a special time when the package of members badges arrived. We held our meetings at lunch times. Members were nominated for president, secretary and treasurer. I would meet with the girls and we would plan the meeting. Students were given the opportunity to show leadership and accept responsibility.

In the mid 1980s meetings were only held when an activity was planned, for example, selling ANZAC stickers, cake stalls, wool drives, knitting lessons and other fundraisers. Meetings later became a fortnightly meeting and then weekly!

In July each year, the children were invited to attend the annual general meeting of the Camden Red Cross branch in December. This was always a very valued activity for the members. Reports of our group's yearly activities were delivered by the children and were written into the minutes of the branch, which are now held at the Camden museum. In 1996 Jessica Ross, the president, gave a report on the activities to the branch:

> 'Good morning ladies and gentlemen. I am Jessica Ross, the president of Camden Public School Red Cross Group and this is Jennifer Matheson, the secretary. Today Jennifer and I are going to tell you about some different events we have participated in or will be participating in. Last year we had a cake stall and raised $39. We sold some Christmas calendars for 50cents and raised $72. This year we had a red and white mufti-day. Everybody brought in a silver coin and in return got to wear something red and white and we raised $65.20. For Anzac Day we sold some Remembrance tokens. We raised $35.90. We have also had a trash and treasure. We sold books, dolls and many other things. Everything was sold and we made $115.10. Miss Davies was one of our best customers. During the trash and treasure we were very lucky to have two ladies from Red Cross House, Sydney to join us. We also received this certificate from them. We are planning to have a silver coin disco. The children will bring in a silver coin and get to go to a party during lunch. We are also planning to have an international luncheon. Next term everybody will bring in food from a different country. Thank you for listening and thank you for inviting us to share your meeting'. [1]

My choir would sing and the members would give the children a handmade gift. A cool drink and sweets were always a treat! Our members were always well received by the branch and I was acknowledged for my efforts by the presidents including Miss Llewella Davies and Mrs Shirley Wells. They encouraged us to continue our support for Red Cross.

Junior Red Cross groups across the state were supported with resources including *Cross Words* and later a national magazine called *JRC News*. It was

Camden Public School Junior Red Cross at Camden Red Cross AGM, Camden High School Hall 1996. Front: Donald Howard, Llewella Davies; Rear: JRC Jennifer Matheson, Jessica Ross (Photo P Love-Lipinski)

always very special when our group featured with an article and photo, as occurred in 2003 edition of *Junior Red Cross News* and 2005 edition of *Humanity*.[2]

The Junior Red Cross has been a state-wide organisation and tried to remain relevant to an ever changing world. In the mid 1980s the themes that the Junior Red Cross promoted were:
- Friendship
- Community Service

Health and Safety

These were later expanded to include 'International Friendship' and 'The Work of Red Cross'. These changes reflected global understanding and social change.

A snapshot of many of the activities by the Camden JRC under these themes gives an idea of the scope of the children's efforts.

Community service

Camden Public School Junior Red Cross in Grand Parade at the Camden Show 2003. The children are carrying trauma teddies made by Shirley Wells, Camden RC branch. (Photo P Love-Lipinski)

- Red and White mufti day (March Red Cross Calling month) silver coin to wear red and white to school uniform.
- Talent Shows. Students performed and donated 20 cents to enjoy the lunch time entertainment.
- Fashion Parades. Members wore favourite clothes and walked down the catwalk.
- Used Stamp Collection Boxes.
- Annual Art Show. Students prepared artworks and the artworks were judged by local artists Mr George Sayers and Mrs Nan Howard.
- Craft Activities, Mother's Day, Father's Day, friendship gifts.
- Wool Drives. Collecting wool for knitting squares for warm blankets. Mrs June Holdsworth was a support for our group.
- Camden Show (2003) and Fisher's Ghost Festival (2005). Members were invited to be part of the parade.
- Collection of toiletries. For the Glen Mervyn homes and asylum seekers program.
- Trash and Treasure. Members donated pre-loved toys and little treasures

Camden Public School Junior Red Cross helping out with afternoon tea at Camden RC branch, CPS Hall.. (Photo P Love-Lipinski)

and sold them to the students (from 5 cents up to $1.00).
Cake Stalls. Selling sweet treats from homemade cupcakes to toffees were always an easy fundraiser.

Health and safety

- Tissue Drive. A collection of tissue boxes was distributed to all classrooms.
- Posters (donated from Red Cross) copies of pictures showing good healthy habits and safety were coloured and displayed around the school.
- Healthy Eating . Talks about healthy breakfasts to support The Breakfast Club which Red Cross initiated.
- First Aid Kits. Our group received kits for our school.
- Safety Plays. Members organised skits with a safety message and these were performed in our school assemblies.

International friendship

For many years (perhaps up until 1998) this theme was Friendship. As stated earlier all primary age children could be members. I personally would ask

**Camden Public School Junior Red Cross 2000, Ruby E Storey Memorial Shield.
R –L Helen Ingram, Amy Ingram, Mitchell Trench, Penny Love-Lipinski
(Photo P Love-Lipinski)**

"new" students to come for a visit to our meetings. It was the feeling of "belonging to a group" that can be an important part of children's lives.

- Friendship Chains. Members designed their names on cardboard strips and joined them together.
- Friendship Lucky Names. This activity was similar to a lucky door prize! Everyone loves to be a winner!
- International Games. Members organised games from different countries and displayed flags. Students were in mixed groups and had "lots of fun".
- International Lunch. This was an annual event and everyone's favourite. Member chose a country and prepared foods for sharing.
- Red Cross Poster Competitions. Members were invited to participate. Themes were "Making a Difference".
- International Projects. Each year a country was chosen for a study. In 2006 donations were sent to Sudan.
- Visiting teachers from Japan. For 6 years our school was involved with a cultural program. Each visiting teacher had an invitation to attend our meet-

Camden Public School Junior Red Cross International Lunch 1996. L-R Kristy Matheson, Jennifer Matheson, Katie Sweedman. (Photo P Love-Lipinski)

ings.
- Friendship Albums. Members were involved in making albums with photos and personal profiles. These were distributed by Red Cross.

The work of the Red Cross

This theme involved the members in understanding the work of Red Cross throughout the world.
- Members researched facts about Red Cross, using the suggested Red Cross websites.
- Members viewed the DVD 'The Work of Red Cross and Red Crescent'. Members celebrated World Red Cross Day each year on May 8, with a group recess, sharing food and making a coin donation.

The themes of the Junior Red Cross have been celebrated each year with the Ruby E Storey Memorial Shield. Miss Storey was a foundation member of Australian Red Cross and served on the New South Wales Junior Red Cross committee. The aim of the shield was to reward two Junior Red Cross groups (one metropolitan and one country) which actively participated in and supported the themes of friendship, health and safety and community service. Our group (Camden JRC) was awarded this prestigious award in 2000, 2001, 2004, 2005 and 2006. (The presentation books with photos and articles will be given to the Camden Historical Society)

The children were asked from time to time to say how they felt about their experience in the Junior Red Cross. These are some comments:

> Abbey Macdonald (2007), 'I am in Junior Red Cross because I like being with my friends and helping other people. Our leaders are really nice people and they make everyone have lots of fun'.
>
> Jamie-Lee Turner (2007), 'I am in Red Cross because I like to know that I have done something good to help people. My friend, Abbey, introduced me to Red Cross and I have loved it ever since. Red Cross is a great organisation, that helps people from all over the world. To be a part of such a great organisation makes me feel special all over. I'd hate to know that Red Cross would be cancelled. Red Cross the biggest and best organisation in the world'.
>
> Guinevere Medbury (2007), 'I am the longest surviving member at Camden Public School. I join[ed] Red Cross to be 3rd in Red Cross in the girl side [of] my family. My Mum, Kaylene Medbury was in Red Cross as well as my Nana'.
>
> Anna Samuela (2007), 'I like doing Red Cross because my older sister Rebecca told me it was fun so I did it and it's the best!'

Fundraising for the Junior Red Cross was an important aspect of our activities but not the only principle for the continued success of our group. Members of the Junior Red Cross raised money from their efforts and we only requested gold/silver coin donations for the annual Red & White Mufti Day. This was held in March each year and was part of Red Cross Calling Month. Other fundraisers included talent shows (20 cents donation), fashion parades (20 cents donation), Silver coins to fill in a Red Cross outline, Trash and Treasure (prices ranging from 5 – 50 cents), just to mention a few of the many activities our group initiated. There were also donations for toiletries, including soaps, toothpastes, toothbrushes, wool drives, tissue drives, used stamps, winter clothes appeal, toy packages (eg, Cyclone Larry victims). These were always well supported over the years. It was important to show members how there are many ways we can help others in need. Over the years the children raised a considerable amount of money for Red Cross purposes, and between 1995 and 2008 this amounted to $5278.18.[3][4]

While I held the position as leader I received support and encouragement from Red Cross House in Sydney. There was a contact person for the school programs and a Schools Program Co-ordinator. The efforts of our group were recognised with certificates of appreciation and thank you letters attached to our donation receipts. There were also visits to our meetings and often a presentation by a Red Cross official at our school assembly.

Elizabeth Couch from Red Cross House in Clarence Street notified the Camden Junior Red Cross that 'Red Cross will not be reproducing any more materials under the Junior Red Cross logo. We encourage schools to participate as Red Cross Youth using materials from the Speaker Network and Y Challenge'.

The final meeting of the Camden Junior Red Cross was held on Thursday 4 December 2008. Mr Johl Storey, the Red Cross youth programs coordinator, presented all the members with a participation certificate and thanked the 30 active members for their efforts.

Now the Junior Red Cross is only a memory. As I am surrounded with papers, photos, letters, certificates and presentation books, I remember only happy and busy moments. For me being a part of Red Cross was sharing opportunities that were given to me and taking responsibility to do something to help someone else to make a difference. I feel proud to have taken the role as the JRC leader for as many years as I did. It as been a privilege to have involved so many children and achieved "what we did".

It is to be acknowledged that the Department of Education and Training encouraged schools to support the Junior Red Cross. The school principals from 1982 to 2008 encouraged and supported the Junior Red Cross principle of 'children helping children'.

One parent from the school, Mrs Helen Ingram, became an active support leader to our group. She encouraged and showed kindness to all members. On a personal level I thank her for her help and friendship.

Mrs Alba Pullman and Mrs Nicole Barlow, both classroom teachers also gave their time to help me with Junior Red Cross groups. We had lots of fun too and I valued their efforts. Mrs Robyne Meek, a parent and school canteen supervisor, shared the last two years volunteering her time to work with our group. Mrs Meek had wonderful contacts and friendships with all the members.

Some of the young members are now - 'young ladies and men" - and I am sure they too can remember their time as a Junior Red Cross member and I hope they can feel proud of the contribution they made as a member of the biggest humanity organisation in the world.

Editor's note

Penny Love-Lipinski has had many accolades for her efforts with the Junior Red Cross at the Camden Public School.

In 2002 the Minister for Education and Training, John Watkins MP, congratulated Penny on her success with the group. He stated that 'your commitment to this activity in the interests of the students at Camden Public School has led to the outstanding success of the schools support for this important charity'. He particularly noted the school's success winning the Ruby E Storey Memorial Shield for the second year in a row, which he claimed was 'positive promotion of public education with the community [and] brings credit not only to your school but also to the whole system'.

The Ruby E Storey Memorial Shield has been a state-wide award amongst all schools that conducted Junior Red Cross groups for promoting the aims of the Junior Red Cross. In 2006 the Camden group, under the leadership of Penny and Alba Pullman, won the award for the fifth time against 74 other schools.[4]

In 2006 Doss Duscher, the National Youth Program Coodinator for the Australian Red Cross, stated that 'I think your leader is to be congratulated for her dedication to Junior Red Cross. She has been supporting the program for over 20 years. That is pretty fantastic!' Further in 2008 Paula Taylor, the National Program Coordinator – Y Challenge, stated, 'Penny, I would also like to take this opportunity to thank you for your enthusiastic involvement with Red Cross and for everything you have done on behalf of the organisation. It really is greatly appreciated'.

Endnotes

[1] Jessica Ross, President, Camden Public School Junior Red Cross, Address to AGM Camden Branch Red Cross, Camden, December 1996.
[2] 'Lets Look at Junior Red Cross, Mrs Penny Love Lipinski', and Images of Trauma Teddy walk, *Junior Red Cross News*, Issue 3, 2003, p.6. 'One Enchanted Evening, The Night a City Stopped for Red Cross and Royalty, Souvenir Liftout', *Humanity*, Edition 16, Winter 2005, p. 13.
[3] Minutes, Camden Junior Red Cross, Camden
[4] Clipping, Jackie Meyers, 'School wins a fifth award', *Camden Advertiser*, date unknown, 2006

Macarthurs' Village of Camden

P.J. Mylrea

John Macarthur's sons, James and William, wanted to establish a village on part of the Macarthur land immediately to the west of the Nepean River. Their father, John Macarthur, would not agree to the proposal because he was 'apprehensive that the formation of a Town on my property at Camden, would in the present state of this Colony, greatly endanger the security of the whole establishment on that Estate [Camden].'[1] However John Macarthur, being mortal, died in 1834 and this allowed his sons to proceed with their idea.

From about 1805 access to the Camden district was by the Cowpasture Road. This route was improved by the building of the first bridge across the Nepean River at Camden in 1826 and the construction of a road across Razorback in 1832. The new name for the road was The Great South Road.

James and William Macarthur designed their village so it would lie on both sides of The Great South Road immediately to the west of the Cowpasture Bridge. This placed the village in a very good strategic position because all traffic to and from the south of the colony had to pass through the village along that part of The Great South Road which they named Argyle Street. This situation was to continue until 1974 when the Camden Bypass was constructed.

The auction sale of land in 1841

Once the plan of the village had been determined the Macarthurs appointed Mr Samuel Lyons, an auctioneer in Sydney, to conduct an auction sale of land in the village. In his advertisements leading up to the auction he gave considerable details about Camden and the allotments offered for sale.[2] The land on offer had been cleared and stumped and in the village there were established a wheelwright, a cooper, a master builder, a brick maker and other 'mechanics' and an inn was being built – all on land which the Macarthurs still owned.

The conditions for payment for land were given in the advertisements:

> The terms too are the most liberal, namely ten per cent, cash deposit on the fall of the hammer, ten per cent. at twelve months, and the residue at five years, bearing interest for the last two years at ten per cent, with security on the property if required.

The village area was divided into sections and into lots within sections. In preparation for the sale Mr Lyons had a plan prepared and on the ground the blocks were marked and the streets named.

The auction sale was held on 23 July 1841. Fifty allotments were offered for sale. Forty five were sold at prices per lot from £135 to £18, for a total return of £2185.[3] The 1841 auction was the only such sale held. Thereafter sales of land were mostly by private arrangements between the Macarthurs (vendors) and the purchasers.

A description of the village two years after the sale was given by Hood.[4] There was 'an inn, a court room, a post office, and a few scattered wooden houses' and a very substantial and neat bridge across the Nepean River.

Anglican and Catholic churches

One reason for the success of the development of Camden was the support given by James and William Macarthur. A manifestation of this was their attitude towards churches and the colonial government. They sold land to these groups at nominal costs which were much less than the prices paid at the auction sale.

The first registered land title in Camden was for a sale by James and William Macarthur to the [Anglican] Bishop of Australia. It was dated the 8 May 1841 and the price was a nominal ten shillings. The land was to become the site of St John's Church. Construction of the church started in 1840 but it was not consecrated until 1849. It was on a large block of over five acres. Included in the sale was a small area about three miles south of the church 'which contains the cemetery of John Macarthur Esquire deceased and is appropriated as a vault and cemetery for the family of the said John Macarthur' (Book V Number 938).[5] This cemetery still exists and is now part of the Belgenny Farm Trust complex.

St Paul's Catholic Church built in 1859. Photo taken about 1880.

A little later, on 28 May 1844, James and William Macarthur sold to the Right Reverend John Bede Polding, Roman Catholic Bishop of Australia, land at the corner of John and Mitchell Streets. In this case the price was £10.[6] This land was the site on which St Paul's Church was to be built in 1859. Over the years, more land along Mitchell Street was purchased and on this St Paul's School was built. In 1987 major extensions were added to the church but the outside of the original church building still remains much as it was when constructed in 1859.

In 1881 William Macarthur and Arthur and Elizabeth Onslow (nee Macarthur) sold more land to the Catholic Church and the purchasers were The Most Reverend Roger Bede Vaughan, Archbishop of Sydney, The Very Reverend John Felix Sheridan, Vicar General of Sydney and The Reverend James Sheridan of Camden Clerk [Cleric] in Holy Orders, to be held 'upon trust for a residence for the Clergyman for the time being in charge of the Roman Catholic Church at Camden'.[7] The price was five shillings to be paid to each of the three vendors. The land was at 28 Hill Street. A weatherboard presbytery was built and used until 1919. In that year a two storey brick building was erected and used as the presbytery until 1959. This building is now occupied by a firm of solicitors.

Colonial government

The first sale to the colonial government was on 31 May 1849 when the Macarthurs made a sale to Her Majesty Queen Victoria, the nominal head of the colonial government. The land had a frontage of 165 feet along John Street opposite the Roman Catholic land. The price was a nominal ten shillings. On this land the Camden Court House was built in 1856 and later the Camden Police Station was erected. The facades of both buildings remain much the same as when they were constructed.

A few months later, on 15 December 1849, the Macarthurs made a second sale to the colonial government. This time it was to the Board of National Education. The land was at the corner of John and Mitchell Streets and it had an area of one acre and the price was ten shillings. The foundation stone for the National School was laid in May 1850 and the new building was opened in January 1851 with 137 students.[9] There has been a school on the site ever since and it is now occupied by the Camden Public School.[10]

Wesleyan Methodist Church

In addition to the Anglicans and the Catholics, the Primitive Methodists and the Wesleyan Methodists were prominent in Camden from its beginning.[11] However to quote from the Rev. S. Raymond Robbins [12] 'from some prejudice the Wesleyans did not receive as liberal treatment as some other denominations.' This is supported by the fact that no records were found of sales of land by the Macarthurs to Methodists.

The first record found of a sale to the Wesleyan Methodists was dated 1861 when

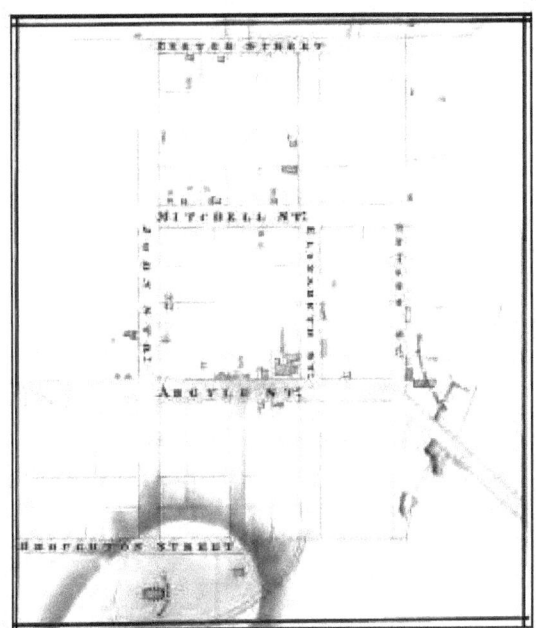

This is part of a 'Plan of the Village of Camden the Property of James and William Macarthur Esq' dated 1847.[8] It shows buildings which had been erected in Camden by 1847. Details of some of them are given later in this article.

The Wesleyan Church and Parsonage in Elizabeth Street between Mitchell and Exeter Streets in the mid 1800s.

Henry Thompson sold a block of land to the Rev. William Clarke who was the Wesleyan Minister.[13] On this land a Chapel and a Parsonage were built. The land was in Elizabeth Street about mid way between Mitchell and Exeter Streets and the price was £50. It was Lot 9 which was originally purchased in 1846 by Joseph Thompson who sold it to his son Henry in 1852.[14]

In 1883 Elizabeth Onslow (nee Macarthur) sold land at the corner of John and Mitchell Streets to the Wesleyan Methodists for £200.[15] Richard Orton was the Wesleyan minister. In 1888 a new church was built on this site. About this time a union of the Wesleyan Methodist Church and the Primitive Methodist occurred and the name Methodist Church came into being.[16] As a consequence the new church was called the Camden Methodist Church.

In 1884 Walter Furner bought from Elizabeth Onslow (nee Macarthur) the block of land on the corner of Hill and Broughton Street (now 33 Hill Street).[17] On this he built a two storey brick house. Then in 1891 he sold the house to the Method-

The Camden Methodist Church erected on the corner of John and Mitchell Streets in 1888.

ists for £1000.[18] The house became the parsonage for the minister. The house still stands and is now a private residence.

Hotels

There have been five hotels in Camden and four of these still exist.

The first hotel in Camden was the Camden Inn located on the corner of Argyle and Elizabeth Streets. It was being built in 1841 by the Macarthurs on land which they owned. Strategically, the hotel was well placed to greet travelers from Sydney as they entered Camden. Joseph Goodluck was the overseer at Camden Park and was the licensee in 1842.[19] The next licensee was John Lakeman from 1843 to 1853. In 1846 Lakeman bought from James and William Macarthur one and a half acres of land 'forming the site of the Camden Inn and its appurtenances' for £1800.[20] The buildings of the inn are shown on the Camden map of 1847. In turn Lakeman sold to John Galvin in 1855 for £4000.[21] Later 54 feet of the frontage on Argyle Street was sold and is now occupied by shops. There have been changes of ownership of the hotel and of its name. At present it is called the 'Merino Tavern'.

The second hotel built in Camden which still exists is the 'Plough and Harrow'. A block of land in Argyle Street, opposite Hill Street, was purchased by Samuel Arnold, wheelwright of Camden, from the Macarthurs in 1849 for £80.[22] Arnold must have built the hotel because in 1855 he leased the land and messuage[23] known as the 'Plough and Harrow Inn' to William Risley, Innkeeper of Camden,

A photo of the front of the Plough and Harrow taken in the early 1900s. The front of the building is still much the same in 2010. The sign reads 'Camden Jockey Club – Tattersalls.'

for a yearly rent of £150.[24]   Probably the inn reverted to the Arnold family because a John Arnold was the licensee from 1866 to 1886.[25]   The name of the hotel persisted from its founding until about 2000 when the name was changed from 'Plough and Harrow' to 'Argyle Inn'.

Another hotel which still exists is the Crown Hotel. Its history is unclear. In 1851 William Stuart Mitchell purchased 2 acres of land in Argyle Street opposite what later became Murray Street.[26]   In 1859 the land passed to his wife Anne Maria Mitchell.[27]   There was no mention of an hotel in either of these deeds but at some time what is now the Crown Hotel was built on part of this land. The first licensee listed for the Crown Inn (hotel) was Charles Walters who held a licence from 1854 to at least 1885 and from 1888 the licence was held by Lucy Waters.

The fourth of the existing hotels is the Camden Hotel. It has had a chequered history which began when Ebenezer Simpson, a Camden farmer, bought a block of land in 1852 for £65. In 1859 Ebenezer's son, William Henry Simpson, inherited the property.[28]   What happened to the land in the next 27 years could not be determined. Then in 1878 S.F. Moore was recorded as the licensee of the Post Office Hotel, Argyle Street and this was the first record of the Post Office Hotel. An important development occurred in 1880 when Charles Page became the licensee.[29]   In 1882 the name was changed from the Post Office Hotel to the Commercial Hotel and Page remained the licensee until at least 1889.[30]   Advertisements for the Commercial Hotel were published in the Camden News up to 1929. Sometime after this the original building was replaced and by 1936 advertisements, including a photograph, began to appear for the Camden Hotel, after another change of name. The front of the hotel has changed little since the mid 1930s.

An early hotel which no longer exist was the Woolpack Inn at the corner of Argyle and John Street. It existed only from 1850 to 1873. In 1850 Thomas Brennan was 'building a fine large house intended for an inn'.[31]   Strangely he did not purchase the land until 1852.[32] He was described in the land title deed as a Licensed Victualler of Narellan. The title deed also records that 'on which premises the said Thomas Brennan hath erected a messuage and certain outbuildings now standing thereon and occupied by him as a Public House '. Brennan sold the inn to Henry Denton, (Sydney, general dealer) who in turn sold it to Samuel Croft (Camden, inn keeper) for £2500.[33]   Samuel Crofts sold it to the Bank of NSW in 1873 for £1,000. It ceased to be a hotel and in 1882 the bank spent £1400 on renovations and improvements.[34]   The building was demolished in 1936 and a new red brick bank was erected on the site. The Bank of NSW (now Westpac) still occupies part of the original site though 88 feet of the original 132 foot frontage on Argyle Street was sold and is now occupied by a block of offices, a shoe shop and the ANZ Bank at 107 to 115 Argyle Street.

As a side issue, it is often stated that the reason for all the hotels in Camden being on the northern side of Argyle Street was to meet the wishes of the Macarthur family. This is unlikely. It is much more probable that it was because this land

The Crown Hotel during the 1898 flood.

The Commercial Hotel before 1888. In that year the Commercial Banking Company moved from their location in the Commercial Hotel into their own building at the corner of Argyle and John Streets (now NAB).

The Bank of NSW building after its renovation in 1882. It was demolished in 1936 and replaced by the present red brick building now called Westpac.

was the first to be made available for purchase. Sale of land south of Argyle Street did not occur till later.

Thompson family

Members of the Thompson family were important land owners in Camden. Joseph Thompson was described as a draper in Sydney. It seems that his interest in Camden was as a land speculator who purchased blocks of land in Elizabeth, John and Exeter Streets.[35] In 1843 he purchased 4 acres of land at the eastern corner of Edward Street and the 'Sydney Road'.[36] By 1845 he had built on this site the 'Camden Steam Flour Mills'.[37] The mill ground and dressed wheat at ten pence per bushel. (Some writers state that it was a water mill but the above name indicates that it was always steam driven.) The site had a frontage on Edward Street of 132 yards and this is now the site of the former milk depot and of Southwell Engineering. It seems likely that Joseph never lived in Camden

Joseph had two sons who had enterprises in Camden. One son, Samuel, purchased a block of land with a 66 foot frontage in Argyle Street in 1849.[38] He ran a shop there until 1854 when he sold his property to Humphrey Weston, a Camden butcher.[39] The block is between the Camden Hotel and the Capitol Arcade and is now occupied by a café, an office block and a pharmacy. Samuel returned to Sydney and had no more direct connection with Camden.

Another son, Henry Thompson, was a prominent business man who lived in Camden from the 1840s until he died in 1872. He was buried in St John's Cemetery.

In 1852 Henry Thompson purchased the four acre parcel of land and the flour mill from his father[40] Then on 1 January 1858 he made a major purchase when he bought a block of land from James and William Macarthur for £2000.[41] It was on the corner of Argyle and View Streets and had an area of eight acres. It was on this site that he built his second flour mill at some time before the wheat disease, rust, destroyed the wheat industry around Camden. After this the building was converted into a woollen tweed mill and continued in this role until it was destroyed by fire on 15 July 1899.[42] The site is now occupied by the Mobil Service Station, shops and industrial buildings.

Lakeman land

In 1849 John Lakeman purchased from James and William Macarthur, 1.5 acres of land bounded by John, Argyle and Oxley Streets. Sections of the land were

Thompson's Mill during the flood of 1898. The photo was probably taken from View Street looking north east.

subsequently sold and on these blocks were erected, amongst other buildings, the Royal Foresters' Hall, the Post Office and the Commercial Banking Company of Sydney (now National Australia Bank). Details of these developments are given in a separate paper by Mylrea.[43]

Residences

There are a number of residences in Camden which still exist and which have histories going back to the mid 1800s.

Bransby's Cottage at 17 Mitchell Street was an early residence which was probably built between 1841 and 1846. It is shown on the 1847 map of Camden on the north side of Mitchell Street near Elizabeth Street. It still exists and was extensively restored by Colin and Agnes Mills in 1996-98. They have recorded the history of land on which it was built, the history of the cottage and of its restoration.[44]

In 1846 Sarah Tiffin bought a block of land from the Macarthurs for £30.[45] This was a large block with a frontage of 165 feet on John Street. Her estate sold the land to Henry Thompson in 1854 for £656. The increase in price suggests that she had erected a building on her land before 1854 and a building on this site is shown on the 1847 map. This could be the cottage which is now at 39 John Street and if this is so, it makes it one of the earliest surviving buildings in Camden..

Henry Thompson built 'Macaria' in 1859-60 on the land which he had purchased from Sarah Tiffin. The building was intended to be a school run by William Gordon but this came to nothing and in 1861 Gordon moved his school to Macquarie Grove.[46] Perhaps Thompson then used Macaria, which was a large house, as his residence to house his family of sixteen children born in Camden between 1846 and 1870.[47] 'Macaria' is a two storey Gothic revival style building which still exists. It has been the residence for a school, a succession of doctors and is now part of the John Street offices of Camden Council.

There is a large two storey brick house on the corner of John and Broughton Streets. It is difficult to determine its early history. It was built by the Macarthurs on land which they owned as part of Camden Park Estate. The house is shown in a drawing of 1887[48] and an advertisement for a land sale in 1893 shows that the building was occupied by a Dr. Jackson.[49] The property was sold by Elizabeth Macarthur Onslow to Abraham Black in 1907 for £1050.[50] Then in 1919 Abraham Black sold the property to Zoe Madeline Crookston, wife of Robert Melville Crookston, medical practitioner, for £1162.[51] There was a later sale about 1980 and the house is now a private residence.

Post Office

In 1841 Mrs Eliza Pearson was appointed by the Macarthurs as Postmistress in Camden.[52] The Macarthurs built a substantial cottage for her on land which they owned and which is now numbered 55-61 Argyle Street. The Post Office was operational by 1843.[53] It continued to operate from this site until 1881 when the Macarthurs sold the land to Charles Smith, a sadler of Camden, for £420.[54] This coincided with the time in 1880 when the colonial government purchased the present day site of the Post Office and postal activities moved to the new site.[55]

Other blocks of land

Some additional information is now given to complete the history of land with frontages on Argyle Street between John and Elizabeth. The land on which the Capitol Arcade and some shops now stand was sold by James and William Macarthur to Thomas Kean, a cooper of Camden, in 1851 for £85,[56] and shops 63-73 in Argyle Street (Campbell's Touch of Class, a lane and other shops) are on land sold to Samuel Ward, a butcher in Camden for £90 in 1854.[57]

Conclusions

This is an incomplete picture of earlier days in Camden. In many cases the records are incomplete or absent so there are gaps in the history. Perhaps someone in the future may be inclined to dig further and continue the story!

The cottage to the left of the photo was built by Sarah Tiffin before 1854 and the house to the right is 'Macaria' built by Henry Thompson about 1860. Both buildings are on the land purchased by Thompson from Tiffin in 1854. A 2010 photo.

Acknowledgements

The comments from Janice Johnson and John Wrigley are acknowledge with thanks.

References

[1] Letter from John Macarthur to Surveyor General (?) dated 3 June 1831.Quoted by James Jervis *Journal of the Royal Australian Historical Society* 1935 p.240.
[2] Sydney Morning Herald 15 July, 17 July, 23 July 1841. Additional information about the establishment and development of the village is given by James Jervis
[3] Sydney Morning Herald 24 July 1841. However registration of sales did not occur until later.
[4] John Hood *Australia and the East- a Journal Narrative of a Voyage to New South Wales 1843.* John Murray, London p. 263.
[5] The titles of land were recorded in the Old System Records in the Land Titles Office. Each registration was identified by a Book Number and a Number within the book.
[6] Book 12 Number 645.
[7] Book 233 Number 695
[8] Mitchell Library. M Series 4 000/1 A 3004/Map 27.
[9] Sydney Morning Herald 17 May 1850, 11 January 1851
[10] Book 17 Number 840
[11] Alan Atkinson *Camden*. Oxford University Press, 1988.
[12] Robbins. Journal and Proceedings of the Australasian Methodist Historical Society, Sydney. 1933 vol 1 part 2 p. 16.
[13] Book 71 Number 240.
[14] Book 13 Number 780; Book 24 Number 730
[15] Book100 Number 280.
[16] James Colwell. *History of Methodism in Australia.* Sydney, 1904 p. 615.
[17] Book 297 Number 984
[18] Book 458 Number 526.
[19] Sydney Morning Herald 15 July 1841,17 July 1841. Certificate by Justices authorising the granting of licences (State Records).
[20] Book 12 Number 622
[21] Book 35 Number 850
[22] Book 18 Number 543.
[23] Messuage – a dwelling house with its adjacent buildings and the land appropriated to the use of the household (Macquarie Dictionary).
[24] Book 51 Number 371.
[25] Lists of Publican Licences published in the Government Gazette annually and State Records microfilm roll 1243.
[26] Book 21 Number 461.
[27] Book 61 Number 503
[28] Book 22 Number 757; Book 60 Number 61.
[29] NSW Government Gazette, Mitchell Library Microfilm Roll 1243.
[30] NSW Government Gazette 1889 p. 5555.
[31] Sydney Morning Herald 6 October 1850.
[32] Book 24 Number 313.
[33] Book 40 Number 776.
[34] Bank of New South Wales Archives. A copy of an article written by the Manager of the Camden Branch in 1965 is held in the Camden Museum Archives.
[35] Section 9 Lots 9,11,13,14.
[36] Book 12 Number 125.
[37] Sydney Morning Herald 23 January 1845 p. 3. This mill is identified and named in the Plan of the Village of Camden, State library of NSW
    M Ser 4 000/1 A 3004/Map 27.
[38] Book 21 Number 163.
[39] Book 34 Number 180
[40] Book 24 Number 730 Book 24 Number 731
[41] Book 61 Number 953
[42] Camden News 20 July 1899
[43] PJ Mylrea *Camden History* 2008 vol. 2 pp. 204-213 and pp. 223-235
[44] Colin and Agnes Mills *Camden History* 2001 vol. 1 pp. 37, 77,116, 129, 193
[45] Book 11 Number 844.
[46] Alan Atkinson *Camden* p. 188
[47] Camden Pioneers Register 3rd edition 2008.
[48] Hardie and Gorman ...
[49] Camden Museum Map Archives
[50] Book 820 Number 727
[51] Book 1173 Number 151.
[52] Alan Atkinson *Camden* p. 48.

[53] Hood p. 263.
[54] Book 220 Number 982
[55] Mylrea *Camden History* 2008, vol. 2 p.228.
[56] Book 2 Number 5.
[57] Book 2 Number 5.

CAMDEN HISTORY

Journal of the Camden Historical Society

September 2011 Volume 3 Number 2

CAMDEN HISTORY
Journal of the Camden Historical Society Inc.
ISSN 1445-1549
Editor: Dr Ian Willis

Management Committee
President: John Wrigley OAM,
Vice Presidents: Dr Ian Willis, Bob Lester
Secretary: Doug Barrett
Assistant Secretary: Julie Wrigley
Treasurer: Ray Herbert
Assistant Treasurer:
Immediate Past President: Cathey Shepherd
General Committee:	Dr Karen Farmer	Sharon Greene
	Rene Rem	Peter Hayward OAM
	Janice Johnson	Robert Wheeler

Honorary Auditor: Russell Dawson
Honorary Solicitors: Bowring, Macaulay and Barrett

Society contact:
P.O. Box 566, Camden, NSW 2570.   Online <http://www.camdenhistory.org.au>

Meetings
Meetings are held at 7.30 p.m. on the second Wednesday of the month except in January. They are held in the Museum. Visitors are always welcome.

Museum
The Museum is located at 40 John Street, Camden, phone 4655 3400 or 46559210. It is open Thursday to Sunday 11 a.m. to 4 p.m., except at Christmas. Visits by schools and groups are encouraged. Please contact the Museum to make arrangements. Entry is free.

Camden History, Journal of the Camden Historical Society Inc
The Journal is published in March and September each year. The Editor would be pleased to receive articles broadly covering the history of the Camden district . Correspondence can be sent to the Society's postal address. The Society takes no responsibility for the contents of articles published in the Journal.

Donations
Donations made to the Society are tax deductible. The accredited value of objects donated to the Society are eligible for tax deduction.

(Cover Edwina Macarthur Stanham outside Camden Park House   Image Courtesy Macarthur Chronicle/Melvyn Knipe,)

CAMDEN HISTORY
Journal of the Camden Historical Society Inc.

Contents

Edwina Macarthur Stanham   185
Ian Willis

Advertisements in the Camden News 1896 - 1914   190
Peter Mylrea

Community partnerships: are they all that they are cracked up to be?
Ian Willis   199

An 1843 Map of Camden   209
Peter Mylrea

Dr Robert Melville Crookston, OBE   214
Pauline Downing

Edwina Macarthur Stanham
talks about life living with her family in historic Camden Park House

Camden Historical Society Meeting
8 June 2011

Ian Willis

Society members were addressed at the June meeting by Edwina Macarthur Stanham. She detailed what it is like living with her husband, John and three children (Will, 21, Victoria, 19, and George, 17) in an early 19th century colonial house. (http://camdenparkhouse.com.au/index.htm)

The family has occupied the house since 1990 after the death of John's mother Antonia in 1989. Before this time John's father Quentin lived in the house and managed the property of Camden Park.

Edwina told the attentive audience that she and John lived in The Old Dairy Cottage on the property after they were married in 1985, after meeting at the University of Sydney.

Edwina Macarthur Stanham grew up on a wheat-sheep property west of Young. She went to Frensham School at Mittagong. Then went to University of Sydney and studied languages. She worked in France for a year, came home and studied art at the National Art School at Darlinghurst.

'Unfortunately John's mother died in her 60s so we moved into the main house earlier than we had expected. Will (their oldest child) was only six months old; it just happened through fate.'

The house, according to Edwina, is a living museum that has been occupied by members of the Macarthur family since it was built in 1835. John's family is the 7th generation of the family that has continuously lived in the house.

'The house has stayed in family since it was built so there's a real tapestry of generations here,' Edwina said in an interview in 2008. 'It's an old house but it's full of such wonderful original pieces of furniture and it's a beautiful setting.'

Edwina has admitted while it has been 'a great honour' to live in the house there is a 'certain responsibility'. In 2009 John Stanham explained their job is that of custodians, and while they are enjoying it, he says that it is like any other house, 'there are ongoing repairs and maintenance work'.

Edwina Macarthur Stanham outside Camden Park House
(Image Courtesy **Macarthur Chronicle**/Melvyn Knipe,)

'We're doing our best to protect and maintain the house,' Edwina explained. The John Verge designed Georgian house was started in early 1830's and finished in 1835. It was located on the original 2025 hectares grant to John Macarthur who had died in 1834.

'The house has 80 rooms and is very much like it was. It has much of the original furniture,' she said. 'What makes it interesting is the original collection. Old uniforms, books and diaries.'

In 2008 the Australian Heritage Database described the house as a two storey Regency mansion constructed of stuccoed sandstock brickwork with sandstone portico and grand colonnade verandah facing garden, sandstone trim and cornices to the shuttered windows. Single storey wings symmetrical about the central block. Large two storey wing (c.1880) added to north main block has hipped slate roof with boxed eaves while remaining roofs are hidden behind Classical parapets in stone.

In the early 20th century there were 15-20 staff to run the house, with some in the garden. 'These days,' said Edwina, 'there are two in the house and two in the garden. Frances [Warner] and Harry [Warner] are our right hand people.'

'The house is from another era. In The 1950s kitchen moved from being at the far end of the house to the main block. The laundry is still at the far end of the house.'

'Nearly every room in the house has its own fireplace, but the only ones used these days are on the main ground floor. The library, drawing room, breakfast room and dining room,' she said.

Frances, who was in the audience, explained 'In the 1960s staff had to wear three different coloured uniforms, blue, pink and grey. Different uniforms for different occasions.'

Two generations of Warner family have lived on Camden Park. Harry started working on the property in 1958. His father worked on Camden Park before him. In 2009 Harry said, 'I love the country, outdoors, farming and animals. Working on such a large and famous property has its perks as Mr Warner found out – he can list movies and television in his resume.' (Often the house and garden is used as a location for films, commercials and fashion shoots)

The property, according to the Camden Park House website, has the largest intact 19th century garden in Australia and includes rare and exotic species, many of which were collected by William Macarthur. The garden demonstrates the informal 'picturesque' style of garden design favoured in the early part of the 19th century. This has been overlaid by a later, more formal, `gardenesque' style. William introduced the Camellia japonica Anenomiflora', today the oldest surviving Camellia in Australia. (see http://www.hortuscamden.com/)

Edwina said 'The garden still contains many of its original rare and exotic species.'

According to Edwina there is no such thing as a typical week. 'There could be a visit from volunteer historians, museum curators, a fashion photo shoot or a visit from a tour group.'

'The house is very busy. There is the open weekend in September where we can get up to 2000 visitors. There can be visitors at all other times. The National Trust used to run the open days in the 1970s. We have done our own thing for the last 30 years,' she said.

' Many people will visit year after year as people love to come back and see what has changed or to tour through the house another time.'

Edwina told the society members that over the years the house has had some interesting and famous visitors. They have included 19th century explorers Ludwig Leichhardt, Duke and Duchess of York in 1927, Princess Anne and Mark Phillips in 1970s, Marie Bashir [New South Wales Governor] in 2010, celebrities Don Burke, Paul Hogan, Rolf Harris, Richard Bonynge and Danny De Vito. A number of movies have been shot in and around the house and have included *My Brilliant Career, Dirt Water Dynasty* and most recently *Sleeping Beauty*. The house is often sought after by the film industry to be portrayed as an English house, for example in the recent Darwin's *Brave New World*.

The many varied unannounced visitors have been an eclectic lot. They have included a hot air balloon on the front lawn on a September open day, some Japanese visitors who thought that the house was open to the public, and a young man who proposed to his girlfriend in the garden.

'The Camden Park Preservation Committee assists us with valuable advice. Our archive people are Janice [Johnson] and John [Wrigley] and Alan Robinson. Greg Martin is our bookbinder. And there are the garden volunteers of the Camden Park Nursery Group headed up by Colin Mills,' said Edwina.

'Recent projects on the house have been external painting, re-roofing and garden work,' she said.

The principal objective of the Stanhams is to maintain the house as a family home. 'It's a home first and foremost,' said John.

'The house is child friendly. The children have just got used to it. They just grew up in it,' said Edwina. 'Our children have been lucky to grow up in the historic surroundings of original furniture, books, paintings and other items.'

'The house is very welcoming,' said Edwina, 'and comes to life with a party. The house has been used for many things, including our son Will's recent 21st birthday party, with all his friends. They all stayed over at the house on Saturday night. All 13 bedrooms were used.'

Frances chirped in that the house had slept 30 plus on the weekend of Will's 21st birthday.

'Camden Park House is a special place,' said Edwina. 'The property of Camden Park has 13 cottages. These are occupied by people who work on the property. I think all who live and work here recognize that Camden Park is a unique place. It is quite a community with many families having lived on the property for long periods of time. We have Christmas drinks to say thank you to volunteers and to recognize that it is a special place and a community.'

Acknowledgements
The author gratefully acknowledges the helpful comments and suggestions of Edwina Macarthur Stanham on an earlier draft of this article.

Additional Sources
Vera Bertola, 'Family's labour of love', *Macarthur Chronicle Camden Edition*, 7 June 2011, p. 9 Online at http://macarthur-chronicle-camden.whereilive.com.au/news/story/edwina-macarthur-stanham-carries-a-big-name/
'Doors open at Camden Park', *District Reporter* 14 September 2009, p. 6.
'Harry remains true to his job', *District Reporter*, 15 June 2009, p. 5.
Iliana Stillitano, 'History's doors flung open', *Camden Advertiser*, 17 September 2008, p.7.
Australian Heritage Database, 'Camden Park, Camden Park Estate Rd, Camden Park, NSW, Australia', Department of Environment, Australian Government. Online at http://www.environment.gov.au/cgi-bin/ahdb. Accessed 12 June 2008.
'Welcome to Camden Park House'. Online at http://camdenparkhouse.com.au/index.htm.

Advertisements in the *Camden News* 1896 - 1914

Peter Mylrea

Advertisements in the *Camden News* give some insight into the services which were available to people living in Camden in the late 1800s and early 1900s. The article is based on advertisements in the local paper, the *Camden News*, from its start in 1896 through to 1914.

There were four hotels in Camden and three of them advertised regularly from 1896. These were the Camden Inn (now called Merino Tavern),

The Plough and Harrow (now Argyle Inn) and the Commercial Hotel (now Camden Hotel). The advertisements gave details of the services offered. The frequency of these advertisements and their details suggest that there was competition between the three hotels which were within 160 metres of each other in Argyle Street. The fourth hotel, The Crown, did not advertise until about 1906. It was located at the far end of Argyle Street and did not have any nearby competition.

Inevitably people in Camden died and had to be buried. Often in country towns a local carpenter was also the undertaker. This happened in Camden where J.D. Rankin, the Mayor of Camden briefly in 1896, advertised himself as a timber merchant etc and as an undertaker who had built a first class hearse. A related tradesman was G. W. Cleveland of Camden Monumental Works.

By 1906 Walter Peters was advertising as an undertaker and embalmer; perhaps he had replaced Rankin. He also advertised that monumental work was carried out on his premises and that a hearse and coaches were available if required.

CAMDEN.

25th. SEPT., 1906.

Sale of first-class property in the centre of Camden.

W. LARKIN

(Late R H Inglis)

WILL sell at his sale yard, Camden on

Tuesday, Sept 25th

at 1 o'clock

On acc the Executor the W of the late MRS ELIZA WH

Large block of land sit O reet, Camden having a f ntage of about 245 feet by a depth of 66ft to that street On this land are erec three cottages, which are at present occupied by Messrs Wiggins, Close, and Mrs Funnell

This sale offers an exceptional opportunity of securing a first class investment, which will return high interest

The Executor is determined to sell right out to wind up the Estate

TITLE FREEHOLD

The Camden Inn,

CAMDEN.

MRS. A. FRENCH,

(Late of Leichhardt, Sydney, and recently of th Commercial Hotel, Camden.)

This FAMILY HOTEL, the oldest and best known hotel in the Camden electorate, has been entirely renovated and refurnished throughout and is the most convenient and best situated in the district with private entrances. Mrs. French giving her personal attention to the comfort of all visitors and everything of the best quality only kept. Luncheon from 1 o'clock daily. Private apartments.

Exceptionally good stabling and paddock. Loose boxes, etc. Horses, carriages and buggies always on hire.

Extensive Billiard Room. Pleasure gardens, etc. Special accommodation for COMMERCIAL TRAVELLERS with spacious sample room.

Plough & Harrow Inn.

ARGYLE STREET, CAMDEN.

M. L. HENNESSY

Having taken the above Hotel from Mr. W. H. McDonald, trusts with civility and cleanliness combined, to receive a fair share of public patronage.

Best brand of Wines, Rum, Whiskey, Brands &c., only kept.

BOARD AND RESIDENCE.

Meals at all hours — First-class stabling, &c.

CHARGS MODERATE.

Champaign always in Stock.

SALE YARDS.

Gravestones made by Cleveland and by Peters can be seen in St John's Cemetery, the Roman Catholic Cemetery at Cawdor, the Uniting Church Cemetery at Cawdor and St Paul's at Cobbitty.

The commercial needs of the town and district required the services of auctioneers. Because dairy farming was the major local industry there was a need to be able to buy and sell cattle. R.H. Inglis met this need. He was an auctioneer with livestock sale yards in Camden and Picton.

In 1906 W. Larkin, a future mayor of Camden, who had been R.H. Inglis' clerk, took over the R.H. Inglis's business and continued as the only auctioneer in Camden. W. Larkin had his saleyard behind the Plough and Harrow Hotel in what is now Larkin Place. In addition to livestock sales both men were general auctioneers who auctioned houses, farm, equipment etc. A Larkin advertisement in 1906 shows an auction sale for land in Oxley Street which is now the site of Woolworths.

There were other advertisements which were more like classified ads, one column wide and only one inch or so deep and consisted only of text. These have not been illustrated in this article.

In 1902 the Public School in Camden was reclassified as Camden Superior Public School. It then provided both primary and post primary education. Alternative education was provided by Mr Oliver who advertised his 'Grammar School- Studley Park, Narellan Camden'. which offered 'a classical, scientific and commercial' education. This school was for day boys and boarders. Girls were not mentioned in his advertisements.

In addition to schools, private tuition was available at a price. In 1896 T.H. Bosworth, teacher of piano, violin and singing, visited Camden weekly and in 1906 Miss Allnut, of the Rectory Cobbitty, advertised elocution lessons for young ladies at one guinea (£2/2/0) per term and ten shillings and sixpence for children. Then came advertisements from two men who were organists at St John's Church. The first was Mr Selby New who advertised in 1908 as a teacher of pipe organ, pianoforte, harmony etc. with pupils prepared for all examinations. He was succeeded in 1914 by Mr Oliver S. Frost who taught organ, piano, harmony, voice production, brass and reed instruments at two guineas per quarter and for junior pupils one guinea.

Up to the early 1900s horse-drawn vehicles, of a variety of types, were the main means of local transport in Camden. In 1911 Butler & Son advertised themselves as Coach and Livery Stable Proprietors and in an ad in 1912 they advised that a coach for Yerranderie left Camden daily (except Sunday) at 6.30 a.m. and from Yerranderie at 7 a.m. They also advertised a Parcel

Commercial Hotel.

C A M D E N.

S. Allingham

PROPRIETOR.

(Late Mrs French.)

This first-class Family Hotel, replete with every possible convenience, and with moderate terms, will in future be conducted in such a manner as to ensure the comfort of every visitor. Only the best of everything kept in stock. A trial is respectfully solicited.

Commercial Travellers and Visitors to Camden will find every home comfort.

FIRST CLASS TABLE.

The Bar is supplied with the best brands of Wines Spirits and Beers, &c.
The Stabling is one of the best in the district.
Loose boxes,
Experienced groom always in attendance.
Buggies and Horses on hire
Bi liards, &c.
Spacious COMMERCIAL and SAMPLE ROOM

Coach between Camden, Nattai and Yerranderie with charges up to five shillings for 112 pounds weight.

However things changed dramatically with the arrival of the motor car. In advertisements in 1914 (2 July 1914) C. Butler & Son now called themselves Motor and Coach Proprietors and they offered transport to Menangle Park Races either in their motor car or in their Dreadnought Coach.

Up to 1914 there were no advertisement for the sale of motor cars in Camden nor is there any information about the number of cars owned in the village. However motor mechanics appeared on the scene to service local cars as seen in F.E. Shaw's 1914 advertisement for his Camden Motor Garage.

For those who did not own cars it was possible to hire vehicles. F.E. Shaw had motor cars for hire which came with 'Careful and experienced drivers' and C. Butler & Son also had a car for hire 'with a competent driver in charge'. Presumably at that time few people knew how to drive or the proprietors were protective of their vehicles. W.J. Keane also had a car for hire, in his case it was a 1914 model.

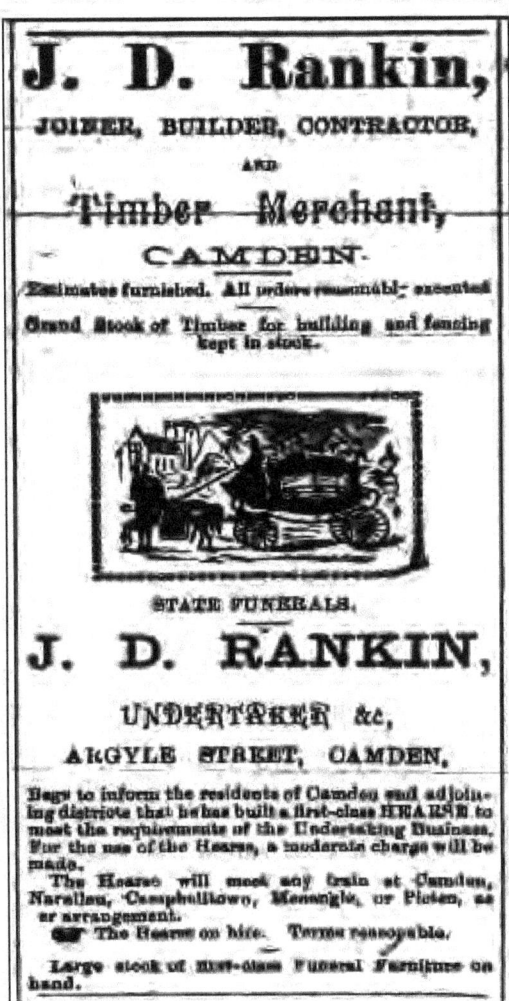

The above advertisements give an idea of some, but not all, of the services available in Camden about the turn of the century. There were also advertisements for dentists, pharmacists, lawyers,, jewellers, watchmakers and many advertisements for shops selling food, clothing, household goods, farming requirements and other goods.

Author's Note

R. H. INGLIS

AUCTIONEER,

HORSE, CATTLE AND PRODUCE SALESMAN.

Weekly Sales held every Tuesday at CAMDEN and every Wednesday at PICTON.

A special HORSE SALE will be held on the 1st Saturday in every month at his Yards, Camden.

BUTLER & SON.

Coach & Livery Stable Proprietors,

CAMDEN

Horses and Vehicles for Hire at Reasonable Rates. Wedding Vehicles supplied.

☞ PARTIES DRIVEN TO ANY PART OF THE DISTRICT.

Our Dreadnought Coach Carrying 19 passengers is just the thing for PICNIC PARTIES to any of the following places:— Bulli Pass, Cataract Dam, Bent's Basin, Burragorang Mountain.

Smaller coaches for hire as well Horses and Sulkies on hand at any time.

Cricketers, Footballers, Dance Parties, Tennis Clubs, Golfers, Rifle Teams, Game Shooters, catered for.

EXPERIENCED DRIVERS ONLY EMPLOYED
NOTHING BUT GOOD HORSES SUPPLIED

That is an important matter.

The Price is the Lowest.

Advertisements used in this article were originally published in the *Camden News*. For those who are interested in further details contact author c/o Camden Historical Society.

Camden Motor Garage.

MOST UP-TO-DATE MOTOR GARAGE WITHIN 100 MILES OF SYDNEY.

F E. SHAW,

MOTOR EXPERT, Argyle Street Camden.

All descriptions of Cars Overhauled, Cleaned and Repaired

Motor accessories kept in stock.   Agent for DUNLOP TYRES.

Motor cars for Hire.

Careful and Experienced Drivers.   Theatre trains met at Campbelltown by appointment.

Camden Motor Garage. F E SHAW,
- PROPRIETOR
(Will store 6 cars.)

CAMDEN MONUMENTAL WORKS

Argyle Street, Camden.

G. W. CLEVELAND,

(LATE H. L. DAVIS)

MONUMENTAL AND GENERAL MASON

Monuments in Marble, Granite, or Freestone.
Over 200 different designs to select from.
Cast and Wrought Iron Tomb Railings.

ENAMELLED FREESTONE A SPECIALITY

☞ Old Stones renovated and inscriptions cut in any Cemetery.

Community partnerships: Are they all that they are cracked up to be?

Ian Willis
Honorary Research Fellow, University of Wollongong.

Paper presented at the 2009 Museums Australia National Conference *Work in Progress* held at Newcastle Town Hall, 17-20 May 2009.

Community partnerships are a form of collaboration between non-profits and government, and business. They are often portrayed as the most successful way for non-profits to proceed in their operation. How true is this in reality? On the positive side partnerships allow community groups, government and business to work collaboratively on common goals, to maximise the available resources and deliver positive outcomes to both parties and the wider community, and build social capital. On the negative side partnerships bring tensions and contradictions. Often they are not as successful as they are portrayed by their supporters.This paper will outline one case study of a community partnership between a local council library and the local historical society which manages a community museum. It will highlight the functioning of the partnership and its success, or not.

In 2007 Peter Scrivener[1] wrote a report for Hawkesbury City Council on community partnerships and in it, he presented a summary of a partnership between the Camden Historical Society and Camden Council. In brief it stated:

> These two parties are proud of the amicable relationship they have nurtured over many years during which time the museum has gained considerable support as an acknowledged 'model' local museum demonstrating exemplary practice. Currently [that is in 2007], the council-owned building is being renovated to share foyer space with the adjacent council library... They have never had a formal arrangement but recently have signed a one-page Memorandum of Understanding... [the memorandum] simply outlines the spirit and intended community outcomes that can flow from greater linkages and integration between the two parties. (Scrivener, 2007)

This partnership is the subject of this paper.

At a local level community partnerships are one form of collaboration between voluntary organisations and councils that can bring measurable benefits to participating stakeholders. They encourage a sustainable solution to the achievement of goals at a time when there are increasing demands on a limited set of resources, while at the same time maintaining that despite their advantages community partnerships are not a silver bullet. They can be compared to a living organism which needs constant attention and nurturing, and if neglected will wither and die.

My interest in community partnerships was initiated by research on the three local historical societies in our area and the role of their local museums in their communities (Willis, 2007b). In that work, which is the subject of a forthcoming paper (Willis, 2009), I maintain that these organisations occupy a privileged place in their community through storytelling and contribute to the development of community identity and place making. They have received the official endorsement of their local councils and in some cases, have entered partnerships with them.

Scholarly work on community partnerships between local councils and historical societies is virtually invisible, although there has been some useful work done by Peter Scrivener (Scrivener, 2007), and others (Sandell, 2004). These limited efforts have shown that these type of community partnerships have mixed results.[2] This field of endeavour deserves the attention of researchers and hopefully this paper will shine some light on a dark corner.

The setting for this case study is the Camden Local Government Area (LGA), which is on the rural-urban interface on south-western fringe of Sydney. The LGA is the fastest growing in New South Wales with a population of 52,000 in 2008 and an annual growth rate that has been in excess of 15 per cent per year. The Camden LGA has a strong community sector with over 250 voluntary organisations (Willis, 2007a: 18).

The two stakeholders in this community partnership are the Camden Historical Society which was founded in 1957 and has 160 members. Its main aim has been the promotion of local history through public education and memorialisation, which includes managing a local museum. The second member of the partnership is Camden Council and its Library Service. The library has two branches, Camden and Narellan, a borrowing collection of 70,000 items and 17 full time equivalent staff. It should be noted that the Camden Family History Society is also part of this arrangement, but is not the subject of this paper. The author also needs to declare his interest in this subject as an insider through his membership of the Camden Historical Society.

This paper will examine the Camden partnership using Jupp's four simple processes that he felt were essential for a successful partnership. They are: 'developing clear objectives; ensuring that each partner benefits individually as well as helping to achieve a common goal; building in evaluation; and finally, developing understanding and trust between partners' (Jupp, 2000, p. 8). The last factor will be treated first.

Understanding and Trust

The basis of the current partnership agreement between the council and the historical society is to be found in the trust and understanding that has developed over the last 52 years between these two organisations.

Since the foundation of the historical society (1957) the council has come to support and endorse the story of Camden as it has been told by the society. From the beginning the society has presented a conservative view of local history based around the pioneer legend and the town's material progress. This view of the world was strengthened in 1970 when the society opened a small pioneer museum, with the assistance of the Camden Rotary Club. The council supported the venture by providing space for the museum rent free. It did this without a formal agreement being put in place. This was followed in short order by society members erecting three public monuments to Camden pioneers located outside the council chambers in 1977, 1978 and 1979. The council then supported the expansion of the museum in 1980, and again in 1999, again without any formal agreement with the historical society.

By promoting an officially sanctioned view of Camden's social history the historical society has achieved a privileged position in the community and become the custodian of the Camden story. In recent years the representation of the Camden story in the museum has broadened, as Australian history has in the remainder of the country, to include Aborigines, women, rural labourers and other aspects of country town life. The museum has also become a site where, according to Robyn Till (Till, 2004), the local community has derived a sense of belonging from story telling, and where a continuity of generations in the one locality, according to Sonya Salamon (Salamon, 2007:3), have contributed to the essence of a strong community identity and sense of place.

Clear Objectives

The next stage in the development of the partnership agreement occurred in 2002 when Camden Council issued a draft strategic plan for the future of Camden library service, called *Vibrant Places, People Spaces*.[3] The aim of the plan was twofold: firstly, the creation of a new community space around the existing library and museum building; and secondly, the formalisation of the existing arrangements between the council and the society to facilitate the building project.

The plan envisaged a new integrated complex as a multi-purpose centre which could function as 'a unified educational, recreational, cultural and tourist complex'.[4] The library was to be a public space that could strengthen community cohesiveness by becoming a 'community hub' and 'communal meeting place'. According to Sonya Salamon, this type of space could act as an arena where the residents could develop a sense of community that bonded them to the place (Salamon, 2007: 13). The library would, according to the council, provide an opportunity for local residents to 'embrace Camden's culture and sense of community' and contribute to place making (Camden Council, 2002: 3).

The new complex was based on the re-adaptive use of two historic buildings: the Camden School of Arts building (1866),which was later the Camden Town Hall then council offices; and secondly the Camden Temperance Hall (1867), which functioned as the Camden Fire Station between 1916-1993. By the end of 2007 the $2.3 million re-development had resulted in a single building with a common street entry after the former laneway between the buildings had been covered with a glass roof to create a galleria. The view of the council's general manager of the completed complex was that it provided 'the community with a stronger sense of belonging and place' and 'a place based and people focused facility'.[5]

In the end the co-location has had a number of advantages for both stakeholders. For the library, according to Kathryn Baget the library services manager, it has meant that it has had one stop convenience, better building maintenance and security, and a sharing of infrastructure with the historical society; a type of convergence, a notion that has received attention in recent times including this conference (Stapleton, 2009).[6] As far as the historical society was concerned it gained a street entrance on John Street, enhanced security, a new lift to the first floor and improved fire safety.

The second part of the strategic planning process was the development of a formal agreement, which was achieved through a memorandum of understanding (MoU). This would be the first time that there had been a formalised relationship between the historical society and the council, and according to the Australian Government is the recommended way to go for community partnerships (DEST, 2004). The purpose of the MoU, according to the council, was to facilitate the building project and to 'promote a stronger working partnership between the Library Service and the Historical Society' (Camden Council, 2006:124).

The MoU was worked up through a number of stages from 2004 and was eventually passed by council in November 2006 (Camden Council, 2006:112). The document is a single page, free of legalese and clearly sets out the objectives of the partnership. The agreement is flexible and open ended. The council maintains that the MoU is 'underpinned by a spirit of co-operation' (Camden Council, 2006: 124) and has reflected the relationship of trust and understanding that has developed over the years between the historical society and the council. The MoU specifically excludes property matters, such as insurance and maintenance, which are addressed through other agreements.

Within the partnership arrangement the formal lines of communication between the library and the historical society are kept open through quarterly partnership meetings chaired by the library's local studies librarian, who also circulates the agenda and minutes. The partnership is reviewed each November with the aim of identifying 'joint programs, projects and funding opportunities for the coming year' (Camden Council, 2006: 112). The formal meeting setting provides the appropriate planning and ongoing communication that Kathryn Baget claims are needed in all partnerships.[7]

The formal linkages within the partnership are supported by leadership from 'community champions' like John Wrigley and Peter Hayward from the historical society, and Kathryn Baget from the library, who have been central to the success of the partnership. They have been involved in the partnership process from the release of the strategic plan in 2002. Their enthusiasm and perseverance has facilitated the progress of the partnership. They have acted as community organisers in a host of areas including meeting facilitation, negotiation and networking, and communicating the vision of the partnership to the wider community, as other people have done elsewhere in Australia (Johns, Kilpatrick and Whelan, 2007: 53-54). John Wrigley maintains that the success of the partnership can only 'work with the positive and willing participation of both partners'. He has stated that he has been 'willing to do anything to ensure the successful continuing operation and improvement of the partnership'.[8] Such enthusiasm has been the basis of the current partnership, and has been fundamental to the development of trust and understanding between council and the historical society for over 50 years.

Just as importantly to the partnership has been the informal linkages between the organisations. For example, some Camden library staff are members of the society and volunteer their time at the museum on weekends. There is also casual interaction between society officers and library staff, both within and outside of the library setting. These informal linkages reflect the strong interpersonal and familial networks which still exist in Camden from earlier decades and help strengthen the formation of social capital.

Common Goals and Benefits

The common goals of all stakeholders to the partnership were outlined by the Camden mayor in March 2007 at the opening of the completed building complex. He stated that the partnership was about 'participation, association and joint interest' and that it captured 'the history, culture and relevance of the community'.[9]

The implementation of these aspirations, as detailed in the MoU, are best characterised by the various joint projects that are undertaken between the library service and the historical society. According to Kathryn Baget, the joint projects have brought a 'new perspective, new ideas and possibly additional resources'.[10] They are part of the story telling process of the historical society and help build a sense of ownership amongst those who participate in this process.

The most important of these projects is **HistoryPix** [now called **Camden Images, Past and Present**] and involves the digitising of the historical society's photographic collection.[11] Photographs are part of the story telling experience by providing the participants to the story with a window on the past. They are a visual aid and can act as a memory prompt when telling a story. They also capture a moment in time, a glimpse of the past, and are a good resource for tracking changes in the local history landscape.

The aim of HistoryPix has been to provide greater public access to the historical society's image collection, which is one of the society's most valuable assets. The project is facilitated by Peter Mylrea, the society's archivist, who has processed over 2500 photographs so far. The society provides the photographs and the photograph captions, the images are digitised by Searchtech (a private company which provides image library software, publishing and scanning services), the council provides the IT and online support, and the library staff handle the sale of photographs and set the charges. According to Doug Barrett, the secretary of the society, the partnership relieves the society of the need to provide a volunteer to deal with enquiries for and supply of copies of photographs to the community and other interested parties.[12] In essence the council funds the project and the society provides the photographs and voluntary labour.

'HistoryPix' has proved to be a valuable public asset and is used by members of the public, local and Sydney media, local businesses and community organisations. Online access to the images is provided through both the websites of the historical society, the library and PictureAustralia. In the last three months of 2008 there were 23,600 hits and 23,700 searches, while in the seven months from April 2008 and January 2009 there were 43,000 hits and 55,000 searches.

More recent joint projects which have been developed within the partnership include, firstly, the **Dictionary of Sydney Project.** This is a local history project which involves writing short histories of different localities in the LGA for the Dictionary of Sydney project. These histories have also been placed on the historical society's website. Secondly, there is the **Camden Area Families Project,** which is an oral history project which encourages local people to tell their stories, provide their photographs and develop a family tree. It was launched in late 2007 by Camden's deputy mayor. The society has supported the project through its Research and Writing Group and recently hosted an oral history training workshop for the community at the museum. Other linkages include w**orkshops and seminars** (history week and heritage week) and **links** between the library catalogue and the historical society library.

Evaluation

The partnership is formally assessed at the end of each year as part of the MoU process as mentioned earlier. Even the preparation of this paper is part of the evaluation process, and has provided an opportunity for some of the partnership stakeholders to reflect on the process associated with its development and success (they are mentioned in the notes at the end of the paper).

More generally though, the partnership has been an opportunity for the historical society to consolidate the position of the museum by formalising its occupation of a council owned building for the first time. This will then provide a strong base for any further development that the society may want to pursue into the future.

The library has better met the guidelines for floor space in a modern library building in the LGA. It is better able to offer modern services in a heritage precinct. It has, according to Kathryn Baget, allowed the library to 'attract a new audience, create unique programs and services for our community'.[13]

There are also considerable benefits for Camden Council. Firstly, it has relieved council of the considerable cost of providing a community museum managed by professional curatorial staff. Secondly, the time and resources that volunteers bring to the museum represents a form of voluntary taxation that benefits the whole community. Further the presence of the society and its archives, according to Wrigley, 'provide a ready source of historical information and advice to council as a virtual unpaid 'heritage branch' of council'. In addition, the museum acts as a 'secure repository for anything important which council wishes to retain of an historical nature'.[14]

The partnership is not without its challenges. Firstly, there is the nonalignment of opening hours between the museum and the library. The library is shut Saturday afternoon and all day Sunday, while the museum is closed between Monday and Wednesday. Secondly, there is the inherent tension between two organisations, one using full-time paid staff, the other using unpaid volunteers.[15] Thirdly, there is the potential political tension if the council and the historical society differ over policy matters related to local history and heritage, and fourthly, the need to ensure a smooth generational change in the administration and implementation of the MoU into the future.

Conclusion

In conclusion I would make some observations about the partnership.

The partnership has brought together the library service and the historical society, whose parallel aims of strengthening community identity and place making, have strengthened community development. This has been achieved by creating a new community space in the Camden LGA where community identity and a sense of place are increasingly being challenged by higher levels of urbanisation.

The success of the partnership has rested on the willingness of all the participants to achieve a common goal and for those involved to ensure that the partnership succeeds. Wrigley has observed that 'so far we have been very fortunate with the enthusiasm and commitment of the people involved from both partners'.[16]

The community partnership has met all expectations made from it so far and given the continuation of the goodwill from all involved should continue to do so into the future.

Finally, the paper has shown, that given the right conditions, community partnerships can be 'what they are cracked up to be'.

Acknowledgements
The author would like to acknowledge the input of John Wrigley, Julie Wrigley, Kathryn Baget, Peter Mylrea, Jo Oliver, Doug Barrett and their comments on this paper.

References
Camden Council, 2002, Draft Vibrant Places, People Spaces, A vision for Camden Council Library Service 2010. Camden: Camden Council.
Camden Council, 2006, Minutes of the Ordinary Council Meeting held on 13 November 2006, Camden: Camden Council, pp. 6, 112-113. Online at http://www.camden.nsw.gov.au/files/2006_minutes/ord_131106.pdf accessed 4 February 2009.
  Department of Education, Science and Training, 2004, *A Community Partnerships Resource: Supporting Young People Through Their Life, Learning and Work Transitions*, Canberra: Australian Government. Online at http://www.dest.gov.au/sectors/career_development/publications_resources/ <http://www.dest.gov.au/NR/rdonlyres/F5328E2A-3806-498D-ADE9-A740F404FCF4/2593/community_partnerships_resources.pdf> . Accessed on 27 February

2009.
Johns, Susan, Sue Kilpatrick and Jessica Whelan, 2007, 'Our Health in Our Hands: Building Effective Community Partnerships for Rural Health Service Provision', *Rural Society*, Vol. 17, No. 1, August, pp. 50-65.
Jupp, Ben, *Working Together, Creating a Better Environment for Cross-Sector Partnerships*, London; Demos. Online at http://www.demos.co.uk/publications/workingtogether Accessed 2 March 2009.
Salamon, Sonya, 2007, *Newcomers to Old Towns, Suburbanization of the Heartland*, Chicago: University of Chicago Press.
Sandell, Claire, 'Local History Collections for the Future: Meaningful Partnerships Between Public Libraries and Community Heritage Groups', Conference paper, Museum Australia Conference, Melbourne, 16-21 May 2004. Online at http://www.museumsaustralia.org.au/site/page313.php Accessed 4 March 2009.
Scrivener, Peter, 2007, *Assessment Report on a Proposed Deed of Agreement between Hawkesbury City Council, Hawkesbury Historical Society and the Friends of Hawkesbury Art Collection and Regional Art Gallery*, Windsor: Hawkesbury City Council.
Stapleton, Maisy, 2009, M&G NSW Convergence Study, Sydney: Museum and Galleries NSW.
Till, Robyn, 2004, 'Propagate or perish: Partnerships, Community Value and Sustainability', Conference paper, Museum Australia Conference, Melbourne, 16-21 May 2004. Online at http://www.museumsaustralia.org.au/site/page313.php Accessed 4 March 2009.
Willis, Ian, 2007a, 'Democracy in Action in Local Government: Camden, NSW', *Australian Quarterly*, Vol. 79, Issue 2, March-April, pp.17-21.
Willis, Ian, 2007b,' Fifty years of local history, the Camden Historical Society, 1957-2007, Address at the 50th Anniversary Meeting of the Camden Historical Society, 12 July, Camden'. *Camden History*, September, Vol 2 No 1, pp. 96-117.
Willis, Ian, 2009, 'Stories and Things, The Role of the Local Historical Society, Campbelltown, Camden and The Oaks', *Journal of the Royal Australian Historical Society*. (forthcoming)

Endnotes

Peter Scrivener, 1999-2000 Parramatta Heritage Centre, 2002-2004 Museums and Galleries NSW, 2004 member of Australian National Committee of International Council of Museums (ICOM Australia), 2006-2008 Museum and Art Gallery of the Northern Territory.
Scrivener gives details of (a) successful partnerships: Wagga Wagga Historical Society; Camden Historical Society; Combined Tweed River Historical Societies; Gilgandra Historical Society; (b) unsuccessful partnerships: Liverpool Regional Museum; Centennial Bakery Museum (Hurstville); Cowra Historical Museum; Peppin Heritage Centre (Denniliquin).
Correspondence, K Baget, Camden Council Library Service to Camden Historical Society, December 2002.
Correspondence, P. Hayward, Camden Historical Society, Camden. 15 February 2005.
General Manager Notes, Schedule, Camden Library Re-opening, 2 March 2007.
Kathryn Baget, Library Partnerships, Discussion Paper, 19 February 2009
Kathryn Baget, Library Partnerships, Discussion Paper, 19 February 2009.
John Wrigley, Camden Library Service – Camden Historical Society Partnership, Discussion Paper, January 2009.
Mayoral Notes, Schedule, Camden Library Re-opening, 2 March 2007.
Kathryn Baget, Library Partnerships, Discussion Paper, 19 February 2009.
'A proposal to put photographs of Camden history on to a computerized system', Draft document, Camden Historical Society, 24 June 2003. The name HistoryPix was a joint suggestion of the library staff and the society.
Interview, Doug Barrett, Camden Historical Society, Camden, 18 February 2009.

Kathryn Baget, Library Partnerships, Discussion Paper, 19 February 2009.
John Wrigley, Camden Library Service – Camden Historical Society Partnership, Discussion Paper, January 2009.
Interview, Doug Barrett, Camden Historical Society, Camden, 18 February 2009.
John Wrigley, Camden Library Service – Camden Historical Society Partnership, Discussion Paper, January 2009.

An 1843 Map of Camden

Peter Mylrea

A copy of a map of Camden dated 1843 has come into the possession of the Camden Historical Society. It showed a number of features which are now of historical interest.

The early 1840s were difficult financial times in the colony of.new South Wales. One of the reasons was the decline in the demand for wool by British mills which resulted in many colonial bankruptcies and much unemployment.[1]
James and William Macarthur, the sons of John Macarthur, may have been affected by this depression and perhaps had to borrow money. They did, in fact, borrow money from their cousin Hannibal Hawkins Macarthur. To cover his financial support Hannibal took out a mortage on Macarthur land and the legal document for this was dated 20 November 1843. The map which is the subject of this article was attached to this mortage document.[2]

The oldest road in Camden

The map shows a road which was the first road built in what was to become Camden. It is shown on the map as the *Road from Camden House*. It passéd to the east of St John's Church and continued into *Elizabeth Street* (now View Street), *Argyle Street* and *Sydney Road* to the Nepean River where there was a ford until the Cowpasture Bridge was built in 1826.

John Macarthur received his first grant of land in Camden in 1805 and probably soon after moved his sheep to Camden from his other properties around Sydney. There is record of Mrs Macarthur visiting the area in 1810 'to look after her farms and numerous flocks of sheep'.[3] By 1820 many of the buildings now called Belgenny Farm had been constructed and Camden House (now Camden Park House) was to be built by 1835.

There would have been a need for an access road to and from the Macarthur properties in Sydney. The route of the road was probably used from the early1800s. It is not known when a well-built road was constructed. This could have been as early as the 1810s because from then on there was considerable movement of people, supplies and wool to and from Sydney.[4].For how long this road was in use could not be determined but it was in use in the 1840s.

The route of the road *From Camden House* is very close to that of the present day Menangle Road. Near the junction with Park Street the original road entered the grounds of St John's Church.

Remains of the road can still be recognised as embankments and shallow cuttings across the grassed paddock. Further on traces of a well built road can be recognised although this section is now heavily overgrown with olive and privet trees. The road continues to the back fence of Number 31 Alpha Road. From there on remains of

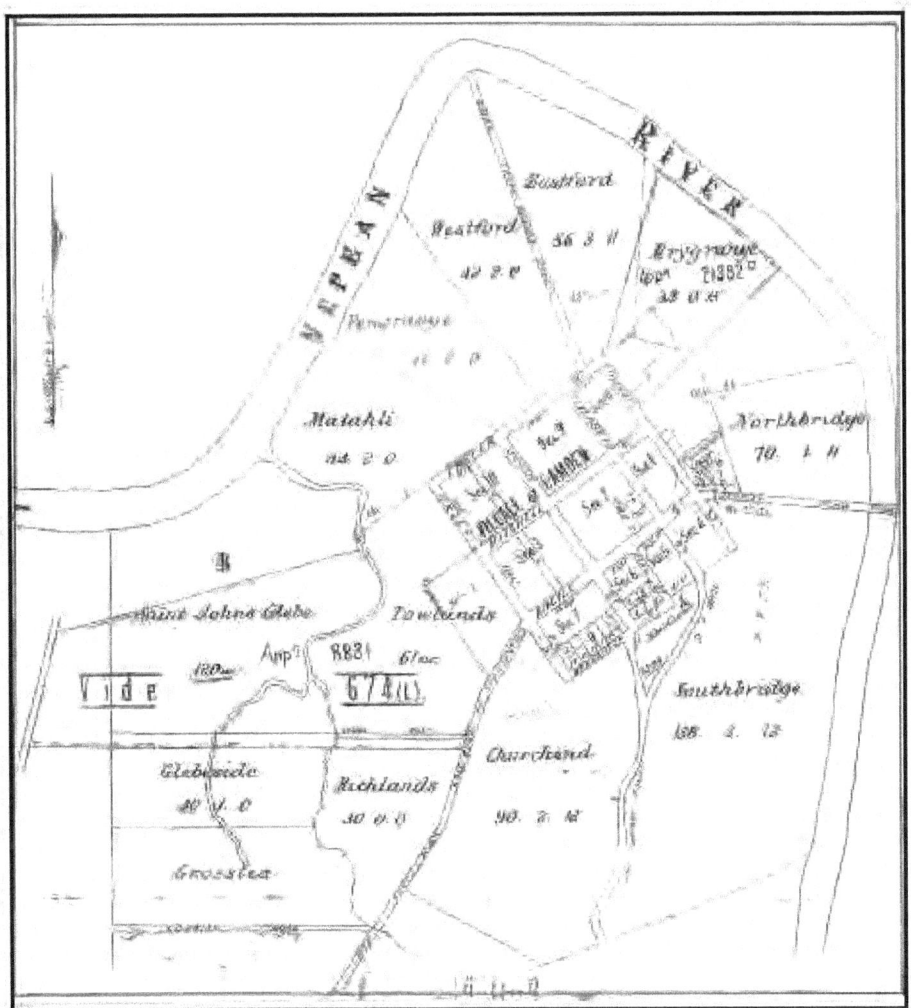

Part of a map dated 20 November 1843 shows developments in the district around Camden at that time.

embankments can still be recognised near the back fences of some of the houses on the upper side of Alpha Road. The road then continued on to what are shown on the map as *Elizabeth Street, Argyle Street* and *Sydney Road.*

The map also shows other roads but these were not constructed until after the road described above was built so they are not as old.

There is a road named on the map as *From Argyle ... Main Road to Sydney.* This road became known as The Great South Road because it gave access to southern

This is a 2011 photo of the remnants of the road in the backyard of a house in Alpha Road. The original road is obvious when viewed on the ground but it is difficult to photograph. The lines drawn on the photo show the original level of the ground, the embankment which has a height of 3 feet and the level part of the road which was 18 feet wide.
Other roads shown on the map

New South Wales and Victoria. The first part of this road to be made ran from the site of the future Camden in a south westerly direction and gave access to the 'wild cattle' stockyards which Governor Macquarie had built at Cawdor sometime between 1815 and 1820.[5] This road continued south after a road over the Razorback Range built in 1832. The first section of the *Great South Road* is now called Cawdor Road and the part over the Razorback Range is now the Old Razorback Road.

In the lower left corner of the map there is a road called *Cobbity Road*. It is shown in an 1842 map leading to a crossing of the Nepean River and then on to Cobbitty.[6] Now days the road starts at the roundabout on Cawdor Road just west of Camden and leads into Sheathers Lane and Werombi Road while the early road shown on the map 1842 is now called Ellis Lane.

Running north from Exeter Street between Edward and Elizabeth Streets is a road bearing the name *Road from Hassall's Ford* now called Macquarie Grove Road. In 1812 Rowland Hassall received a grant of land just across the Nepean River which he called Macquarie Grove and Camden Airport is now on this land. Over the years Rowland and his sons acquired more land by grants or purchases and so were the main land holders north of the ford, hence the name on the map.

After Camden Village was established in the 1840s, a road from the corner of John and Broughton Streets was constructed. It joined the old road described above near the present day Park Street. Later the road was named Menangle Road.

Other features on the map
The map identifies a number of other features which existed in Camden in 1843.

Site of Saint John's Church

The site for Saint St John's Church was sold to William Broughton, the Anglican Bishop of Australia, by James and William Macarthur in 1841 for a nominal ten shillings.[7] Construction of the church started in 1840 but it was not completed until 1849.

Saint John's Glebe [8]

The map also shows *St John's Glebe* and the mortage document contains the following:

All that parcel of land marked Saint Johns Glebe on the said plan being the portion of land granted by the said James Macarthur and William Macarthur as a Glebe for the use of the incumbent of Saint Johns Church aforesaid containing by measurement one hundred and twenty acres more or less situated near the Village of Camden …
This land was later sold by the Church.

Thompson's Steam Mill

In 1843 Joseph Thompson bought the land at the north eastern corner of the Sydney Road and Edward Street. Upon it he built his 'Thompsons Steam Mill' which ground wheat, an important crop in the district at that time.[7]

Village of Camden

A plan for the proposed village of Camden was drawn up in 1836. Sale of land commenced in 1841 and by 1843 some blocks of land had been sold but the details of these blocks are not shown on this map.

Surrounding the village there were many areas which were named and their size given in the old Imperial measurements of acres, roods and perches. Whether these areas were farms or only named paddocks could not be determined. Their names often related to other features on the map. Thus Southbridge and Northbridge related to their proximity to the Cowpasture Bridge and Eastford and Westford were on either side of *Road from Hassall's Ford.*

Acknowledgements
The comments from Peter Hayward and John Wrigley are appreciated.

References
1 Manning Clark *A History of Australia.* Vol. 3, pp.293-5. Melbourne University Press. 1979.
2 Land Titles Office, Old System Titles, Book 5 Number 502; File Plan 192218 SH 1/2.
3 Lachlan Macquarie *Journal of His Tours in New South Wales ... p. 8.*
4 Peter Mylrea *Belgenny Farm 1805-183: The Early Years of the Macarthurs at Camden.* Camden Historical Society 2001.
5 Peter Mylrea *Camden District: A History to the 1840s.* Camden Historical Society 2002.
6 *Chart of the District of Camden* Mitchell Library 4 000/1 A 3004/Map 3.
7 Peter Mylrea *Macarthur's Village of Camden* in *Camden History* March 2011 vol. 3 p.23.
8 Glebe land: Land bequeathed to a specific parish or benefice so that its rental or crops may be employed to augment the income of their incumbents. (Macquarie Dictionary).

Dr Robert Melville Crookston, OBE

Pauline Downing

He was born and raised in Toowoomba, the son of a Moderator General of the Presbyterian Church of Australia. He trained at Melbourne University and graduated with first class honours in medicine and won what was called the exhibition in surgery. He worked at Royal Melbourne Hospital and was later offered a prestigious position assisting one of the most prominent surgeons, but instead chose to come to Sydney and not long after decided to live and work in Camden. He purchased the house in 75 John St Camden in 1913. He continued to live there until his death in 1978 at age 91. His surgery was in the front room of the house. He was a noted surgeon, also the Government Medical Officer for Camden.

He rode a horse to visit patients in the early years, but later purchased a car. Dr Crookston brought modern surgery to Camden. Surgery became his life, it meant everything to him. He was in a busy practice, but had many community interests.

Robert Campbell of Looking Class, Camden at 71 Argyle St, Camden, (pers comm 20.06.2011) said he was dead for 9 minutes during an operation by Dr Crookston for tonsillitis. He was aged 14 at the time in 1964. The anaesthetist from Campbelltown who was to assist was unable to attend the hospital, instead his wife substituted, she was also a doctor, but she overdosed Robert with ether and he died of that overdose. Dr Crookston opened up Robert under his sternum inserted his hand inside and massaged Robert's heart until it began to beat.

Robert was transferred to a city hospital, unconscious for some days. When he woke, he was astonished that there was a large wound in his stomach, He wondered if Dr Crookston had removed his tonsils that way!

Dr Crookston loved Camden, its people and country atmosphere. He was the president of the Camden Show Society between 1957-1962.

Crookston was the mayor of Camden in the 1930s. One of the lasting reminders of his office are the jacaranda trees that are in many of Camden's town streets and line the median strip in Argyle Street.

His second daughter Suzanne (Williams) was a noted horsewoman who in 1954 disappeared when the ship was off Perth, while sailing to England to train for the Olympic horse jumping team. There was a suspicion of murder

**Elsie Pyrke 1929
Dr Crookston's Receptionist
(Camden Images)**

as Mrs Williams had been afraid of being poisoned and along with several other mysterious happenings her parents wanted a charge of foul play or murder to be investigated. Suzanne had married a New Zealand Army officer whom she met on holidays in New Zealand, but he was killed in WWII.

My own personal experience of Dr Crookston began in the late 1960s when my youngest son was burning with fever one day when the outside temperature was well over 100 degrees Fahrenheit. None of the local doctors would see him, and I was very worried about him. As I was rather new in the town I looked up all the doctors in the phone book and called Dr Crookston's surgery. His receptionist, Miss Pyrke, said to come straight away. I remember she was a rather old fashioned older woman with a rather elaborate hair style.

When we entered the large hallway of the house on 75 John Street, the temperature inside was around 25 degrees lower than outside. I noticed that the floor boards were really wide and looked hand adzed.

We waited in the large waiting room on the right hand side of the hallway, then were ushered into his large surgery on the opposite side of the hall. The room had 12 foot (4 metre) ceilings. Dr Crookston was very myopic at that stage of his life, in his 80s and had long given up surgery but was a well respected man still for his knowledge and diagnostic skills. His spectacles had extremely thick lenses to compensate for his failing eyesight.

He became our personal doctor, although my two sons were very much in awe of him (read here rather frightened of a man so old). Dr Crookston was the only medico that fixed my recurring throat infections, in fact the only doctor that looked at my throat after complaining to my previous GPs. He told me I had tonsillitis and then I thought, "He has lost the plot..." and informed him that I had my tonsils out at an early age, as did most of my generation.

Dr Crookston gave me a hard stare and said that maybe so, but the surgeon had not cut them properly and they had grown back, I had a perfectly good, but very inflamed set of tonsils. And I still have them. He told me that day, if I got another episode of tonsillitis I would have to have them extracted. That threat must have worked, I have never had another bout of tonsillitis from that day to this.

Towards the end of his life he became so poor sighted that he was unable to read and I had heard that his family had asked anyone willing to come and read to him.

It was something I really wanted to do, but was too shy or afraid of Mrs Crookston, who was a very well spoken and to me a rather haughty woman and I was afraid she would reject my offer, I had not been in the town for very long and was not a 'local'. Young people are very susceptible to being rejected and I was very afraid of that. I have regretted to this day not knock-

CAMDEN HISTORY

Journal of the Camden Historical Society

September 2012 Volume 3 Number 3

CAMDEN HISTORY
Journal of the Camden Historical Society Inc.
ISSN 1445-1549
Editor: Dr Ian Willis

Management Committee
President: John Wrigley OAM
Vice Presidents: Dr Ian Willis, Bob Lester
Secretary: Doug Barrett
Assistant Secretary: Julie Wrigley
Treasurer: Ray Herbert
Assistant Treasurer:
Immediate Past President: Cathey Shepherd
General Committee: Dr Karen Farmer   Sharon Greene
                    Rene Rem   Peter Hayward OAM
                    Janice Johnson   Robert Wheeler

Honorary Auditor: Jim Hunter
Honorary Solicitors: Bowring, Macaulay and Barrett

Society contact:
P.O. Box 566, Camden, NSW 2570.   Online <http://www.camdenhistory.org.au>

Meetings
Meetings are held at 7.30 p.m. on the second Wednesday of the month except in January. They are held in the Museum. Visitors are always welcome.

Museum
The Museum is located at 40 John Street, Camden, phone 4655 3400 or 46559210. It is open Thursday to Sunday 11 a.m. to 4 p.m., except at Christmas. Visits by schools and groups are encouraged. Please contact the Museum to make arrangements. Entry is free.

Camden History, Journal of the Camden Historical Society Inc
The Journal is published in March and September each year. The Editor would be pleased to receive articles broadly covering the history of the Camden district . Correspondence can be sent to the Society's postal address. The views expressed in articles are expressly those of the authors and are not necessarily endorsed by the society.

Donations
Donations made to the Society are tax deductible. The accredited value of objects donated to the Society are eligible for tax deduction.

(Cover Frances Warner at Camden Park House. Photo Courtesy Camden Narellan Advertiser/Jeff de Pasquale)

CAMDEN HISTORY
Journal of the Camden Historical Society Inc.

September 2012, Vol 3 No 3

Contents

Frances Warner Ian Willis	74
Tracing the Untraceable - Camden's Great War Nurses Laura Cole	79
"Sketches from my Notebook": A Portrait of Sister Hester Morton, Great War Nurse Laura Cole	88
European Explorers in the Camden Region Peter Mylrea	90
A Practical Partnership: library, museum and family history society co-operation at Camden Jo Oliver	97
Camden in the News Janice Johnson	105
Yearning, Longing and the Remaking of Camden's Identity: the myths and reality of 'a country town idyll' Ian Willis	107
Local Government, Camden Municipality and Nepean Shire Peter Mylrea	118

Frances Warner
talks about Camden Park House
Eat History, History Week 2011.
Camden Historical Society, 14 September 2011

Ian Willis

Camden Park housekeeper Frances Warner spoke at the September meeting of the Camden Historical Society about domestic arrangements in the Georgian mansion house.

Frances told the attentive audience that in the colonial days a lot of items for the house came out from England including furniture, books, newspapers, china and porcelain and kitchenware of all sorts. 'The blue and white Coalbrookdale dinner service with the Macarthur crest was purchased by James Macarthur in 1838. This is now in a cabinet outside the main dining room. Many pieces are carefully stored and wrapped in paper. A treasure trove to be enjoyed in many years to come,' Frances said.

'The dining table can seat 14 people with comfort. The chairs are cedar and green leather. These were made for Camden Park House,' she said.

In the early days before Frances arrived at Camden Park things were done a little differently. 'Food preparation at Camden Park House was in the west wing. There were external bakers' ovens in the courtyard area, a butcher shop and food storage. The butcher's block was still in the room. There was a walk-in pantry, a scullery room with wooden sinks, a small store room, the main kitchen and a staff room,' she said.

Camden Park House has had extensive gardens since the 1840s. Nursery gardens were developed by William and James Macarthur, as well as extensive house gardens supplying fruit, vegetables and cut flowers. Milk was supplied to the house from the dairies on the estate.

'The gardeners grew most of the produce used for cooking. Vegetables were grown in the house garden and also in the lower garden, near the dairy, which supplied the milk and cream. Fruit trees were in the house garden and also at the Estate orchard. Rabbits were raised in sheds and later on chickens. The glut of produce was bottled (some still on display in the large cellars) and jars of jams of many varieties. The gardeners also grew many different types of flowers for the house. Each Friday, 'Old Harry', my father-in-law would bring maiden hair ferns from the hot house, to place in the house on the large round tables. In summertime the ferns were placed in the fireplaces,' she said.
'Even in the 1950s and 1960s produce was still grown in the gardens below the house,' she said.

Frances Warner at Camden Park House where she has worked for 45 years.
(Photo Courtesy Camden-Narellan Advertiser/Jeff de Pasquale)

Sir Reginald and Lady Helen Stanham came back to Camden Park House from England in the 1940s. 'Marian McKay, who was in their employ in England, travelled with them. She became the housekeeper until she left to marry Robert Millwood in 1966', she said.

In those days things were more formal. 'All meals were checked before delivery through the serving hatch in the main dining room at the start of the hall in the butler's pantry,' recalls Frances.

'The kitchen was moved up into the main part of the house in the 1950s. A modernised kitchen that was much easier to use. Lady Stanham and Marian set out the menu for each week. A lot of entertaining was done in the main dining room. The brass dinner gong was struck thirty minutes before the dinner service started. A different uniform was worn to prepare the dining room for dinner guests. It was a grey dress with a blue and grey concertina pleated half apron. The staff then changed to a white starched half apron and a ribbon threaded head covering for table service,' she said. 'The breakfast room near the kitchen is now more often used for dining. Lady Stanham had a button under the carpet square. She would step on this. The bell would ring in the cellar and be heard in the kitchen,' Frances said.

Lady Stanham's son Quentin, his wife Antonia (Toni) and children John and Jane Macarthur Stanham lived in the East Wing in the 1960s. 'Meals were served in a small dining room off the kitchen or the children had high tea in the nursery. These were cooked by 'Pinki', Ethel Warner, my mother-in-law. The stove was a coke fuelled Aga,' said Frances.

'Toni enjoyed cooking, but had a number of cooks over time. Some long term or when needed for special functions. One cook was Mrs Louisa Bainbridge, her husband operated the dairy and her daughter, Margaret Mills, was a downstairs cleaner. Madeline Thurston, who was the first Australian Le Cordon Bleu to graduate in Paris. She also gave private cooking in her garden cottage. Dame Helen Blaxland (Toni's mother) cooked from Sydney, and, Joyce and Ruth were invited to help with large functions. Harry Warner would be behind the bar, while I would help with sewing and then busy doing the dishes,' said Frances.

'Quentin's favourites were Red Wine Beef Casserole, Salmon Kedgeree, and Treacle Tart,' she said.

Frances told how she moved into Camden Park House as a newly wed some 45 years ago after she married Harry, the estate gardener. 'I met Harry on a blind date in Camden Hospital,' she said.

'I was nervous on my arrival. I was overwhelmed by the big house,' she said. Frances has worked for many years as the housekeeper. These days a typical week for Frances starts on Monday with 'cleaning and tidying' the library, then moving on to the front hall, along with other duties.

The house has been used for a host of functions over the years. Frances remembers one of them. 'Dame Helen organised a fundraiser for the National Trust, an early colonial dining treat. No electric lighting downstairs, only candle light. Candles on window sills, mantles and any flat surface. Silver candle holders down the centre of the dining room look fantastic. The fire places provided extra light in the dining room, drawing room and library rooms. June Holdsworth and myself were kept busy, keeping the candles aglow and also providing table service. Joyce and Ruth cooked the corned beef, boiled cabbage, mash potato and carrots,' she said.

Open weekends called for special effects. 'One Camden Park House open weekend, Dame Helen had set the dining table as if the diners had just finished their meal. Wine glasses with a little wine in the glass. Some lipstick. Small desert plates with fruit peels, seeds or pips left on the plate. Linen serviettes crumpled, some on the table or fallen onto the floor. And with a lingering whiff of cigar smoke,' she recalled.

The house is now under the guidance of John and Edwina Macarthur Stanham. Edwina, among her many other responsibilities, is in charge of the kitchen. 'What a fantastic organised cook and film crew caterer. Slices, cakes, sandwiches and soup produced in no time for workers or visitors,' Frances said.

Celebrities have been regular visitors to the house as it is often used as a film set. 'I have seen the main dining room used for Robert Morley, Heinz Soup advertisement. As a snooker games room for *The Empty Beach* (Aust, 1985, thriller) with Bryan Brown, *Gosford Park* (USA, 2001, TV) setting for the *Australian Women's Weekly*,' she said.

The house also hosts important political dignitaries. 'I have served cucumber sandwiches and anchovy paste toast fingers and tea to Prime Minister Malcolm Fraser and Tamie Fraser in June 1982. They were going to the Camden Civic Centre for a Liberal Party Conference. I helped with morning tea for Her Excellency, Professor Marie Bashir in November 2010. Harry was invited to have a cup of tea and he did!' she said.

Frances and Harry raised their family of three children on the estate. 'Harry and I have been employed by the Macarthur family for over 90 years of combined service. Camden Park House is more than a job, it is being part of the family,' she said.

Acknowledgements
The author gratefully acknowledges the helpful comments and suggestions of Frances Warner on an earlier draft of this article.

Additional Sources
Iliana Stillitano. 'Tours add sparkle to housekeeper's role', *Wollondilly Advertiser,* 14 September 2011. Online @ http://www.wollondillyadvertiser.com.au/news/local/news/general/tours-add-sparkle-to-housekeepers-role/2290525.aspx?src=rss
'Sharing of festive memories', *Macarthur Chronicle, Camden Edition,* 13 December 2011, p. 7. Online @ http://macarthur-chronicle-camden.whereilive.com.au/news/story/camden-historical-society-shares-festive-memories/

Tracing the Untraceable - Camden's Great War Nurses

Laura Cole

Introduction

Historian E.H Carr argued that "there is no more significant pointer to the character of a society than the kind of history it writes or fails to write".[1] Wartime editions of *Camden News* afford readers significant understanding of local characters, news and gossip, both from the frontline (via letters and correspondence) and in the community. Given this, it is somewhat surprising that there remains an almost total absence of nurses' narratives. It is this premise which underpinned this study, which provides a meaningful snapshot of the lives of four ordinary nurses from Camden that served in the Great War; narratives which are largely overlooked in local archival material.

The following demonstrates that missing data and an absence of personal narrative has, in many cases, raised more questions than answers. Although personal journals and letters have come to dominate historical scholarship about the Great War, in the case of Camden's four nurses, this material was largely lacking. As such, the portraits of Camden's four nurses are largely constructed from military service records, newspaper records, local archival material and cemetery listings. In doing so, this project will provide support for the contention that the contribution of the ordinary Australian nurse in World War One, has been poorly recorded and as a result remains largely under-valued, particularly where there is an absence of personal narrative.

Camden's Nurses

Mary Theresa Morton McAnene
(1880- August 24, 1924)

The picture that can be constructed from archival material of the life of Mary Morton McAnene, although fragmented, is the most complete of the four nurses in this project, most likely by virtue of her position as Matron of Camden District Hospital from circa 1913.

Born in Kiama in 1880, McAnene joined the staff of Camden Hospital initially as a probationer nurse, expected not only to nurse, bathe and feed patients but also to scrub the floors, clean the wards, instruments and dressings, working from 6am to 8am and earning around £52 a year. In 1902, the hospital had twelve beds, an operating theatre and cottage for infectious diseases. Although records do not show exactly when McAnene joined the staff, it is most likely the hospital was running at a similar capacity when she joined. Furthermore, it is unknown when McAnene progressed to Matron, with archives only indicating she was afforded the position when the Matron of the time took extended leave to go to France.

Nursing staff at Camden Hospital 1910 (Camden Images/Camden Historical Society)

To put the scope of her pre-work as Matron in perspective, it is necessary to consider that by 1913, Camden District Hospital was treating more than 200 patients a year, with a staff made up of Matron, Nurse, three Probationer Nurses and two Resident Doctors. Despite new accommodation being built, many nurses didn't stay long and preferred to go to larger training hospitals where they could obtain their training certificates; something that perhaps provides some insight into why McAnene was afforded the position as Matron in the first instance. Camden initially couldn't become a training hospital because McAnene was not part of the the ATNU (Australian Trained Nurses Union), but was invited to sit for her exams. As a consequence, by March 1915, it was admitted as a training hospital.

In January of that year, records indicated that McAnene took extended leave with full pay for three months. Her service record indicates that she joined the AANS (Australian Army Nursing Service) in mid June 1915 at age 35, with her sister Rose appointed as acting Matron in her absence. The only Roman Catholic nurse in this project, McAnene embarked from Australia on July 14, but was seemingly not despatched for duty until November. An article in the *British Nursing Journal* discusses the arrival of McAnene and others on September 11, 1915, with McAnene listed in the contingent of 42 nurses to be sent to convalescent depots while the remainder of the unit was assigned to hospital ships.

Indeed, McAnene was initially appointed No. 3 AGH (Australian General Hospital), where she worked for almost two years (until August 1917) until she was sent to work with No 1 AAH (Australian Army Hospital) in Harefield, United Kingdom, a seemingly chaotic convalescent depot growing to the size of a normal military hospital (described by Butler as an example of "casual improvisation",[2] awkward to manage and difficult to command). The patients at Harefield were mainly surgical cases (often heavy surgical and blinded cases), with a capacity for over 1000 beds for casualties from France. Her service record indicates that she worked without incident until early December, when she was sick and sent to the Australian Nurses Hospital in Southwell Gardens and never quite recovered. She was admitted to Southwell Gardens again in mid January, then marched out for return to Australia on Mt Balmoral Castle on February 1, 1918.

The medical report in her service record suggests that although she was "much improved by voyage" she still felt unfit to go on duty, accounting for her return to Australia. Furthermore, it notes:

> In January had been feeling tired and ill for some time. Had often experienced similar weakness and could not carry when work was very heavy. She had some pain in left chest. Some pain in left axilla (?) was noted. Improved with next 2 months, but still feels and looked unfit for work.

The cause for this illness was attributed to natural debility combined with the strain of work. This is pertinent when considering the reparation payments she received post war, whereby she was to receive £2/2/- per week for twelve months from February 24, 1921, with her pension totalling £4/4/- per week exclusive of a pension for maintenance in an approved Sanatorium "in view of the fact that there are no facilities for treating that class of patient in Departmental institutions".[3]

In regards to her position as Matron at Camden Hospital, *Camden News* gives an account of her first visit to the Hospital in May 1918 after her return from active service, noting her "great pleasure"[4] at all the structural improvements and additional equipment supplied to the hospital in her absence. McAnene continued to suffer from health problems, with hospital records showing that in 1919 she requested two months leave. Similarly, in March, her appointment to the AANS was officially terminated. Later, in July 1920, the local newspaper reported the continued ill health of Matron McAnene, indicating that it was "not the desire of the board"[5] to accept her resignation, unanimously deciding to grant her an extended leave of absence, however, in 1921, McAnene's appointment as Matron was officially terminated due to illness.

The only record about McAnene that exists past this point are the notices placed in both the local newspaper and the *Sydney Morning Herald* upon her death on August 25, 1924 at her residence Shalvah Private Hospital, Wentworth Falls. The death notice in the latter[6] (placed on September 1, 1924) interestingly attributes her death as "the effect of war service". Her file at the National Archives,[7] on the other hand, lists the cause of death being *Pulmonary Tuberculosis and Tubercular Meningitis*.

McAnene's grave is listed in the Faulconbridge General Cemetery Heritage Report, suggesting it is a site of historical significance. Bearing the AIF insignia, it is understood that the grave was erected by the Australian War Graves Office and is maintained in perpetuity by the Office. Contrary to many headstones at this time, this meant that no separate application was needed to use the AIF insignia; as such- no further file exists for former Matron McAnene. McAnene's contribution to the AANS is also commemorated locally in Camden, with her name listed along with Ethel Lloyd and Hester Morton's, on the Memorial Gates leading in to Macarthur Park.

Rebecca Margaret Williams Stafford (1882-?)

Born in Camden in 1882, Williams joined the AANS on August 15, 1915 as part of the No 10 AGH. Australian Trained Nurses Association (ATNA) records suggest that previous to this, Williams trained at Claremore Private Hospital, Sydney (February 1908 to February 1912). Inconsistencies in her service record present difficulties in ascertaining an accurate timeline of her service with the AANS. This said, it is nevertheless clear that unlike the other three nurses in the study, who served mostly in England, Williams worked almost solely in France.

Her service record seems to indicate that upon disembarkation, Williams proceeded for duty to No.1 AGH in Heliopolis in March 1916. On July 12, she proceeded for duty at No 32 Stn. Hospital, then on August 2, 1916, reported for duty at No 2 AGH, Wimereux, France, where she worked until March 19, when she was sent to hospital with suspected German measles. No 2 AGH was a large hospital with a capacity for 1900 beds, and dealt with general battle casualties. It came to specialise in the treatment of fractures, with its fractured femur ward known as the 'Carpenters Shop'.[8]

After being treated for German measles, she rejoined her unit from hospital, only to be re-hospitalised on April 29 and sent to a convalescent home in Boulogne, France, on May 7, 1917. Although she rejoined her unit on May 19, on the 27th, a medical board held at the Boulogne base recommended 21 days of sick leave to England, finding that she was suffering from debility following a severe attack of Erythema Multiforme (a type of hypersensitivity reaction in response to medications, infections, or illness). On July 19, her records indicate that she was retained in England for health reasons and was promptly assigned to No 3 AAH. In August it seems as though Williams worked for a period at No 1 Birmingham War Hospital, until she was detached from there to work at No. 3 AAH. In October she was promoted to Sister, returning to Australia on March 31, 1919, seemingly working her passage home as part of the nursing staff on Hospital Ship 'Benalla'. Arriving in Australia on May 31, Williams was reported to be in good condition, with her Medical report noting "Measles. France 1917/ Mumps Egypt 1915/ Erythema France 1917", despite little evidence that Williams served in Egypt at this time.

Any other details about Williams' life or service were not found, making it difficult to draw many meaningful conclusions about her work. The only other source that does provide a degree of insight into Williams' home life is the correspondence from her mother (in Williams' service record) who enquired to the military base in March 1919 about information concerning her daughters return to Australia. Most pertinent to this study of Williams is her mothers first letter, dated March 19, 1919, Mrs E. Williams cites "urgent domestic reasons" as the principle reason for the enquiry. While the nature of this emergency is unknown, it would provide an interesting point for study should additional sources become available.

Hester Louise Mars Morton
(May 25, 1878- January 1976)

Born in Camden, to parents Dr Selby Mars Morton and Ann Isabel Horsely Lord, Hester is unique from the other three nurses in this study in that she trained not as a nurse, but as a masseuse.

The youngest of six siblings, Hester Louise Mars was the only child of Selby and Ann to be born in Camden, with local records suggesting Selby's medical posting in the area was relatively short. Around 1881, for example, the family seems to have been based in Goulburn, with Selby and four of his children buried at St Saviours, the local Anglican Church.

A number of sources give insight into the high societal position held by her family. Firstly, marriage notice from the *Sydney Morning Herald*[9] notes her father's membership in the Royal College of Surgery and his father John Morton's previous post as superintending Surgeon in the Honourable East India Company Service (HEICS). Similarly, University of Sydney records indicate that Selby Morton was one of only two students who graduated in 1874 with a Bachelor of Medicine, then again in 1877 with a Doctor of Medicine.[10]

Hester graduated from the University of Sydney herself in 1910 as a massage student, later joining the AANS on October 22, 1915, as part of the Masseurs No 2 Unit General Hospital. For reasons unknown, she lists her age as 30, despite family genealogy records indicating she would have been 37. Similarly, in her writings for the official record[11] Hester says that she joined the AANS early in November 1915 and left Sydney later that month on the *Orsova*, calling at Freemantle en route to Egypt. Much of her account, including descriptions of her leave in Perth reads very much like a travel journal, as do her first impressions of Egypt, where she marvels at the decorations and architecture of Gazera Palace, where she was stationed for four months. As far as work was concerned she describes how there was not a great deal, but "just enough" massage. After leaving Gazera she went to the Sporting Club for two weeks then transferred to Luna Park for two weeks- 'the work at the former was very light but very heavy at the last... many bad and heavy cases passed through during that time, fractures of different kinds and injured backs'. Furthermore, she describes how the high spirits of the men made their workload seem lighter.

Hester's departure from Egypt was, in her own words 'rather hurried'. Given marching orders to proceed to France, Morton was assigned to No 6 Imperial Hospital at Rouen, France, then transferred a month later to No 1 AGH, where she was sent to help as a Staff Nurse, given there was very little massage to be done. She describes a great influx of trench foot and how the nurses were working double the ordinary hours for a number of months (No 1 AGH had a capacity for 1300 beds during the Big Push), before a hospital ship relieved them of most of their most acute cases.

After five months in France, Morton was transferred to England and went to No 3 AAH in Dartford, Kent in January 1917. No 3 AAH was an Infectious Diseases Hospital specialising in nerve surgery and the treatment of war related nerves and neuroses. It grew to 1400 beds, and was most likely near or at this peak whilst Morton was nursing there. Morton's account ends in June 1919, where she describes the workload as "normal and our hours much less". Discharged on June 25, 1919, Morton returned to Australia on September 23rd, from England.

Little is known about Morton's post war life, beyond the fact that she made a claim for reparation benefits in June 1964.

Ethel Graham Lloyd
(c.1891- ?)

The name of Ethel Graham Lloyd is on the Macarthur Park Memorial Gates. In comparison to Hester Morton, whereby her narrative in the Butler archives, adds significant insight into her life and service, very little is known about Lloyd beyond her service record.[12] Born in Charters Towers, Queensland, Lloyd enlisted AANS quite late in comparison with the other nurses in this study, in April 1917. Listing her age as 25, Lloyd identifies herself as being part of the AANS 1st Military District since December 29, 1916.

Embarking from Sydney on May 9, 1917 and disembarking at Plymouth from Australian HMAT (His Majesty's Australian Transport) 'A38', her service record indicates that she was first posted to Croydon War Hospital, where she worked for a number of months (late August to mid December 1917). In mid December, she reported for duty at No 3 AAH in Dartford, which, as aforementioned, specialised in the treatment of war related nerves and neuroses. In July 1918- she was detached from duty with No 3. AAH, and sent to the No 38 Stationary Hospital in Italy, returning to duty at No. 3 AAH on September 28. In December, Lloyd took four days leave to go to Rome, with her service record noting that she disembarked at Southampton from Italy to Administrative HQ in London on January 22, 1919. On February 9, Lloyd was detached from duty with No 3. AAH and transferred to No. 2 AAH for duty. Located in Southall, No 2 AAH was originally designed to cope with limbless soldiers from the battlefields of the Somme, but by 1917-18 was exclusively treating amputees and fitting artificial limbs.

In March, Lloyd was admitted sick to Southwell Hospital in South Kensington, although no medical reports are attached to her service record in relation to this period. She remained at Southwell for two weeks, when she was discharged to duty with No. 2 AAH, where she was promoted from Sister from Staff Nurse on July 1st and where she worked until her return to Australia on July 23, 1919.

While her record indicates that her appointment with the AANS was terminated on November 1919, unfortunately, no other records about Lloyd other than this service record, seem to exist.

What this means

The stories of Camden's four nurses, though far from complete, are made all the more significant not only for the scholarship they add to local studies research, but because of the length of time they have gone unnoticed in the archives. Stories of ordinary nurses like McAnene, Morton, Lloyd and Williams that are largely devoid of first hand narrative material, are excluded in academia, with historians instead seeking to focus on the hardships and psychological effects of war on Australian nurses, supporting their narratives with first person accounts. The experiences of the ordinary undecorated nurse have been largely excluded or generalised in historical narrative due to a preoccupation with the nurse as a war icon; focusing largely on nursing as a whole, making differences between individuals difficult to determine.

It is not surprising that this research raises many more questions than it perhaps answers. It provides significant scope for further research, both in terms of local history as well as the commemoration of war nurses in wider society- why was the ordinary nurse largely forgotten upon her return to Australia? Was her contribution to the war merely overshadowed by the soldier and decorated nurse or matron or were there other issues at play? Was it her choice; did she want to be celebrated? Of course, academics like Dr. Ruth Rae and others have touched briefly upon these issues in their research, but it would be worth considering them on a deeper level, particularly in line with the historical void around war reparation for nurses. While the amateur research skills of the author leave this study flawed with a lot of missing data, it provides a base from which further study can continue.

Endnotes
1. Carr, EH *What is History*? (2nd ed.), Penguin Books, London, 1990, p.53. 2. Cited in Goodman, R "Our War Nurses" p56
3. *A2487* 1924/8715 *[Mary M McAnene - Correspondence re special allowances for ex-members of the Australian Army Nursing Service while under treatment]*
4. Camden News, May 2, 1918
5. *Camden News,* July 18, 1920
6. "Deaths" *The Sydney Morning Herald (NSW : 1842 - 1954),* Monday 1 September 1924, page 8
7. "Mary M McAnene - Correspondence re special allowances for ex-members of the Australian Army Nursing Service while under treatment (1920-24)" file A2487, National Archives of Australia, Canberra
8. Rae, R *Veiled Lives* p156
9. *Sydney Morning Herald* Thursday 21 December 1865, p7
10 "Alumni by Name" Sydney Medical School, University of Sydney, March 2010
11. See AWM41
12. Ethel Graham Lloyd, AIF (AANS), *Attestation Papers,* Australian Archives, Canberra, 1917

Bibliography
'Alumni by Name,' Sydney Medical School, University of Sydney. Accessed online in March 2010 @ http://sydney.edu.au/medicine/people/alumni/alumnibyname.php?ln=M&groupby=y
'Arrival of Nurses of the Australian Army Nursing Service,' *The British Journal of Nursing* September 11, 1915, p211
Barker, M. *Nightingales in the Mud- the Digger Sisters of the Great War 1914-18* Sydney: Allen and Unwin, 1989.
Butler Papers, *Nurses Narratives: Hester Morton* AWM Box 41, Australian War Memorial, Canberra.
Camden Museum Archives, files 'World War One,' 'Camden Hospital'
'Camden, Saturday,' *The Sydney Morning Herald (NSW : 1842 - 1954),* Monday 5 July 1915, page 11.
Carr, E.H. *What is History?* Penguin Books, London, 1990.
'Deaths,' *The Sydney Morning Herald (NSW : 1842 - 1954),* Monday 1 September 1924, p8
Melanie Sbroja, Email Correspondence, Office of Australian War Graves to author, 4 October 2011
Judith Cornell, Email, Archivist at Australian College of Nursing Library to author, 21 October 2011
Ruth Rae, Email correspondence to author, August- October 2011
Ethel Graham Lloyd, AIF (AANS), *Attestation Papers,* Australian Archives, Canberra, 1917
Faulconbridge Conservation Management Plan, *Hubert Architects, Blue Mountains Cemeteries* April 2003 p42
Goodman, R. *Our War Nurses– The History of the Royal Australian Army Nursing Corps,* Boolarong Publications, Brisbane, 1988.
Hester Louise Mars Morton AIF (AANS), *Attestation Papers,* Australian Archives, Canberra,1916
Mary Morton McAnene, AIF (AANS), *Attestation Papers,* Australian Archives, Canberra,1915
"Mary M McAnene - Correspondence re special allowances for ex-members of the Australian Army Nursing Service while under treatment (1920-24)" file A2487, National Archives of Australia, Canberra
Mary McAnene gravestone photograph. Accessed online on 15 September 2011 @ http://www.flickr.com/photos/orange-tim/4102231169/ ()
Rae, R *Australian World War One Nurse Leaders — Missing in Action* Burwood: College of Nursing: 2006
Rae, Ruth "Reading between unwritten lines: Australian Army nurses in India, 1916-19" *Journal of the Australian War Memorial,* May 2002 (36). Online @ http://www.awm.gov.au/journal/j36/nurses.asp
Rae, Ruth *Veiled Lives: Threading Nursing History into the Fabric of the First World War* Burwood: The College of Nursing, 2009
Rebecca Margaret Williams Stafford AIF (AANS), *Attestation Papers,* Australian Archives, Canberra, 1915
Rees, Peter. *The Other Anzacs: Nurses at War 1914-1918.* Sydney: Allen and Unwin, 2008
"The Monaro Pioneers Project - Pioneers and Settlers Database", data base, RootsWeb Family Trees. Online @ http://wc.rootsweb.ancestry.com/cgi-bin/igm.cgi?op=GET&db=monaropioneers&id=I71771

Biography
Laura Cole is a Camden local and a University of Wollongong graduate with a BA (Deans Scholars) in History/European Studies, minoring in Spanish. Her current research interests include war commemora-

tion and memorial building, European immigration and language policy.

"Sketches from my Notebook": A Portrait of Sister Hester Morton, Great War Nurse

Laura Cole

There is now a wealth of literature devoted to the nurses who served during the First World War. Despite this, it is curious to note the almost total absence of local histories that focus on the ordinary nurse. Sister Hester Morton was one of a number of nurses from the Camden area to join the Australian Army Nursing Service. This study has uncovered a wealth of information about her service hidden within her personal narrative in the Australian War Memorial's Butler Papers, which consist of a series of nurses' narratives collected by Australian Army Medical Services Historian, A.G Butler. The AWM have generously allowed this previously unrealised source to be published here in full; allowing for great insight into Great War Nursing.

Particularly interesting in these 'Sketches' is Morton's tendency to mostly exclude unpleasant experiences in her writings for the official record and the subsequent great length at which she writes of her experience as a tourist on leave. Another issue raised by Morton's narrative is the fact that the service in Egypt that she discusses, is absent from her service record- but why? Historian Ruth Rae (author of a number of books about Australian war nursing) suggests that it was not uncommon for nurses to be requisitioned on route to England by the Matron-In-Chief to assist nurses in Egypt if there was a particularly heavy time putting pressure on the nurses in Egypt; Morton arrived in Egypt when the Gallipoli evacuation was being planned, with the nursing leaders preparing for the worst. Rae did, however, indicate that it is somewhat surprising her service is not mentioned given that there were no Australian soldiers in Europe until after the evacuation of Gallipoli.

Sketches from my Notebook

I joined the AANS early in November 1915 and left Sydney in that month on the Orsova, calling at Fremantle where we had leave from 11am to 4pm. Motoring to and from Perth we saw every thing of interest in and around these two cities- King's Park and the Swan River were the most attractive to us. We continued our journey that night and had a most delightful trip to Aden where we stopped to take in coal. We did not get leave there however, but this was not a disappointment as the sight of the place from the boat was by no means enticing. The boat was surrounded by natives in different kinds of craft selling their wares, they formed a good deal of amusement in their bantering and particularly when the ships crew turned the hose on them when they....fled so many rats.

Our next stop was Suez where we landed and trained from Cairo. From the first Egypt just fascinated me, all the bright harmonious colours of the cast formed a sight of perpetual delight to me. I was stationed at Gazera Palace for four months. This place as one time used as a Palace and later as a Hotel. It had a wonderful marble staircase, I believe built for the time of Princess Eugene visited Egypt. The rest of the building had a good deal of Coptic decorations and mosaics. As far as our work was *concerned, we had normal times there, not a great deal of massage but just enough. During my stay at the Palace I had a trip to Luxor. Four most delightful days visiting tombs and ruins, I thoroughly enjoyed the opportunity of this to its fullest extent. After leaving Gazera I went to the Sporting Club for two weeks when I was transferred to Luna Park for two weeks, the work at the former was very light but very heavy at the last named. Many bad and heavy cases passed through during that time. Fractures of different kinds and injured backs. I found the men simply splendid, their spirits never drooped under the most severe suffering, they were always bright, witty. This of course made our labours seem lighter. I then received marching orders to proceed to France. My departure was rather hurried, but I had a couple of days at Alexandria. I saw most of the sights in the town and was much impressed at the old buildings and gardens. We left in the Salta and arrived at Marseilles in April 1916, we were not allowed off the boat for some days and were then at one of the hotels for a couple of days. It rained most of the time and our baggage was piled up on the pavement in the street and when we wanted anything from our cabin trunks had to open them to the full view of every French man woman or child who happened to be about and there were always crows, it was anything but pleasant. We enjoyed seeing everything we could in the limited time we had and think we did wonders in the couple of days. We trained to Rouen the journey being rather a trying one it occupied two days and one night and at some of the stations where we stopped we found difficulty in obtaining food. It was very cold and we arrived at Rouen in in the pouring rain and immediately sent to the different Imp. Hospitals. Six of us went to no ! Imperial Hospital. A month later I was transferred to no 1 AGH. There was very little massage to be done and the Sisters were very busy so Matron sent me to keep them as Staff Nurse. I was only there a month when I was again sent back to No. 6. I had a very busy time there may very acute but interesting cases came through. There was a great influx of trench feet, some very bad. I found the boys here very cheerful both Australians and English. After five months in France I was transferred to England and went to Dartford in Kent, I had two years very busy but most interesting work. When I was transferred to 1st AGH Sutton Veny. At first the work was extremely heavy. We were working first double the ordinary hours. This lasted about two months when a Hospital boat took most of our heavy cases home, relieving us of a good deal of the worst cases. At present the work is about normal and our hours much less.*

H. Mars Morton (AANS)
no 1 AGH
27-6-19 Sutton Veny

Nurses Narratives, H Mars Morton, 1919. AWM41/1014/5172259. With permission Australian War Memorial 31 January 2012.

European Explorers in the Camden Region

Peter Mylrea

Aboriginals have lived in the lands to the south west of Sydney for thousands of years.[1] In contrast it was only 222 years ago that European men first came into this area.

The first European explorers were Tench, Dawes and Worgan in 1790. They were followed by Governor Hunter's parties in 1795 and 1796 and by George Bass in 1796 and 1797.

Tench, Dawes and Worgan

The Tench, Dawes and Worgan exploration took place in the very early days after the founding of the settlement at Port Jackson. It was the first time any European men had travelled to the south west part of the colony.

The route of the expedition is shown in Maps 1 and 2. The party started from Rose Hill (Parramatta) on 1 August 1790.[2] They walked about ten kilometres on this day and made their first night's camp south of Prospect Hill.[3] On the second day they walked about 21 kilometres to their second camp (2 August). After walking about five kilometres on day 3 they came to the Nepean River and thus were the first European men to see this part of the Nepean. They crossed the river and walked up Navigation Creek for about 2 kilometres to their camp site (3 August).[4] This placed them at the foot hill of Razorback range and they climbed a small hill which, because of its shape, they called Pyramid Hill.[5] Navigation Creek is in the shallow valley between Belgenny Farm and Camden Park House. It joins the Nepean River about one kilometre upstream from the Macarthur Bridge

From this camp they walked on 4 August 1790 down stream on the right bank of the Nepean River. They walked through what was to become the suburbs of Spring Farm (western part), Elderslie and the western part of Kirkham.

They camped that night a little down stream from the present Macquarie Grove Bridge.

Dawes's map shows the course of the Nepean River between Navigation Creek and Macquarie Grove Road. His map is surprisingly accuractely when it is compared with modern day maps, especially considering he made all his observations in one day.

An indication of the type of country they walked through is given by Peter Cunningham who wrote in 1827 'The banks of the Cowpasture [Nepean] river near Narellan [Camden] are high, sandy, and clothed with goodly gum-trees, swamp oaks and scrubby brushwood'[6] Nowdays most of this country has been cleared for farming.

After camping at Macquarie Grove on the night of 4 August they started their return journey to Prospect Hill in a direction about 30 degrees east of north. This took

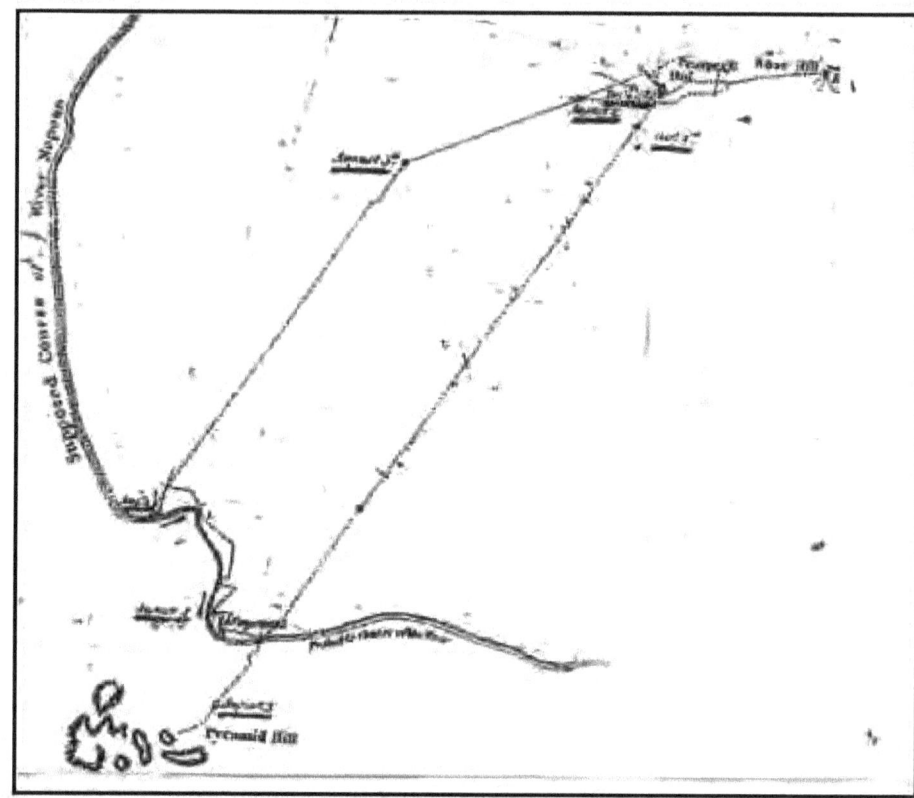

Map 1. Part of the Dawes's map of 1792 showing the route taken by Tench, Dawes and Worgan in their exploration in August 1790.

them through the land of the future suburbs of Cobbitty (eastern part), Harrington Park (northern part) and Oran Park.

Their route is shown on the map as straight lines. As the country through which they passed had no prominent topographical features it was probably necessary to do a compass march noting directions and distances. This would have been within Dawes's surveying skills and would allow them to find their way home. As far as can be estimated from present day maps they walked at least 90 kilometres during the seven days they were 'out'.

These three explorers were naval men, aged 28 to 32 years old at the time of their exploration.
Captain-Lieutenant Watkin Tench was the commanding officer of one of the four marines companies which sailed in the First Fleet and arrived in Botany Bay on 20 January 1788. He was a keen explorer and when not engaged in his military duties he spent his leisure as a member or leader of expeditions to the west and south west of the settlement, one of which is described above. He left Australia after nearly four

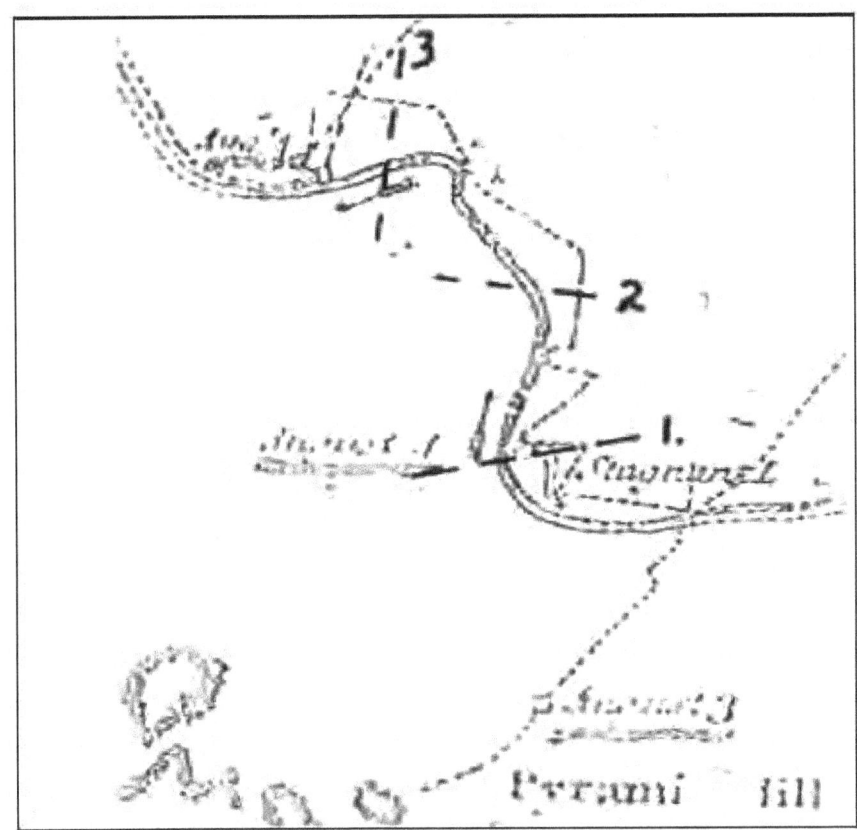

Map 2. A section of Dawes's map showing in more detail their route (dotted line) through future suburbs in the Camden district. The approximate location of present day structures are superimposed as broken lines; 1. Macarthur Bridge and Camden Bypass, 2. Cowpasture Bridge and Camden Valley Way, 3. Macquarie Grove Bridge and Macquarie Grove Road.

years when the marines returned to England with Governor Phillip in December 1791.[7]

William Dawes was a second lieutenant in the marines and arrived in the settlement in January 1788. Because of his professional skills he was employed on shore as an engineer and surveyor from March 1788. He accompanied a number of exploratory expeditions. He sailed for England with the marines in December 1791.[8]

George Boucher Worgan was a naval surgeon who served aboard the *Sirius* for a number of years including its voyage to Australia with the First Fleet. In the colony he joined a number of expeditions. Surprisingly he brought a piano with him on the *Sirius*. On his return to England in 1791 he left the piano with Mrs Elizabeth Macarthur, the wife of John Macarthur.[9]

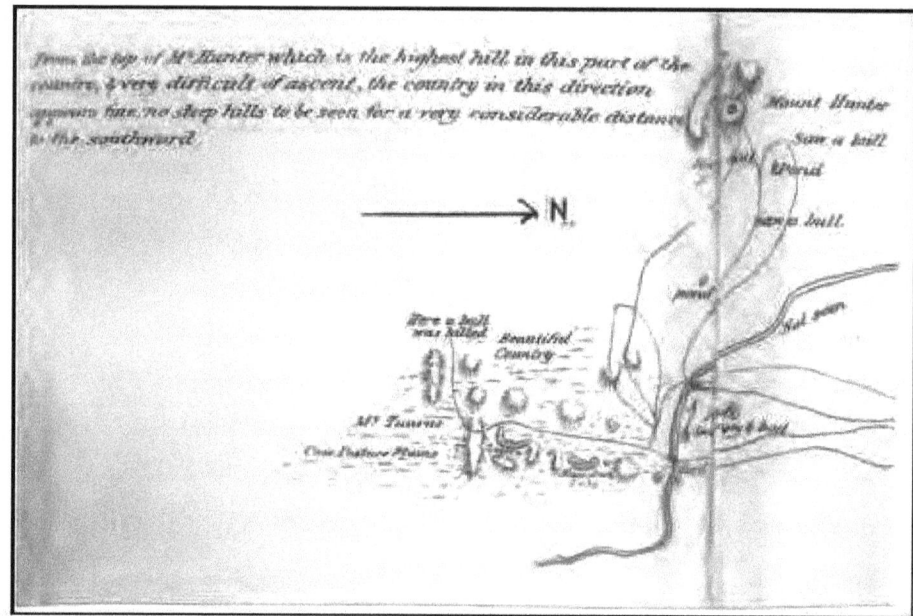

Map 3. Part of Governor Hunter's map of November 1796 showing his routes on Razorback Range in 1795 and 1796.

Governor Hunter

Cattle imported on board the First Fleet in 1788 escaped from the new settlement in Sydney and after some searching they were given up as lost. Nothing more was known about them for the next seven years but there were rumours that cattle had been sighted to the south west of the settlement. To confirm this Governor Hunter dispatched Henry Hacking in 1795 to investigate and he confirmed the presence of wild cattle.

Hunter wanted to see the cattle for himself and he led two expeditions to the Razorback Range. The first was in November 1795, two months after he became governor. He was accompanied by David Collins, the Judge Advocate, George Bass and Captain Waterhouse. They started from Parramatta and in the first section of their expedition they walked to the Nepean River. For this part of their journey they had the knowledge and maps from the expedition of Tench, Dawes and Worgan who had passed this way in 1790. From thereon they were in unexplored country. Hunter's map suggests that they followed Navigation Creek to its headwaters and in the process ascended the Razorback Range. The top of the Range is, in effect, a plateau about thirteen kilometres long and up to two kilometres wide. To the south was Mount Taurus and to the west Mount Hunter (now called Mount Prudhoe) both of which were named by Governor Hunter.[10]

The explorers saw many mobs of cattle which Hunter recognized as having the physical features of the cattle which the First Fleet had procured in Cape Town and which had escaped from the settlement. On his map Hunter marked an area as the 'Cow Pasture Plains' and so he was the first man to use the term 'Cow Pasture'.

Governor Hunter's second expedition was in June 1796. Again he ascended the Razorback Range. In November 1796 he produced a map which gave details of his routes and findings in both explorations.[11]

Captain John Hunter served in the navy and had been captain of *Sirius* in the First Fleet. He was also granted a dormant commission as successor to Governor Phillip in the case of Phillip's death. Hunter served in the settlement until he returned to England in 1792. He returned to the colony in September 1795 and was Governor of the colony from September 1795 to September 1800. He was a keen explorer, naturalist and a competent artist. [12]

George Bass

Bass was a member of Governor Hunter's expedition in 1795 to the Razorback. This was only two months after he arrived in Sydney. It introduced him to the Australian bush, information which he used in two explorations which he led in the next two years. One of these was to the west of Razorback Range and the other to the east.

The first exploration started about June 1796 when Bass and two companions set out from Mount Hunter (on the Razorback Range). They travelled in a westerly direction and passed near the sites of the present day The Oaks and Oakdale. They continued on and descended into the Burragorang Valley possibly near Brimstone Creek and crossed the Wollondilly River. They were the first Europeans to traverse this country. The exploration took fifteen days and during this they suffered from lack of water and shortage of food. [13, 14, 15, 16]

Notwithstanding his experiences on the first expedition Bass, with Mr Williamson, the Acting Commissary, undertook a second exploration. This time it was to the east of the Razorback. In September 1797 [17] they walked east from Mount Taurus (on the Razorback Range) to the coast. Their course is shown in Map 4 which was drawn by Governor Hunter and dated 1798.[18]

Bass and Williamson were the first European men to traverse the country between the Razorback Range and the Appin district. After leaving Mount Taurus they travelled a little south of east on a route which was about four kilometres south of present day Menangle and three kilometres north of Appin. The map describes this land as level to gentle ascents with good grass and pasturage, a description which fits reasonably with its present nature.

East of Appin they crossed the Georges River. From there on the country was 'mountainous and brushy land'. and involved crossing deep gorges on the Georges River, Stokes Creek, O'Hares Creek and Woronora River. They had intended covering twenty five miles in one day but it took them two days. When they reached the coast they rendezvoued with a whale boat the presence of which had been prear-

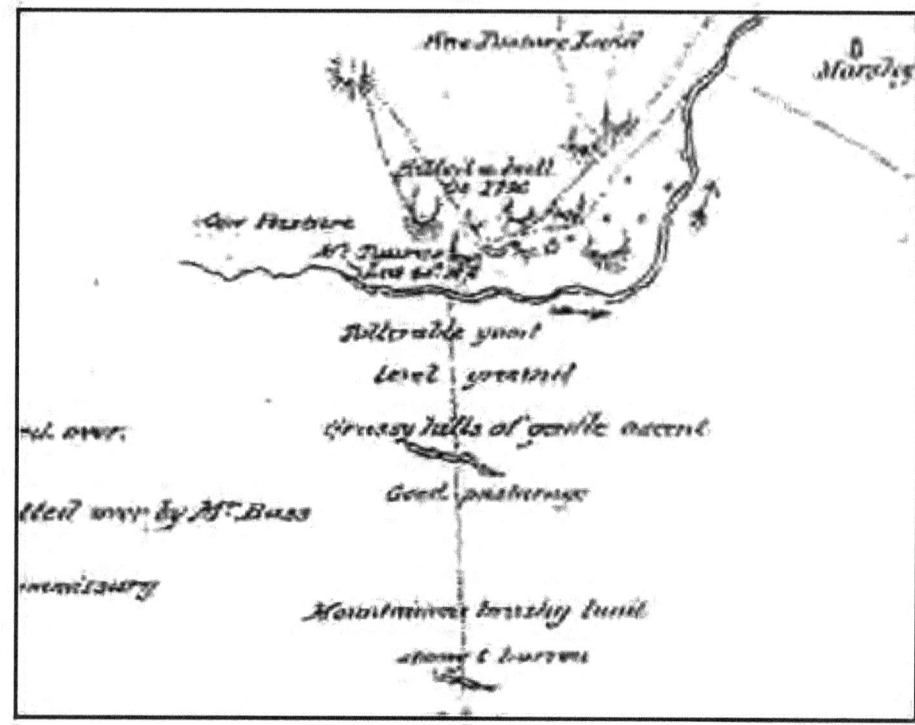

Map 4. Part of Governor's map of 1798 showing Bass's route between Mount Taurus and the Appin district on route to the coast.

ranged. This took them back to Sydney.

George Bass was a naval surgeon who arrived in Sydney in September 1795 on the same ship as did Hunter who was returning to the colony as Governor. Bass is best known for his sea explorations, often with Flinders. However he was also involved in a number of land explorations in Tasmania and in the Sydney region. He left Sydney in May 1799.

Others

The above men can be classed as the explorers of the Camden region. After them those who came into the Camden area were entering a region which was becoming well known. Barralier passed through the area on his explorations into the Burragorang Valley in 1802 [19] and George Caley made a number of visits to the region mainly collecting biological specimens. In 1803 Governor King, Hunter's successor, and Mrs King came on a tour of inspection [20] and in 1804 'a party of Ladies and Gentlemen with servants' rode to the top of the Razorback Range.[21]

References

1 Val Attenbrow *Sydney's Aboriginal Past.* University New South Wales Press, 2002.
2 Watkin Tench *Sydney's First Four Years.* Library of Australian History, 1979 pp. 74-75. Contains an introduction and annotation by L.F. Fitzhardinge.
3 Dawes did not give a scale on his map so the distances quoted are estimates based on present day maps.
4 Navigation Creek is in the shallow valley between Belgenny Farm and Camden Park House and is crossed by a bridge on the road.
5 See Mylrea *Camden History vol 1, pp. 87-92*
6 Cunningham, P. *Two Years in New South Wales* London 1827.
7 *Australian Dictionary of Biography.* Volume. 2
8 *Australian Dictionary of Biography* Volume 1.
9 *Australian Dictionary of Biography.* Volume 2.
10 David Collins *Account of the English Colony in New South Wales.* Vol. 1, p. 365.
11 Hunter *Historical Records of Australia.* vol. 1 p. 550; *Historical Records of NSW.* Vol. 3, p. 71.
12 *Australian Dictionary of Biography* Vol. 1.
13 Hunter *Historical Records of Australia* vol. 1, p. 550; *Historical Records of NSW* vol. 3 p. 71.
14 *Australian Dictionary of Biography.* Vol. 1.
15 Collins vol. 2 p.37; Else Mitchell. R. *Journal of the Royal Australian Historical Society* 1951, vol.37, pp 245-248.
16 Collins vol. 2 p. 37.
17 Hunter *Historical Records of Australia* vol. 2 p.117.
18 *Australian Dictionary of Biography,* vol. 1.
19 Peter Mylrea *Camden District – A history to 1840.* Camden historical Society.
20 *Sydney Gazette* 11 December 1803.
21 *Sydney Gazette* 24 February 1804.

A Practical Partnership: library, museum and family history society co-operation at Camden

Jo Oliver
Local Studies Librarian, Camden Council Library Service

The local library, historical society and family history society at Camden NSW work together in partnership to preserve & celebrate local history and develop a sense of place for local people. The partnership is guided by a memorandum of understanding and includes joint contribution to and referral of enquires, planning a yearly program of events and a number of shared ongoing projects.

Camden Library, Camden Museum and the Camden Area Family History Society room are co-located in the heart of the town of Camden on the southwest semi-rural fringe of Sydney metropolitan area. After thousands of years of indigenous land use along the Nepean River it was cattle escaped from the early Sydney colony who found their way to pasture on the river flats bringing the area to the notice of Europeans. In 1806 John Macarthur received a land grant of 5,000 acres and planned the village of Camden in 1841.

The Camden Local Government Area is the location of a projected population growth of 390.8% between 2011 and 2036, the highest in NSW. In light of this rapid change it is important that the existing history of the area is preserved and celebrated and a sense of place is developed and shared with new residents.

This paper outlines how the local library and two community groups seek to achieve these aims through a practical partnership based on co-location, co-operation and continuity.

Co-location

Camden Council Library Strategic Plan 2003 - 2010 describes Camden library as 'a focal point, a community hub, a centre of activity and a natural meeting place in much the same way as a village square provided a focal point in the past'.[1] When Camden Library was renovated in 2007 it was decided it should be 'a working country town library with a strong heritage and cultural focus'[2] and 'retain the heritage façade'.[3] The Camden Museum (1970, 1980, 1999) was located behind the library building (1867,1964) and a former fire station, originally Camden Temperance Hall (1867), also owned by council, was next door. The refurbishment planned that 'the existing library be physically linked with the Camden Museum and Fire Station to create an exciting cultural heritage precinct',[4] the library contain a local studies room and an adjoining room be provided rent free to Camden Area Family History Society.

The $2.3 million new complex resulting from these plans was opened in 2007 and joins the Camden library, museum and former fire station in a building with a common street entrance, a glassed roof galleria between previously separate buildings and the capacity to open and close different sections to allow for varying opening

Camden Library Museum Complex (Photo I Willis)

hours. In the view of Camden Council's General Manager the completed complex provided 'the community with a stronger sense of belonging and place' and 'a place based and people focused facility'.[5] This view matches recent comments from the public from feedback comments from Library Lover's Day February 2011 'I love my library because it's such a warm and welcoming place, and it's the true heart of my town. Marilyn. I love my library because it brings the world to me and I can give it to my family. Jennifer. I love my library because it feels like home. Joanne'.[6]

Camden Library, including its Local Studies Room, is open business hours Monday to Friday with two later night openings and Saturday mornings. Camden Museum is open Thursday to Sunday 11am - 4pm and the Camden Area Family History room is open Thursdays to Saturdays 10am – 3pm. Each group is able to change and adapt their hours without inconvenience to the other parts of the facility. Each group has individual responsibility for their own service and collection and at any one time a least one of the sections of the facility is open and able to take enquiries.

'Advantages of the co-location also include one stop convenience, better building maintenance and security and a sharing of infrastructure; a type of convergence'.[7]

Co-operation

At the same time as the Camden Library/ Museum refurbishment, a new Local Studies Librarian position was created and a partnership established between the three groups to 'share expertise, time and collections'.[8]

Sandall comments: 'the value of partnerships between public libraries and heritage groups should not be underestimated. It is a relationship that nurtures the ability of cultural institutions to sustain themselves as well as increasing their capabilities in improving the cultural sustainability of the community'.[9]

Jupp suggests, 'at the centre of the idea of partnership is collaboration. Partners retain separate identities, but they work together to meet a common goal. They share both objectives and rewards.' He comments 'partnership working remains a good idea but incredibly difficult in practice' and suggests, 'four processes common to successful partnerships: developing clear objectives, ensuring each partner also benefits individually as well as helping to achieve a common goal, building in evaluation, developing understanding and trust between partners'.[10]

Willis describes: 'the basis of the current partnership agreement between Camden Council and Camden Historical Society is to be found in the trust and understanding that has developed over the last 52 years between these two organizations'.[11] This relationship was formalized in a Memorandum of Understanding signed by both parties in November 2006, a few months before the joint facility was opened. The agreement is a succinct two page document and excludes property matters such as insurance and maintenance which are covered in other agreements. At the same time, a similar MoU between Camden Council and Camden Area Family History Society was signed.[12]

'Within the partnership arrangement the formal lines of communication between library, historical society and family history society are kept open through quarterly meetings chaired by the Local Studies Librarian who also circulates agenda and minutes. The partnership is reviewed each year with the aim of identifying joint programs, projects and funding opportunities for the coming year'.[13] The formal meetings provide an opportunity for planning and ongoing communication including discussion of any issues or areas of concern.

'Just as important to the partnership are the informal linkages between the organizations. There is casual interaction between society officers and library staff both within and outside the library/museum setting. The informal linkages reflect the strong interpersonal and familial networks which still exist in Camden from earlier decades and help strengthen the formation of social capital'.[14] Introducing new residents to these networks will assist in the development of a sense of place for those who have moved more recently to the area.

Camden Council Library Service Local Studies, Camden Historical Society and Camden Area Family History Society contribute to and refer enquiries received by any one of the three groups. This is achieved by use of a referral form and email. The form can be used by library staff and volunteers to document the enquirer's contact details, nature of the enquiry and what assistance has been given. The paper format is easy to use by staff and museum and family history volunteers some of whom are not familiar with computer technology. Email is also used between the groups to refer or add to answers to enquiries. This co-operative system gives the enquirer the benefit of access to all three collections and areas of expertise without multiple visits to heritage services. Each group can add to the work of another and the system minimizes duplication of searches and information provision without necessitating access to collections under the jurisdiction of other groups. Enquiry forms are transferred between groups by mail trays based at the library.

The library, historical society and family history partnership plan a yearly calendar of events centred on the yearly themes in National Trust NSW Heritage Festival in April and NSW Heritage Office History Week in September. Each group contributes two or three activities to each program complementing each other in activity type, date and time. The programs are registered with the state organization to appear in their official program and flyers and media release of the local program are produced by the library and publicized in the local media and through members and contacts of each group. Events include book launches, lectures, workshops, walking tours, exhibitions and children's activities.

The library, historical society and family history society also undertake joint projects. The largest to date is Camden Images: Past and Present, an online image database previously called HistoryPix which contains nearly 3,000 digitised images from the museum and library collections and adds around 200 new images each year. The images are archived in the museum.
(http://www.library.camden.nsw.gov.au/camdenimages)

Camden Images has a collection development policy instrumented by a selection committee including the library's Local Studies Librarian and representatives from Camden Historical Society. This group identifies targeted themes for collection each year and seeks images for donation or loan from the public through local media and library and museum websites and newsletters. Images are also taken by each group of local people, events and the changing built and natural landscapes. The library also has a Flickr site and a Flickr group called Changing Places and Faces of Camden from which additional images may come for more permanent archiving on Camden Images. (http://www.flickr.com/groups/969898@N23/) Images sent by the public to one of the local newspapers are sent on to the library for potential selection and the Flickr group site is highlighted in this newspaper each week.

Donations of images to the library or historical society are accompanied by similar but separate donation forms both giving permission for placement on the Camden Images database. Image numbers reflect the ownership of each image. This arrangement allows each group to retain ownership and responsibility for their collection.

This project of the partnership operates with the contribution of library staff time, library funds and voluntary labour. Volunteers from Camden Historical Society have written descriptions for text accompanying images online and the upload of these files and scanning of images has been outsourced to a commercial company. The library budgets for the cost of this work. An ordering service for images is operated by the library using a printed form and online facilities.

Recently library staff have begun to add further subject headings and tags to images working with Australian Pictorial Thesaurus, LC subject headings and local studies vertical file headings. These keywords enhance the accessibility of the database with particular attention to generic words used by students. A recent upgrade of the software used for Camden Images also enables library staff to add images electronically.

Another project with the joint contribution of the library, historical society and family history society is the Camden Memories of Your Suburb weblog. (http://camdenmemoriesofyoursuburb.blogspot.com/) This site initiated by the library and linked to the websites of each organization contains historic and current information on each suburb in the Camden Local Government Area derived from the records of each group. In the comments area of each suburb posting, people are encouraged to add their memories of suburbs. The blog is a social history site to which members of the public may contribute with comments moderated by library staff.

Both the Camden Memories of Your Suburb blog and Changing Faces and Places of Camden Flickr group help to foster the sense of place of old and new residents by encouraging them to contribute their experiences, interpretations and images of their local place. These technologies also appeal to younger generations and enhance the connections between older and younger members of the community.

The oral history project Camden Voices undertaken by Camden Council Library Service in 2009 – 2010 also involved contribution by members of the historical and family history societies.
(http://www.library.camden.nsw.gov.au/camdenvoices/) Both societies contributed

suggestions and contacts of people to be interviewed. The library sought volunteers from these groups and the general public and trained a group of people in undertaking and recording oral histories. Thirty local people were interviewed and extracts from the interviews were placed on a new website Camden Voices Online, hosted by the library. CD copies of the interviews are being added to the library collection and full transcripts are being typed by volunteers.

In September 2010 the library and museum began a new program called Mini Discoverers. The program is aimed at 2 to 5 year olds and their parents/carers and is held quarterly at a usual storytime time and day. Each session involves a free hour of stories, craft and songs in which children get to play with, touch and see items from the museum. The themes to date have been: 'Discover…Communication', 'Discover….Toys' and 'Discover…Home'.

The library is developing a Camden Kid's Passport for use by school tours to the joint facility. The booklet includes questions relating to the library, museum and family history and when each section is completed children receive a stamp in their passport.

Camden Council Library Service, Camden Historical Society and Camden Area Family History Society each hold individual and distinct collections which are housed and catalogued separately by each group. Each organization is responsible for the selection and maintenance of their collection. In order to facilitate access to records and sharing of information contained in each collection the library has included electronic links in the library catalogue to pdf lists of museum and family history society library and file holdings. This linkage gives online enquirers access to the listings of all the organizations as part of one online search. The local studies page of the library website also has links to the shared website of the historical and family history societies and there are also links to and from Camden Images, Camden Voices, Flickr sites and Camden Memories blog. (http://www.library.camden.nsw.gov.au/localStudies.aspx)

Continuity

Continuity of the services provided by member organizations of the partnership is preserved across changes in library staff, society membership, committees and technology through the application of written policies and procedures. These documents aim to be practical and succinct. They seek to describe and guide rather than prescribe. They have inbuilt flexibilities and are adapted and changed where necessary. They provide working documents to facilitate the collection management and service provision of the three organizations involved. They describe the aims and goals of the partnership and the ways they operate together to preserve and celebrate the existing history of the area and develop and share a sense of place with new residents.

Evaluation is an important check for the work of the partnership. At quarterly meetings the previous event program is evaluated, operating issues are discussed and where necessary changes are made to policies and procedures. The meetings provide a place where concerns of members of the volunteer organizations can be made known through their representatives.

At the end of each year the Memorandum of Understanding between each volunteer group and the library is evaluated. To date evaluation has been very positive and no changes have been necessary.

Willis comments 'the partnership has brought together the library service and historical society whose parallel aims of strengthening community identity and place making have strengthened community development and capacity. The success of the partnership has rested on the willingness of all participants to achieve a common goal. Wrigley has observed that so far we have been very fortunate with the enthusiasm and commitment of the people involved'.[15]

Much has been achieved by the partnership between Camden Council Library Service, Camden Historical Society and Camden Area Family History Society with 2 ½ days of library staff time and the committed and enthusiastic contribution of volunteers. The success of this practical partnership owes much to the co-location of services, co-operation to achieve shared goals and continuity maintained across change by policies and procedures. Underpinning these factors are the relationships of mutual respect and appreciation between all those involved in the venture.

Acknowledgements

Paper presented at the Auslib Press *A Sense of Place, Local Studies in Australia and New Zealand* Conference at the State Library of New South Wales 5-6 May 2011.

Endnotes

1. Camden Council, *Library Strategic Plan 2003-2010; Vibrant Places – People Places*, Camden, 2005 p.6
2. *Ibid*, p.22
3. *Ibid*, p10
4. *Ibid*, p.22
5. General Manager, Notes, Schedule, Camden Library Re-opening, 2 March 2007
6. Camden Council Library Service, Library Lovers Day response sheets, 14 February 2011
7. Willis, I, *Community partnerships: Are they all they are cracked up to be?* Conference Paper Museums Australia National Conference, Newcastle, 17-20 May 2009, p.3
8. Camden Council, *Library Strategic Plan 2003-2010: Vibrant Places – People Places, op.cit*, p.22
9. Sandell, Claire, *Local History Collections for the Future: Meaningful Partnerships between Public Libraries and Community Heritage Groups* Conference Paper, Museum Australia Conference, Melbourne, 16-21 May 2004, p.4
10. Jupp, Ben, *Working together: creating a better environment for cross-sector partnerships*, Demos, London. Online at http://www.demos.co.uk/publications/workingtogether accessed 2 March 2009
11. Willis, I *op.cit*, p.3
12. Camden Council, Memorandum of Understanding between Camden Council and Camden Historical Society Incorporated.
13. Willis, I, *op.cit*, p.6
14. *Ibid*, p.7
15. Willis, I *op. cit*, p.10

Camden in the News

Janice Johnson

Have you ever used Trove to follow up unusual stories of Camden's past? It can be a very interesting and at times rewarding experience. The following story came to my attention when I read the following in *The Sydney Herald* March 29, 1839 - '*A most horrible murder was committed at Cobbitty on St Patrick's Eve, by a blacksmith named Magee, who, in a fit of brutal intoxication, actually cut his wife into two parts with a spade...*' This story led me to follow up with the Court case, as it provided information as to the name of Catherine Magee's husband and how she had died on March 18, 1839. Catherine is buried in St. Paul's Cobbitty.

As with today's news reports, the newspapers of yesteryear often exaggerated the story. The correct story was revealed during the court case and told in *The Sydney Herald,* May 22, 1839:-

Henry Magee was indicted for the wilful murder of Catherine Magee, at the Cowpasture, on the 18th March, by beating her on the head with a spade. The principal witness in this case was a man who resided in the prisoner's house, named, Gill. He stated that the prisoner returned to his own house about twelve o'clock on the night of the 18th March, and made his wife get up to give him his supper. She got up and came out of the room in which she was lying asleep with her children when the prisoner knocked her down and reproached her with some previous ill conduct with respect to a black fellow; when she got up he struck her on the head with a spade; she had a child in her arms which Gill took from her when the prisoner made a blow at him with the spade; Gill got out of the house when he heard several other blows given. Shortly afterwards he returned to the house accompanied by a person named Murphy, when they found Mrs. Magee lying on the floor. They were about moving her when Magee said let her be there until she gets sober, but Gill and Murphy lifted her up and laid her on the bed. Shortly afterwards Magee went to lie down on the bed and told his wife to move over, and as she did not he said she was sulky, and went to move her himself, when he found she was dead. Mr. Clarke, a surgeon, residing near Penrith, stated that the skull and arm of the deceased were fractured, and that there were several other injuries on her person. The defence which the prisoner's Counsel attempted to set up by his cross examination, was, that when he went home his wife was in bed with Gill, but Gill denied it. His Honor told the Jury that if they believed that the prisoner did find his wife, in bed with Gill, and under the excitement produced by that circumstance, committed the deed when he could scarcely be said to be master of his own actions, it would reduce the crime from murder to manslaughter. The Jury retired a few minutes and returned a verdict of Guilty of Murder, His Honor passed sentence of death upon the prisoner, to be carried into execution on such day as the Governor may direct..

Henry Magee's death warrant was issued June 1st 1839 and he was hanged 7 days later still proclaiming that he was innocent.

Source: http://trove.nla.gov.au/ndp/del/page/1525531

Yearning, Longing and the Remaking of Camden's Identity: the myths and reality of 'a country town idyll'.

Ian Willis
Honorary Research Fellow, University of Wollongong.

Paper presented at the 2007 Australian Historical Association Regional Conference Engaging Histories *held at the University of New England, Armidale, 23-26 September 2007.*

In May 2007 the headline on the front page of the *Macarthur Chronicle* screamed 'Home Invasion'. The report warned that

> The rural landscape surrounding Camden will be engulfed by suburbia when the construction starts on the Oran Park and Turner Rd precincts early next year. More than 30,000 will occupy 11,500 homes in the two precincts, which form part of the South West Growth Centre. By 2030 Camden will be surrounded by new suburbs consisting of up to 181,000 homes as dense as some of Sydney's most populated areas.[1]

Sydney's urban expansion into the local area has challenged the community's identity and threatened to suffocate Camden's sense of place. In the face of this onslaught many in Camden yearn for a lost past when Sydney was further away, times were simpler, and life was slower. A type of rural arcadia, which I have called 'a country town idyll'. The purpose of this paper is to examine the idyll and show how its supporters have used history as a community asset to remake Camden's identity.

Initially the paper will define the 'country town idyll' and then show that its origins are drawn from the broader traditions within rural studies. The discussion will then move on to examine the development of the idyll and investigate its validity in its contemporary context. This will be done by exploring its values and how it has been adopted by local government, businesses, land developers and community organisations, and used variously as a political weapon, a marketing tool and a tourist promotion. So, what is meant by the term 'country town idyll'.

What is the country town idyll?

For the purpose of this paper the 'country town idyll' is defined as an idealised version of a country town from an imagined past which uses history to construct imagery based on Camden's heritage buildings and other material fabric. At the heart of the idyll is the view that Camden should retain its iconic imagery of a picturesque country town with the church on the hill, surrounded by a rustic rural landscape made up of the landed estates of the colonial gentry. The idyll has been created by its supporters in an attempt to isolate Camden, like an island, in the sea of urbanisation and development that has enveloped the town. The imagery is firmly located in 'the country' that Kerrie-Elizabeth Allen maintains is a location of nostalgia where one can experience an idyllic existence. Central to this notion is a nostalgia for the past and an escape from the present, where rural life was associated with an uncomplicated, innocent, genuine society in which traditional values persisted, and a place where lives were real and relationships were seen as honest and authentic.[2]

These are the values that the supporters of Camden's 'country town idyll' have encouraged and then expressed in the language they used to describe it. They talk about the retention of Camden's 'country town atmosphere', or retaining 'Camden's country charm', or 'country town character'. They describe the town as being 'picturesque', or having 'charming cottages'. To them Camden is 'a working country town', or is simply 'my country town'. These elements are evocative of an emotional attachment to a place that existed in the past, when Camden was a small quiet country town that relied on farming for its existence. So, where did the idyll come from?

The origins of the idyll

The origins of the 'country town idyll' are to be found in the rural ethos that is drawn from within the nineteenth century rural traditions brought from Great Britain, where there was a romantic view of the country, that had an ordered, stable, comfortable organic small community in harmony with the natural surroundings.[3] Elements of this rural culture have been variously described as 'countrymindedness',[4] 'rural ideology',[5] 'rural ethos',[6] 'ruralism',[7] and a 'rural idyll'.[8] They have been a pre-occupation of many scholars,[9] including contemporary writers, like the Australian poet Les Murray.[10] Within this tradition there is an Arcadian notion of a romantic view of rural life where there is a distinction drawn between the metropolis and the village, commonly known as the town/country divide. This was the essence of pre-war Camden (a town of around 2000) where rural culture provided the stability of a closed community which was suspicious of outsiders, especially those from the city, with life ordered by social rank, personal contacts and familial links. It was confined by conservatism, patriarchy and an Anglo-centric view of the world. Camden's 'rural culture' reached a watershed during the 1960s, after which social, economic and political conditions combined to permanently change Camden's rurality.

The historical development of the country town idyll and its contemporary use by its supporters

The conditions for the development of the idyll were set by the planned post-war urban growth of Greater Sydney. Sydney planning authorities had earmarked Camden as part of the Greater Sydney Area and the County of Cumberland Plan as early as 1948. The idea was to form a girdle of countryside around Sydney (a rural-urban fringe) and for Camden to be part of it. In 1968 Camden was included as part of Sydney's outer rural area in the Sydney Region Outline Plan.[11] While Camden may have been part of each of these plans, they had little direct effect on the township or its rural identity, but this was about to change.

For many the release of The Three Cities Structure Plan in 1973 was a direct assault on Camden's 'rural character'. The plan covered Campbelltown, Camden and Wollondilly local government areas which according to the plan were destined to become part of Sydney's urban sprawl. For one Liz Kernohan, the structure plan rang alarm bells. She was an agricultural scientist, who worked at the University of Sydney Farms at Cobbitty, west of Camden.[12] She was a 'city type', an outsider, who came to Camden in 1960 and became a strident advocate for the retention of Camden's country town charm (that is, Camden's country town idyll) The release of the structure plan prompted her to stand for election to Camden Municipal Council. She based her election platform on the retention of Camden's 'rural character', and while she was not the first to take an interest in these values her election to Camden Council in 1973 helped crystallise the idyll in the minds of many in Camden for the first time.

Kernohan used the values within the idyll as a constant theme throughout her political career, including her election to the New South Wales Parliament in 1991. In her maiden speech to parliament, she stated that her constituents wanted a semi-rural lifestyle, and that 'explosions of suburbia' did not constitute progress.[13] Kernohan maintained that Camden's identity and sense of place was built on the town's place in history, and was exemplified by *Camden Park* (the colonial property of John Macarthur and his descendants) and the Camden museum (managed by the Camden Historical Society). Kernohan used the values within the idyll to create a direct link between Camden's history and an idealised landscape from the past. She maintained that:

> The Camden district [had] the unique history of being the area where the wool and wine industries were developed by the Macarthur family. Camden municipal council [sic] wants to retain the area's rural heritage and environment, and is encouraging developers to enhance the country town image and take cognisance of the history of the area.[14]

Kernohan's political activity in the early 1970s helped the development of the idyll and contributed to the formation of the Camden Resident Action Group (CRAG). CRAG was one of first organisations in Camden to publicly advocate the values within the country town idyll and it received strong support from Kernohan. The members of CRAG felt that Camden's rural culture was being undermined by urban growth, and set out with the aim of effectively isolating Camden from Sydney's urbanisation. The members of CRAG sort historical links through time to strengthen their sense of belonging and participation in space and place. Janice Newton has maintained that these types of progress associations were more nostalgic and defensive and looked to conservation as their ideal, as opposed to progress associations of earlier times that were positive and supported development.[15] The Camden Historical Society, which fitted the same mould as CRAG, fostered interest in local history and memorialised Camden's pioneering past with a number civic monuments in the early 1970s.

Newton quotes British research which has shown that these 'peripheral communities have a consciousness and valuing of difference',[16] that is, an identity of separatedness. The identity of difference is one of the main values within the country town idyll. The local community has long held an animosity to Sydney based decision makers dating back to the nineteenth century, and was expressed as the town/country divide. Kernohan encapsulated these values when she stated that,

> Camden will be happy to be known as that large country town on the outskirts of Sydney with its own suburbs; it does not want to become part of suburban Sydney'.[17]

Geographers readily identify this difference as exurbanisation. According to US research exurbs are 'places just beyond the suburbs where the country looks like the country'.[18] This is the rural landscape on Sydney's rural-urban fringe that Camden offers its new arrivals. A rural landscape that promises the new arrivals lots of 'country town charm'. These city types are looking for greener pastures on the rural-urban fringe where they can escape the city, but interestingly not the city's attractions. The values brought to Camden by these new arrivals, including the search for separatedness, have altered the community's subjectivity (the feeling of the community about themselves) and forced a re-evaluation of how the community sees itself, and this is expressed as the country town idyll. Interestingly the desire by the new arrivals for difference is similar to the values of separatedness that exist in gated estates, where residents are trying to isolate themselves from the outside world and the perceived evils of the city.[19] For Camden's new arrivals the Camden township is a metaphorical gated estate with the Nepean floodplain acting as the fence surrounding the estate. They are protected from the evils of the city, such as crime and congestion, by open space in their 'contemporary country living'. All part of the country town idyll.

Difference and exclusivity within the idyll are supported by Gleeson's view that areas of new land releases on the fringe of the Sydney Metropolitan Area (like Camden) have become part of an 'edge city…existing largely in isolation and antipathy to the older cities'.[20] Exclusivity certainly appealed to Camden's new arrivals who, Kernohan claimed had come to Camden to 'escape city conditions', and were, according to Matt Leighton, the president of the Narellan Chamber of Commerce, 'refugees' from the city.[21] Leighton felt that they had graduated 'a step up' by making their home in Camden. While others wanted Camden to become the 'Bowral of Western Sydney' by 'attempting to stay out of the fast lane',[22] or maintaining that it should become the 'Double Bay of the South Western Sector' of Sydney.[23] Gleeson maintains that the new arrivals were looking for the creation of new 'urban villages' which, he claims, is a part of a 'postmodern angst' where 'contemporary suburbanisation in Australia is shaped by the mounting anxiety and insecurity among Australia's urban middle class'. He argues that all this has been fuelled by 'neo-liberal restructuring' of the last 20 years and the 'new political emphasis on self-provision'. Gleeson claims that this is creating 'aspirational communities' on the fringe of the city with a high degree of 'cultural homogeneity'.[24] In other words, Gleeson would maintain that Camden's new arrivals were looking for a safe and secure environment with predictable lifestyle outcomes, in an Anglofile community where their lifetime investment in housing was protected from the threats of the city. This fitted Kernohan's Camden and the country town idyll she advocated.

Kernohan was strong supporter of the idyll until her death in 2004 and her successes were due, in part at least, to her recognition of the processes associated with the development of the idyll which have contributed to the changes in Camden's identity and sense of place. Kernohan was able to encapsulate this process in the language of Camden's conservative rural tradition and successfully used it in her political platform. She harnessed Camden's rurality (or what was left of it) and pragmatically voiced the underlying aspirations of Camden's old and new residents for some sense of stability in the face of constant demographic change in an ideal past. She did this very effectively in 1994 when she opposed a land release by Industrial Equity. Industrial Equity planned a land release at South Camden (Cawdor) of 4900 lots. There were protests and a public meeting was called in July, which attracted over 300 people.[25] Kernohan campaigned to keep the area 'pristine' and had the number of lots reduced to 777 (of between 0.4 and 1.0 hectare) and the provision of public housing stopped. The threat from public housing tenants, real or otherwise, would, it was maintained, would undermine the values of privately owned properties on the estate. Industrial Equity's development was rejected, and still remains undeveloped.[26] Yet, eight years later, in 2002, Stockland successfully promoted a land release adjacent to this area called Bridgewater. The Bridgewater development is typical of the development found in 'exurbia' or Gleeson's 'edge city' that have fostered the country town idyll in Camden.

Over the last five years the developers of the Bridgewater land release have used the idyll to sell their allotments to locals and city types. It has been advertised as 'contemporary rural lifestyle' and stridently maintained in its press releases that it was not 'suburbia'. Stockland have claimed that the estate was within an hour of the city where 'second and third homebuyers who were looking to upgrade their lifestyle' and be able to enjoy large parklands.[27] Stockland claimed in its 2006 advertising that its development at South Camden was

> An idyllic community bordered by undulating countryside, Bridgewater offers the ultimate country lifestyle a mere 50 minutes from the Sydney CBD.[28]

The promotional literature for the Bridgewater land release used images of blond haired young children frolicking in a idyllic rural vista in the late afternoon light. The images draw heavily on the nostalgia of a care-free child hood in the country free from the evils of city-life. In other promotional literature Stockland claimed that their estate was

> Set in the charming rural enclave of South Camden on Sydney's metropolitan fringe. Bridgewater offers you the chance to create a new contemporary country lifestyle. Surrounded by the unique heritage and ambience of 19th century farm buildings and homesteads, Bridgewater is the epitome of modern country style, providing innovative, contemporary living in a truly historical Australian setting.[29]

The promotional article is supported by panoramic vistas of Camden's rural countryside.

Formalisation of the idyll

The first formalisation of the idyll occurred in 1999 with the development of Camden council's strategic plan. The strategic plan, which captured community sentiment, was drawn up 'in consultation with the community',[30] and drew heavily on the values of the idyll. It acknowledged the threat of Sydney's urban sprawl and the desire for separatedness by the community through the use of local history. In the introduction to the plan it states that

> Camden has retained many of the traditional qualities of a rural lifestyle and environment and is characterised by historic towns, country villages and new suburban areas. This has been achieved whilst accommodating the fastest urban growth in the Sydney Region. Importantly, it is not a mere extension of the suburban sprawl by Sydney.

It further maintains that

> Camden's unique rural landscapes and vistas have been retained and improved… [and that]…Camden town has retained its country town atmosphere and culture.

The plan claims that the council recognised the aspirations of the community and the role of the idyll in urban planning within the local government area. It maintains that

> Council recognised that economic prosperity and quality of life are linked to its rural identity. The attributes of safety, friendliness and close knit community associated with rural lifestyle also contribute to the amenity of Camden as a place to live and enjoy.

The council acknowledged that 'newer residents are attracted by the rural nature of Camden' and that 'the rural landscape is an important factor in the lifestyle of the Camden community'.[31]

The idyll received a significant boost in 2004 with the completion of the Camden Draft Heritage Plan. While the plan does not formally acknowledge the country town idyll it uses history, and its heritage, to recognise the special status of Camden. The plan identified a number of special qualities about the Camden town area which supported the idyll. They included: the town's reputation as one of the few original Cumberland Plain country towns still intact; the town's early farming and settlement history; the area's large early colonial landed estates; the town's association with the Macarthur family; the layout of the town that still reflects its original purpose; the arrangement of the town which took advantage of the views and vistas of St Johns Church on the hill. The report recommended the adoption of the Camden Township Conservation Area based on: the original grid plan for the town, which still exists; the mix of colonial buildings in the town area; the mix of residential, commercial, retail and industrial activity in the town area; the rural properties that still exist on the edge of the town centre; the location of the Nepean River floodplain wrapping around three sides of the town; St Johns Church on the hill; and the historical development of the town that is still evident in the properties and usage of the buildings in central Camden.

Two aspects of the Draft Heritage Plan[32] warrant special attention as they are critical to understanding the contemporary use of the idyll in Camden, the Nepean River floodplain and the St John's church. Each have a special historical, moral, social and psychological significance within the idyll. The supporters of the idyll have used both the Nepean floodplain and St Johns Church and the history associated with them as a political weapon, a tourist promotion and part of the construction of heritage iconography. The floodplain is the site of a number of activities which act to re-enforce Camden's rural past, they include the Camden Town Farm (an old dairy farm), Bicentennial Park (an old dairy farm) and Camden Showground, the old milk factory of the Macarthurs on the northern approach to the town and the Camden saleyards, which still operate.

Firstly, the moral imperative of the church on the hill that is St Johns underpins the values of the idyll and the development of the romantic notions surrounding the town and its past. The church was built on the highest point of the town in 1840 and provides an important psychological and spiritual focus for the community by dominating the town's skyline. St Johns is a sacred site associated with the pioneering heritage of the colonial period of the town and the role of the Macarthur family in it. The Macarthur family ruled over Camden for over a 150 years and the church was central to the Macarthur's moral view of the world and how that should be played out in the town.[33] The town was their metaphysical castle and they were the squires, especially between 1890 and 1943, when power rested with two Macarthur women, Elizabeth and Sibella Macarthur Onslow. The social authority of these women was absolute. They ensured that the village of Camden reflected as much as possible their view of the world. Nothing escaped their scrutiny or influence and St Johns was central to their view of the world in Camden. Elizabeth Macarthur Onslow encouraged the maintenance of the proprietaries of life, moral order, and good works, as well as memorialising her family by donating a clock and bells to St Johns Church in 1897.[34] She also memorialised the memory of her late husband by providing a public park, which was named after her husband (Onslow Park), and is now the Camden Showground. This is one of the sites in Camden that celebrates the idyll each year at the Camden Show. A prominent member of the show committee, Dick Inglis, who was past

St Johns Church has dominated the town's landscape from the hill since it was built in the 1840s (Source: Camden Images/Camden Historical Society/R Driscoll)

president (1962-1974), member of the firm William Inglis and Sons (auctioneers, stock and station and bloodstock agents) and a member of a prominent Camden colonial family, claimed that he was proud that the Camden Show was 'still a country show' and he hoped that it stayed that way.[35]

Secondly, the geography of the Nepean River floodplain creates a sense of openness around the town, or ruralness, that engenders a 'country' mindset of those who live, or would like to live, in the local area. The landscape creates a physical and psychological separation from the city. The rural landscape symbolised traditional values that have been embraced by the local community and used in local tourist promotions and by the developers of the new land releases to voice the difference between the local and the metropolitan. This imagery uses nostalgia to connect with Camden's earlier days when the town was a small rural community and promotes Camden's ruralness as a positive difference for new comers to the area. The inundation of the floodplain by the waters of the Nepean River provides a physical and psychological barrier to Sydney's urbanisation. The floodplain around Camden has been seen as a buffer zone against the onslaught of the city. A moat surrounding the metaphorical castle, that is the country town.

Both the Nepean River floodplain the St Johns Church were invoked within the idyll to defeat a proposal to build a multi-storey carpark in central Camden in 2006. The supporters of the carpark, principally the Camden Chamber of Commerce, wanted additional car parking places in central Camden as early as 1995 because they felt that their financial viability was threatened by competition from Narellan Town Centre, a shopping mall. They thought that a multi-storey carpark would solve their problems. The council considered three possible sites. Two sites were between St John's church on the hill in cental Camden and Camden's main street (Argyle Street), the third on the floodplain. Camden Council approved a site near St Johns Church in early 2006. The project was eventually defeated because it was felt that any development on the elevated southern sites compromised the vista of the St John's Church from the Nepean River floodplain. The church was located on the hill behind the proposed John Street sites. This vista was part of the iconic imagery of Camden that has been an important part of the town's cultural landscape and identity from colonial times.[36] The carpark supporters, the Camden Chamber of Commerce, did not contest this position, but felt that the final design of the carpark did not compromise these values, needless to say, Camden Residents Action Group, the historical society and a council commissioned heritage architect did not agree. The heritage architects felt that the proposal compromised the integrity of the 'most intact country town on the Cumberland Plain'.[37]

Tourist promotions of Camden have drawn on the historic nature of central Camden, including St Johns church, and the vistas of the floodplain and the values of the idyll. This has occurred in brochures, promotions and a recent webpage, which is part of heritage tourism, which allows visitors 'to experience places and activities that authentically represent the stories and people of the past and present'.[38] The website states that,

> Camden's heritage precinct is dominated by the church on the hill, St John's Church (1840) and the adjacent rectory (1859). Across the road is Macarthur Park (1905), arguably one of the best Victorian-style urban parks in the country. In the neighbouring streets there are a number of charming Federation and Californian bungalows.

The webpage continues in a similar vain.

> The picturesque rural landscapes that surround Camden were once part of the large estates of the landed gentry and their grand houses. A number of these privately owned houses are still dotted throughout the local area. Some examples are *Camden Park* (1835), *Brownlow Hill* (1828), *Denbigh* (1822), *Oran Park* (c1850), *Camelot* (1888), *Studley Park* (c1870s), *Wivenhoe* (c1837) and *Kirkham Stables* (1816). The rural vistas are enhanced by the Nepean River floodplain that surrounds the town and provides the visitor with a sense of the town's farming heritage.[39]

Camden Council in partnership with Camden Historical Society produced a brochure for a walking tour of Camden and under the heading 'Camden Town, A Place in History' states that,

> The historic township of Camden, on the south-western outskirts of Sydney, is the cultural heart of a region that enjoys a unique place in our nation's history… This rich rural heritage is evidenced around the town in the presence of live stock sale yards, vineyard, equestrian park and dairy facilities, giving Camden a unique 'working country town' atmosphere and flavour.[40]

St Johns Church has been used on cups and saucers, mugs and various other ephemera over the years.

The same imagery within the idyll is used to promote local businesses. One stockfeed supplier claims to be 'Keeping Camden Country'.[41] Another business has released a DVD with a slide show with a backing track that uses the values of the idyll in the lyrics of a song that was written by a local Camden singer/songwriter. The song is called *Still My Country Home* and is the backing track for a DVD called *Camden, Still My Country Home*. It has been developed to promote a local business and has all the characteristics of the country town idyll.

Is the idyll still relevant?

Despite the apparent strength of the idyll in Camden, cracks are starting to appear. For example, the use of the idyll as a political weapon appears to have disappeared, at least in the March 2007 state election. Both local candidates from the major political parties, Chris Patterson (Liberal), and Geoff Corrigan (ALP), one the present mayor and one a former mayor of Camden, dropped references to the retention of Camden's country town atmosphere. This contrasts with earlier election campaigns that involved Liz Kernohan, where these values were central to her campaigns for state parliament. This change may be partly reflected by both changes to the boundaries to the state seat of Camden and the inclusion of new suburbs in the northern part of the local government area that are a result of Sydney's urban growth. In addition, Stockland removed references to 'contemporary country living' from promotional literature early in 2007, and the latest land release at East Camden (Elderslie) called Vantage Point makes no mention to the idyll.

Yet a development application in May 2007 by McDonalds for a new restaurant in South Camden has seen the idyll used as a potent political weapon. Protesters invoked the idyll and the flood of objections from the community centred around concerns that were evocative of the evils of the city coming to invade the country town. One resident complained that he had witnessed drunkenness, throwing bottles, loutish behaviour and burnouts in the carpark by McDonalds customers at an outlet in Narellan. He further claimed that all incidents went unchecked by McDonald's staff, security or police.[42] Helen Stockheim, a local resident, claimed that she moved to area because she liked the 'country town atmosphere' and the area was 'McDonalds free'.[43] The *Camden Advertiser* ran an editorial titled 'Let's treasure our beautiful area'.[44] McDonalds are the 'outsiders' in this story and bring the 'evils of the city' in the form of globalisation, cultural integration and market domination to Camden. They directly challenge the community's identity and the values that are represented by the idyll such as honesty, simplicity and authenticity of family run businesses. The global corporation is the representative of everything that the country town idyll is not.

The future relevance of the idyll to the Camden community is still an open question. The encroachment of Sydney's urban sprawl is reshaping Camden's identity in ways which are not yet clearly discernible. Yet many want the rural vistas and the historic buildings that create the separatedness of Camden from Sydney's urbanisation. They are the ones who are trying to hold on the values of the small town in the form of the country town idyll.

References

1. *Macarthur Chronicle* 15 May 2007.

2. Kerrie-Elizabeth Allen, 'The Social Space(s) of Rural Women', *Rural Society*, v.12, no.1, 2002.
3. PJ Waller, *Town, City and Nation 1850-1914*, Oxford University Press, Oxford, 1983.
4. Aitkin, Don, '"Countrymindedness" - The Spread of an Idea', *Australian Cultural History*, 4, 1985.
5. Gretchen Poiner, *The Good Old Rule, Gender and Other Power Relationships in a Rural Community*, Sydney University Press/Oxford University Press, South Melbourne, 1990. Margaret Alston, *Women on the Land, The Hidden Heart of Rural Australia*, University New South Wales Press, Kensington, 1995.
6. Elizabeth Kenworthy Teather, 'Mandate of the Country Women's Association of New South Wales',*Australian Journal of Social Issues*, 31, 1, February 1996.
7. Neutze, Max, 'City, Country, Town: Australian Pecularities',*Australian Cultural History*, 4, 1985.
8. Jim Ward & Greg Smith, (eds), *The Vanishing Village, A Small Australian Town in Transition*, Quartet, Melbourne, 1978. Leonore Davidoff, *World's Between, Historical Perspective on Gender and Class*, Polity Press, Cambridge, 1995. Kerrie-Elizabeth Allen, 'The Social Space(s) of Rural Women', Rural Society, v.12, no.1, 2002.
9. Ward & Smith, *The Vanishing Village*.
10. Murray's Boeotia and Athens (city and the bush).Helen Lambert, 'A Draft Preamble: Les Murray and the Politics of Poetry'. Accessed 14 May 2007 online @ http://www.api-network.com/main/index.php?ap-ply=scholars&webpage=default&flexedit=&flex_password=&menu_label=&menuID=homely&menubox=&scholar=58
11. Bunker Raymond and Darren Holloway, 'More than fringe benefits: the values, policies, issues and expectations embedded in Sydney's rural-urban fringe', *Australian Planner*, Vol. 39, No. 2, 2002.
12. L Copeland (ed), *1910-1985 Celebrating 75 Years of Agriculture at the University of Sydney*, Sydney: University of Sydney, 1985.
13. *New South Wales Legislative Assembly Parliamentary Debates*, 16 October 1991, pp.2293
14. *NSWLAPD*, 16 October 1991, pp.2293-2294
15. Janice Newton, 'Rejecting Suburban Identity on the Fringes of Melbourne', *The Australian Journal of Anthropology*, 1999, 10:3, pp. 320-336.
16. Newton, 'Rejecting Suburban Identity'.
17. *NSWLAPD*, 16 October 1991, pp.2293-2294
18. Tom Foreman, 'Exurb growth challenges US cities', *CNN.com* Accessed on 25 May 2007 online @ http://www.cnn.com/2005/us/03/27/urban.sprawl/
19. Jane Cadzow, 'Do Fence Me In', *Good Weekend*, 5 May 2007.
20. Bridgewater brochure.
21. Brendan Gleeson, 'What's Driving Suburban Australia?' in *Griffith Review*, special edition 'Dreams of Land', Summer 2003-2004.
22. *Macarthur Advertiser* 16 August 1995; *Camden News* 22 August 1973.
23. *Macarthur Advertiser* 16 August 1995.
24. *Camden Crier* 18 March 1981.
25. Brendan Gleeson, 'What's Driving Suburban Australia?' in *Griffith Review*, special edition 'Dreams of Land', Summer 2003-2004.
26. *Camden Crier* 17 August 1994.
27. *Camden and Wollondilly Times* 14 September 1994; 'Mini City Proposal Stopped', Pamphlet, August 1994, Kernohan File, Camden Historical Society Archives.
28. *Macarthur Advertiser* 11 September 2002.
29. Stockland, *Upgrade Your Lifestyle*, (Stockland Sales and Information Centre, 2006, Advertising Brochure)
30. Stockland, 'Bridgewater, Contemporary Country Living', *Aspect NSW*, Spring/Summer 2005, pp. 36-37. (Advertising Literature).
31. Camden Council, *Statement of Affairs*, Camden: The Council of Camden, 2007.
32. Camden Council, *Camden 2025, A Strategic Plan For Camden*, (Camden: Camden Council 1999). Accessed on 14 December 2006 online @ http://www.camden.nsw.gov.au
33. Camden Council adopted the Camden Draft Heritage Report in December 2006.
34. Atkinson, Alan, *Camden, Farm and Village Life in Early New South Wales*, Oxford University Press, Melbourne, 1988. Ian Willis, 'The Gentry and the Village, Camden, NSW, 1800-1939', AQ Australian Quarterly, Vol 78, Issue 4, July-August 2006.
35. RE Nixon & PC Hayward (eds), *The Anglican Church of St John the Evangelist Camden, New South Wales*, Camden: Anglican Parish of Camden, 1999.
36. *The District Reporter*, 24 August 2007.
37. Paul Power's *A Century of Change, One Hundred Years of Local Government in Camden*, (Camden: Macarthur Independent Promotions, 1989).
38. *Camden Advertiser* 28 June 2006.
39. National Trust for Historic Preservation , 'Heritage Tourism'. Accessed on 4 April 2007 online @ http://www.nationaltrust.org/heritage_tourism/index.html
40. Ian Willis, 'Camden, the best preserved country town on the Cumberland Plain', *Heritage Tourism*. Accessed on 23 May 2007 online @ http://www.heritagetourism.com.au/camden-the-best-preserved-country-town-on-the-cumberland-plain-nsw/
41. Camden Council, *Heritage Walking Tour of Camden Town*, (Camden: Camden Council, 2001)
42. *The District Reporter* 24 August 2007.
43. *Camden Advertiser*, 27 June 2007.
44. *The District Reporter*, 1 June 2007.
45. *Camden Advertiser* 27 June 2007.

Local Government, Camden Municipality and Nepean Shire

Peter Mylrea

The village of Camden was established by James and William Macarthur. It was planned in 1836 and the first land sales were held in 1841. Because it was established on land owned by the Macarthurs it was classed as a 'private' village in contrast to Narellan which was built on government land and classed as a 'government' village. By 1885 many blocks of land and houses in Camden were privately owned and there were public buildings in the village such as schools, churches and hotels. Despite this development the village was still called a private village in 1885.[1] Perhaps this meant that the Macarthurs had a controlling interest in many aspects of the running of the village. This situation would not change until Camden was constituted as a municipality.

Camden Municipal Council 1889 to 1948

Prior to 1867 there were only thirty five Sydney suburbs and country towns which had any form of local government and this number did not include Camden. There was no local government in the rest of New South Wales.

On 23 December 1867 the Municipalities Act of 1867 was passed by the colonial parliament. Clause 10 of the Act read as follows

> The Governor on receipt of a petition signed by no fewer than fifty persons … and stating the number of the inhabitants resident therein and praying that the same may be declared a Borough or Municipal District under this Act.

Twenty years after the passing of this Act there was a move in Camden to seek local Government. To this end a petition was submitted to the Colonial Secretary which contained the names and addresses of 89 men (but no women!) and a statement that the population of the proposed municipality was 'not less than 900 persons'.[2]

The petition was accepted and by a proclamation dated 6 February 1889 the 'Municipal District of Camden' was created. Soon after, it was announced that Francis Ferguson, Esquire, J.P. of Camden was to be the Returning Officer and that the polling booth would be at the Camden Court House.[3] The election was held on 12 April 1889 and

> The following gentlemen were this day duly elected Aldermen at the first election for this Municipality. Frederick Henry Burns, Charles Thomas Whiteman, Thomas Huxley Wasson, James Hayter, George Frederick Furner, Samuel Ellis, William John Cranfield, Joseph Doust.
> Returning Officer. F. Ferguson
> Camden 12 April 1889.[4]

The new Municipality had an area much smaller than that of the present day Council. It did not include the villages of Narellan and Cobbitty but did cover what in the future would be the suburbs of Elderslie, Camden, Camden South, Bickley Vale, Grasmere and Ellis Lane. The Municipality remained this size until it was enlarged by an Act of Parliament in 1948.

Nepean Shire 1906 to 1948

Up to 1906 there were many parts of New South Wales which did not have any form of local government. This included areas around Narellan and Cobbitty and districts further north such as Bringelly and Leppington.

To overcome such a situation the Local Government (Shires) Act was passed in 1905. It prescribed that the whole of the State of New South Wales, apart from areas which had municipal councils, was to be divided into shires with defined boundaries and given names.

This is how the Nepean Shire came into being. In a proclamation of 7 March 1906 the Nepean Shire was created, along with many other shires in the State.

The same Act appointed five temporary councillors in each shire. The main task of the Temporary Council was to compile a list of eligible voters and arrange for a council election. The temporary councillors were: Thomas Barker, Bringelly; Frederick Firth, Hoxton Park; Walter Furner, Elderslie; David Nott, Narellan and Thomas Sheil, The Grove.[5] The first meeting of the Temporary Council was held on 15 June 1906 and David Nott was elected Chairman.[6]

An election for the permanent council members was held on 24 November 1906. D. Nott (Narellan) and T. Barker (Bringelly) had been Temporary Councillors and the new councillors were A. Heydon, R. Fitzroy, T.G. Scott, G.A. Church and T. Baker. They held their first meeting on 12 December 1906 and D. Nott (Narellan) was elected President.[7]

The new Shire was larger in area than the Camden Municipality at that time. It lay between the municipalities of Camden and Campbelltown in the south and Liverpool and Mulgoa in the north and included the villages of Narellan and Cobbitty. The meetings of the Temporary Council had been held in Narellan but the new Council moved the Council offices to 1191 The Northern Road, Bringelly, where they remained until the Shire was abolished.

Camden Council from 1948 [8]

The next change occurred when the Local Government (Areas) Act of 1948 was passed. This Act abolished the Nepean Shire and the areas which it covered were transferred to surrounding councils. The 'C' Riding [ward] of the Nepean Shire was amalgamated with Camden Municipality, while 'A' Riding was allotted to Penrith Council and 'B' Riding went to Liverpool Council.

This amalgamation greatly increased the size of Camden Municipality. It also meant that Cobbitty and Narellan became, for the first time, part of Camden Municipality. The 'C' Riding extended north from Narellan to the Bringelly Road and included Cobbitty, Catherine Fields, Leppington and parts of Rossmore and Bringelly. Later the newer suburbs of Oran Park, Harrington Park, Gregory Hills, Currans Hill, Mount Annan, Narellan Vale and Spring Farm would be established in the Camden Council area.

References

1 Government Gazette 20 March 1885.
2 Government Gazette 12 June 1888.
3 Government Gazette19 March 1889.
4 Government Gazette 16 April 1889.
5 Camden News 14 June 1906.
6 Camden News 21 June 1906.
7 Camden News 19 December 1906.
8 The name of the municipality changed over the years. Originally it was the Municipal District of Camden, then Camden Municipal Council and currently it is Camden Council.

CAMDEN HISTORY

Journal of the Camden Historical Society

September 2012 Volume 3 Number 4

CAMDEN HISTORY
Journal of the Camden Historical Society Inc.
ISSN 1445-1549
Editor: Dr Ian Willis

Management Committee
President: Bob Lester
Vice Presidents: Dr Ian Willis, Cathey Shepherd
Secretary: Doug Barrett
Assistant Secretary: Julie Wrigley
Treasurer: Ray Herbert
Assistant Treasurer:
Immediate Past President: John Wrigley OAM
General Committee: Sharon Greene   Robert Wheeler
                    Peter Hayward OAM   Rene Rem
                    Janice Johnson   Julie Wrigley

Honorary Auditor: Jim Hunter
Honorary Solicitors: Bowring, Macaulay and Barrett

Society contact:
P.O. Box 566, Camden, NSW 2570.   Online <http://www.camdenhistory.org.au>

Meetings
Meetings are held at 7.30 p.m. on the second Wednesday of the month except in January. They are held in the Museum. Visitors are always welcome.

Museum
The Museum is located at 40 John Street, Camden, phone 4655 3400 or 46559210. It is open Thursday to Sunday 11 a.m. to 4 p.m., except at Christmas. Visits by schools and groups are encouraged. Please contact the Museum to make arrangements. Entry is free.

Camden History, Journal of the Camden Historical Society Inc
The Journal is published in March and September each year. The Editor would be pleased to receive articles broadly covering the history of the Camden district . Correspondence can be sent to the Society's postal address. The views expressed in articles in this journal are solely those of the authors and do reflect any endorsement by the society.

Donations
Donations made to the Society are tax deductible. The accredited value of objects donated to the Society are eligible for tax deduction.

Cover John Southwell

CAMDEN HISTORY
Journal of the Camden Historical Society Inc.

September 2012 Vol 3 No 4

Contents

John Carlyle Southwell OAM, RFD, ED Ian Willis	124
Camden Historical Society, Annual Report, 2011-2012 John Wrigley	129
Elderslie Robert Wheeler	132
The Original Village of Cawdor Peter Mylrea	137
Development of Law Courts in Cawdor, Picton and Camden Peter. Mylrea	139

John Carlyle Southwell OAM, RFD, ED

Ian Willis

John Southwell, engineer, businessman, soldier, community worker and gardener, has been an enduring local identity in the Camden district for over 70 years. During his lifetime John has seen Camden change from a small country town to became part of Sydney's rural-urban fringe.

John was born in Turramurra on 7 January 1930 to Howard Carlyle (Dick) Southwell (1900-1951) and Alma Edith (Edith) Southwell (1901-1977), a child of the Depression. His parents had moved to the Camden area in 1928, and John grew up living in 'Nepean House', 1 Mitchell Street, Camden. After being home-schooled by his mother until third class, John was educated at Camden Central School, Homebush Boys High School, Sydney University for a year of Arts, and then University of New South Wales, where he graduated in mechanical engineering in 1952. From 1942 to 1952 John travelled on Pansy, the Camden train, leaving Camden station at 6.45 a.m. and returning home at 5.30 p.m.

John married Susan Le Good in 1964 and has 3 children, Bridget, Andrew and James; and 2 grandchildren, Charlotte and Louis.

Business

From an early age John was interested in making or restoring things: steam engines, carts, harnesses, trains and furniture, so it was natural for him to become a mechanical engineer and follow in his father's business. In 1928 John's father had started the Menangle Sand Company, which supplied concrete sand for the construction of the Sydney Harbour Bridge and for the depression employment project building the Hume Highway from Liverpool to Narellan. A large steam-driven suction dredge lifted sand from the Nepean River via a light-rail steam locomotive to the Menangle Rail siding. The sand dredge closed in 1936 and after the war his father founded H C Southwell Pty Ltd.

After his father's death in 1951 John became managing director of H.C. Southwells (later Southwell Engineering Pty Ltd) and remained a director until his retirement in 1997. John was responsible for expanding the company group. The agricultural sales business, which was managed by John's brother David, was added to the engineering business, which was managed by John. In 1985 the family company was split into Southwell Agricultural Sales Pty

Ltd, managed by David Southwell and John's nephew Hugh Southwell, and Southwell Engineering Pty Ltd, managed by John, so that each company's activities were clearly defined.

Army
John is a retired Lieutenant Colonel. In 1952 he first joined the University of New South Wales Regiment, now the Army Reserve Unit which was then the Citizen Military Forces (CMF). The aim of the regiment was, and still is, to teach skills in leadership, management, and personnel administration and to train members in command. As a training officer John did a tour of New Guinea with the Pacific Island Regiment and served in Vietnam in 1969, attached to the 5th Battalion, Royal Australian Regiment. He spent three years with Eastern Command at Victoria Barracks in the 1970s and became Commander of the 17th Battalion Royal NSW Regiment, retiring in 1982. He was appointed Honorary Colonel of the University of New South Wales Regiment.

Community organisation	Community service
1st Camden Scouts	Senior Scout, and Scoutmaster from 1950 to 1955
Camden RSL Youth Club	President 1976 to 1978, managing the erection of the Youth Club building
Camden Apex Club	1954 to 1960
Camden Rotary Club	1960, and awarded Paul Harris Fellowship in 1993
Camden Show Society	John joined in 1962, and served on the Committee for 36 years (1962 – 1998). He was President of the Show Society from 1986 to 1989. As President he increased the organizational professionalism of the Show and its financial accounting. One of his outstanding memories is of the 1986 Show Ball attended by 1200 people, and the great party of that night. In 1994 John was made a Life Member of the Show Society.
Carrington Centennial Trust	1974 to 2000; Chairman of Board of Directors 1990-1993; a Trustee from 1980 to 2000
Campbelltown Group Metal Trades Industry Association	Chairman from 1979 to 1981
Camden Sub-Branch Returned Services League (RSL)	Vice President
Salvation Army Red Shield Appeal	Chairman, 1986
Legacy	1989 to 1998
University of NSW Foundation	Fellow, 1997

In 1998 John recalls an interesting task was being a guard attachment commander for the 1953 Queen's visit to Sydney. Again in 1971 as Commanding Officer 17th Battalion, his troops were on general duties at the Opera House at its opening by the Queen.

Community Service

In 2003 John received the Medal of the Order of Australia (OAM) for service to the Camden community through a range of aged care, service and veteran groups. Other awards John has been given include the Queen's Silver Jubilee Medal in 1977, the National Medal, and the Commonwealth Seniors Recognition Award in 1999 (see attached table for community service).

Over the years he has contributed thousands of hours of service to the Camden community, starting with the Scouts in the 1940s and later serving as Scoutmaster in the 1950s. John maintains that 'service is the basis of worthy enterprise' and that he 'always wanted to help the community by putting service above self'. John has taken leadership roles in a number of Camden organisations.

John has supported many community organisations, providing truck transport, cranes or metal fabrication when needed for sporting and community projects. He has generously supported the Camden Historical Society and the museum.

Gardener

In recent years John has had considerable success in the Camden Garden Prize with the charming garden on his property "Benwerrin". He won Grand Champion in 2007 and 2010. John has stated that his garden takes a lot of work and that he is supported in his efforts by his son Andrew. John enjoys spending time in his garden, and says that gardening is like life – a mixture of fulfillment and disappointment.

Conclusion

John takes a casual approach to sport, but he has enjoyed some activities including navigating and sailing. At one stage he sailed his own yacht 'Benwerrin'. His quirky sense of humour often catches his friends and associates unawares. John's deliberately provocative statements often come as a surprise to those who do not know him well. His love of travel and adventure has taken him to many unusual places including up the Sepik River in Papua New Guinea and many parts of the world. In retirement he has developed a liking for luxury sea cruises especially on the Queen Elizabeth II liner. He likes to travel first class and to dress formally for dinner. Friends have stated that John should be buried in his dinner suit!

Acknowledgements

The author gratefully acknowledges the helpful comments and suggestions of John Southwell and John Wrigley on an earlier draft of this article.

Additional Sources

'A drop of good advice', *Camden Advertiser,* 26 November 2003.
'Southwell gets an OAM', *Camden & Wollondilly Advertiser*, 10 June 2003.
'Help on the farm or around home', *Camden & Wollondilly Times*, 17 September 1997.
'John's retirement brings a company to a Head', *The Crier*, 11 June 1997.
'Forty-eight years in business', *The Crier*, 13 September 1993.
Farah Abdurahman, 'Soil toil earns acclaim again', *Camden Narellan Advertiser,* 27 October 2010.
Vera Bertola, 'Honours bookend his name', *Macarthur Chronicle Camden Edition,* 27 April 2010.
Neville Clissold, *Camden Show 1886-2011, The People, The Stories*, Camden, The Camden Show Society, 2011.
Joseph Correy, 'Sharing wonder of nature', *Macarthur Chronicle,* 23 October 2007.
Jeff McGill, 'John gets steamed up about his hobby', *Macarthur Advertiser*, 13 October 1993.
University of New South Wales Regiment. Online @ https://my.unsw.edu.au/student/atoz/Regiment.html
Joanne Vella, 'Camden takes pride of place for this scout', *Macarthur Chronicle,* 10 June 2003.

Camden Historical Society Annual Report 2011 – 2012

John Wrigley

I am pleased to present the annual report of the Camden Historical Society for the year 2011 – 2012. This report covers the activities of the Society itself and of the Camden Museum.

In both areas the year has been a very successful one. The Society has continued to hold its monthly meetings and to be involved in a number of community events. The Museum has continued to improve and to attract many appreciative visitors. The continuing support of Camden Council is much appreciated.

Our monthly meetings had an average attendance of about 35 members and visitors each month and our membership stood at 130 members at the end of the financial year. The following guest speakers kindly donated their time to make our meetings entertaining and informative:
- Mick Starr - Raptors on Camden Park (July 2011)
- Members of the Society on 'Eat History' (Sep 2011)
- Colin Mills - Bransby Cottage (Oct 2011)
- Vince Capaldi - Camden Cemetery (Nov 2011)
- Members of the Society on Memories of Christmas (Dec 2011)
- Lorraine Iddon – The Tea Ceremony (Feb 2012)
- Ian Willis - Camden on the Rural-Urban Fringe (March 2012)
- Lu Papi – 'Innovation and Invention' (April 2012)
- Elizabeth Villy - The Razorback Road (May 2012)
- Ken Newton - Camden International Friendship Association (June 2012)

The Society continued its advocacy role in heritage protection and town planning matters with several letters being submitted on specific Development Applications. These included the proposed St John's Hall extension and buildings in John Street. Meetings were held with Camden Council planning staff.

Our partnership with the Camden Library Service has continued to be productive and helpful to both organisations. Regular quarterly partnership meetings were held. The Society acknowledges the effective hard work of the Local Studies Librarian Jo Oliver in this work particularly during the successful festival programs in 'Eat History' History Week September 2011 and the 'Innovation and Invention' National Trust Festival April 2012.

Grants were received from Camden Council for new textile display and storage cabinets and from the Federal Government for a Red Cross Centenary project to be developed in 2013-14. Congratulations to Bob Lester and Ian Willis for arranging these grants. A range of donated objects to the Museum collection were accepted during the year. These included the 1953 QE2 Coronation Medal awarded to the well known Camden character and community worker Ben Hodge; an 1846 lithograph portrait image of Lord Camden after whom John Macarthur's land grant and the town are named; and an original letter handwritten by Sir Evan Nepean, after whom the Nepean River was named.

The Museum was able to be open four days a week from Thursday to Sunday thanks to the dedication of fifty-three volunteers. The Museum is always looking for more volunteers to join our merry band. A willing team of members helped organize the displays in the research room of Camden Weddings in 2011, and Camden Christening Gowns in 2012. A generous donation from Quota was used to conserve the 1899 wedding gown of Maud Hodge. Other exhibitions were for Naidoc Week and an interesting display of old maps and plans.

Thanks to the enthusiasm of Secretary Doug Barrett and members, 5,465 visitors attended the Museum and many complimentary remarks were placed in our Visitors' Book. Our policy of having free entry to the Museum, while encouraging visitors to make a donation or to consider purchasing items from the Museum Shop, continues to be successful. The joint operation the Mini Discoverers program with the Camden Youth Librarian has meant a lot of fun for young visitors. Several local schools have made good use of the museum in their history activities and excursions.

I would like to acknowledge the work of the various office bearers and committee members in achieving the success of the past year. In particular the good works of Secretary Doug Barrett, Treasurer Ray Herbert, and Volunteer Coordinator Bob Lester have been exceptional. Vice President Ian Willis has continued to edit the excellent Newsletter and Journal to a very high standard. Publications by Peter Mylrea on Narellan and by Janice Johnson on Early Reminiscences have been well received during the year.

I will be standing down as president at this meeting and I wish the incoming executive and committee every success. I will continue to work for and support the Society wherever I can. I encourage all members to support the committee in the various activities during the coming year.

John Wrigley OAM
8 August 2012

Elderslie

Robert Wheeler

Elderslie is the suburb in the Camden local government area where I having been living for the past twenty three years.

It took its name from John Oxley's second land grant of 332ha (820 acres) of June 1816, adjacent to his first land grant and home, Kirkham and fronting the then Cow Pasture Road. However, the name on his land grant was 'Ellerslie' so the search began as to firstly, why the spelling change? and secondly, why did John Oxley choose this name?

Well my first call was to 'Google' which revealed that in Scotland both names are interchangeable with the meaning of 'field of elder trees'. However, there were no Elder trees on his land grant or nearby.

Kirkham, in Yorkshire, England was the birth place of John Oxley (born in 1783) and again searching the internet didn't reveal any close association of an Ellerslie where he grew up. Also he left home early at sixteen to join the Royal Navy in 1799 and probably hadn't travelled far from home, that is, until his naval career, where he sailed to the West Indies, Cadiz and Gibraltar and NSW in 1802 returning home to England in 1807. He sailed back to Port Jackson in November 1808 as first lieutenant on the 'Porpoise' and returned to England in May 1810 with the ex Governor Bligh.

Oxley had taken a liking to the Colony after his several visits with the Navy. He had obtained an order for a land grant of 243ha (600 acres) near the Nepean River from the Colonial Office. However during this last visit the acting governor, Lieutenant-Governor William Paterson, (filling in between Bligh and Macquarie) gave land grants to the officers of the 'Porpoise'. Oxley received 405ha (1,000 acres) in February 1809.

When Governor Macquarie arrived in January 1810 this land grant was cancelled but regranted as 243ha (600 acres) in May 1810 with the name of 'Kirkham Park', in the same area based on the recommendation from England. This was just as well as Oxley had purchased stock for his land. Oxley's first land grant eventually was finalised in June 1815, when the grant from Macquarie was cancelled and he received the original 405ha (1,000 acres), again in the same area and Oxley named it this time as 'Kirkham'.

Oxley was discharged from the Navy in 1811, when he had arrived back to England. He was appointed as Surveyor-General, effective from 1 January

1812, but it was not until 25 October 1812 before he arrived back in NSW to take up his new position.

Further searching on the name of his second land grant, revealed that there was an Elderslie just out of Glasgow and it was famous as the family estate of Sir William Wallace, the famous Scottish knight who is known for leading a resistance during the Wars of Scottish Independence and is remembered in Scotland as a patriot and national hero and today as 'Braveheart'. He defeated an English army at the battle of Stirling Bridge, and became Guardian of Scotland, serving until his defeat at the Battle of Falkirk. Later he was captured near Glasgow and handed over to King Edward 1 of England, who had him executed for treason in 1305.

Again what was the association with John Oxley? I had noticed when researching Sir William Wallace, that in 1810 a novel had been written about him by a Miss Jane Porter, called 'The Scottish Chiefs – A Romance'. Apparently it was a best seller and has been reprinted many times. Downloading a copy from the Gutenberg Project, revealed that on page one, Ellerslie was mentioned and that Chapter 3 was called 'Ellerslie'.

As John Oxley travelled out from England in 1812 to take up his new position, it was probable that that he had some reading matter and as Miss Porter's book was new and popular there would have been a copy on board the ship.

I decided to look for a second hand copy (easier to read) and found one in Goulburn, in fact there were a lot for sale on the internet, especially in America. The edition I bought was published about the 1900's and to my surprise the name Ellerslie had become Elderslie. The next step was to find a first edition. The Fisher Library at Sydney University had a copy, which would have been the edition that John Oxley read on the ship. 'Ellerslie' was used in this original version.

Unfortunately when Oxley died at the early age of 45 in1828, he was not in a good financial position and his library and household furniture were sold at his town house at the corner of Macquarie and King Streets, which Oxley firstly leased from D'Arcy Wentworth in about 1819 and later from the Government in 1821 after the Government purchased the building. Oxley used the house for both his office and Sydney home.

A catalogue of his library was presented at the book auction in August 1828, and whilst a copy of Miss Porter's book was not listed Oxley may have lent his copy and it was not returned, or he may have borrowed the book from someone in the Colony to read.

A variation to the above hypothesis is that the naming of Oxley's second land grant in 1816, which was much larger than those generally Governor Macquarie preferred to grant, usually less than 40ha, was the pattern of using place names to please the 'people of influence', that is the Governor and/or the Colonial Office in England.

Governor Macquarie was born on the Isle of Ulva, on the west coast of Scotland and spent thirty three years in military service, before coming to NSW as governor in 1810. Again it would be expected that with the then recent publication of 'The Scottish Chiefs – A Romance', re-establishing the hero status of Sir William Wallace that Oxley's use of Wallace's family estate name 'Ellerslie' would have won him some 'Brownie Points' with the governor of NSW.

Oxley's third land grant of 255ha was located at Appin and called 'Malton', after a town close to his family home at Kirkham, England.

Two more land grants were given to Oxley in June 1823. Firstly, 243ha near St Marys, now the suburb of Oxley Park, which he called 'Bathurst' after the Earl of Bathurst, who was then the Colonial Secretary, and 971ha located at Bowral, which he called 'Weston'.

The earliest reference to Elderslie that I could find, appears in the 'The Sydney Gazette' on Tuesday 7 April, 1829, where hay was advertised for sale at Elderslie, Cowpastures.

The early maps for this area adjacent to the 'Cowpastures', that is to the north of the Nepean River, showed both names were used. This would relate to the draughtsman using the name as shown on the land grant and the use of 'Elderslie' either that it was easier to pronounce and/or clearer to read on a plan, or just that it was the Anglicisation of the word.

However, the earliest map (Parish Plan, a copy is attached) that I could find is dated 1834 that has used the 'Elderslie' spelling.

Whilst there can be no specific correlation for the derivation of my suburb's name, it is very satisfying that John Oxley has had his naming of his second land grant fixed in our local history. Also, it has been very gratifying journey to have had the opportunity to research one of Australia's earliest explorer and senior public servants, who left a significant imprint to our local area and country.

References:

Jane Porter, The Scottish Chiefs – A Romance, first edition 1810 Vol. 1 of 5;
Jane Porter, The Scottish Chiefs, 1910;
The Sydney Gazette 7 April 1829;
Richard Johnson The search for the inland sea – John Oxley, explorer, 1783-1828 (2001);
Richard Johnson The Library of John Oxley, Esq.(1982);
PJ Mylrea, Camden District – A History to the 1840's (2002);
MH Ellis, Lachlan Macquarie fourth edition (1965);
Frank Clune, Serenade to Sydney (1967);
Terry Kass, Sails to Satellites – The Surveyors General of NSW 1786-2007 (2010);
EV Crampton, …remembering the forgotten – The untold stories of John Oxley's 1817 & 1818 Expeditions(E-book);
NSW Department of Lands;
Australian National Library internet site 'Trove'.

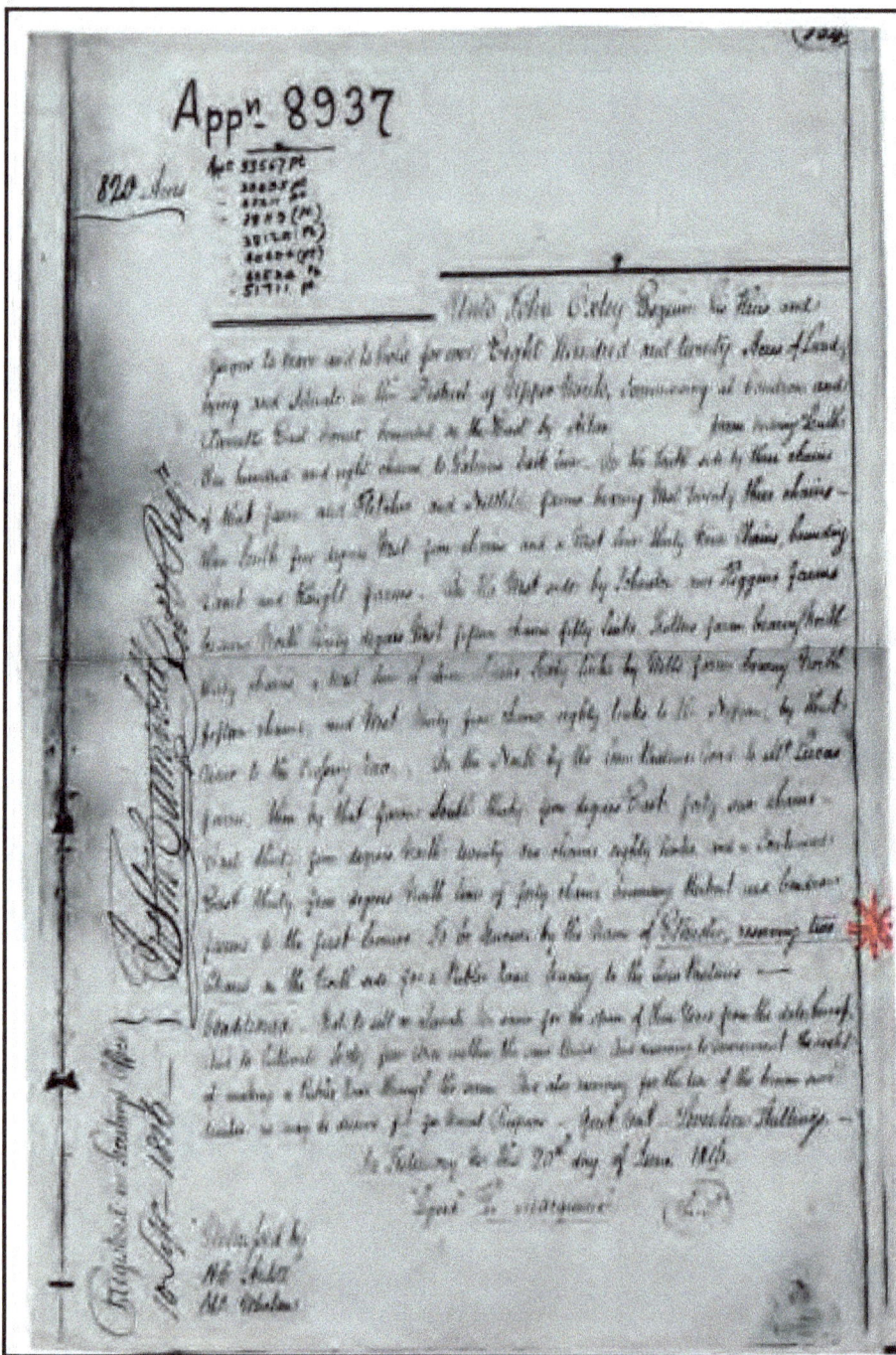

The Original Village of Cawdor

Peter Mylrea

The small village of Cawdor is mentioned in various historical documents from the 1820s to 1841. These cover the establishment of the village, activities in the village and its fading away in the early 1840s.

The early development of Cawdor came about because of the presence of the 'Wild Cattle' in the Cowpastures. These were descendants of cattle which had escaped from the settlement of Sydney soon after it was established. Their existence was known from about 1895 but it was not until Macquarie became Governor that attempts were made to tame and manage these cattle. In June 1813 Macquarie issued instructions for the erection of 'Substantial Strong Stock Yards' in the Cowpastures [1] and in present day terms these were on the western side of Cawdor Road just to the north of Westbrook Road. [2]

On this site by 1822 there was a brick house for the Superintendent of Government Stock and the Overseer of Government Stock, a weather-boarded house for the stockmen, four large paddocks each of one hundred acres with strong fences and a tanning house. [3] The name of Cawdor was given by Governor Macquarie during his tour in 1820 in honour of his wife's birthplace in Scotland. The settlement was known as the Government Establishment. By 1825 John Macarthur had received his final land grants. These surrounded the 'Government Establishment' at Cawdor but the land and buildings were retained by the government.

The Wild Cattle were sold and the site and buildings became the centre of government activities in the region. First there was the Bench of Magistrates, followed by a Court of Petty Sessions and a little later by a Post Office.

The Bench of Magistrates was established at Cawdor in 1825 and this was the first court of law in this part of the colony. It continued to function until 1828 when the Bench was transferred to Stonequarry (later called Picton). In 1832 another type of court, a Court of Petty Sessions, was established at Cawdor. It functioned at Cawdor until 1841 when it was transferred to the new village of Camden.[4]

A later development was the establishment of the Cawdor Post Office. In 1832 a road was built from Cawdor over the Razorback Range going south. This facilitated access to more southerly districts of the colony and was much used by people and for the transport of goods. One example was a mail ser-

vice which ran between Sydney and Bong Bong [Goulburn] three times a week. In May 1836 a post office was established on this mail route at Cawdor.[5] It continued to operate until 1841 when it too was transferred to Camden
Once these changes had taken place and the village of Camden began to develop there was little reason for Cawdor to continue to exist and so the village faded away.

One and half kilometres away from the site of the original village of Cawdor and many years later other buildings appeared in the district. These had no connection with the site of the original Government Establishment. First, was the opening of the Cawdor Public School and teacher's residence in 1888[6], then came the Wesleyan Church [now the Uniting Church] built in 1902 and third was the building of St Jeromes Anglican Church about 1900. All four of these buildings still exist today.

References

1 Historical Records of Australia (HRA) vol.7 p. 745
2 The site is shown on a map drawn before 1825. It is catalogued in the Mitchell Library as M Ser 4 0001 A30004 map 20.
3 HRA vol. 10 pp. 694-5.
4 Mylrea *Camden History* September 2012, vol.3.
5 Sydney Gazette 24 May 1836.
6 Letter from John Fletcher, Teacher, to the Chief Inspector dated November 1888. A copy is as Attachment 14 in Sue Davis *Chapters of Cawdor, 2008.*

Development of Law Courts in Cawdor, Picton and Camden

Peter Mylrea

The Camden region has been well served by Courts of Law over the last 190 years. First was the Bench of Magistrates at Cawdor which was followed by a similar Bench at Stonequarry (Picton). These were presided over by Justices of the Peace who were mostly the major land owners in the district. Most of the people brought before the Courts were convicts often those in the service of land owners. By present day standards most of the charges were minor but the sentences passed were draconian. In 1832 the names of the courts at Cawdor and Picton were changed to Courts of Petty Sessions. In the first years they differed little from the preceding Benches of Magistrates. They were still presided over by the same Justices and the charges and sentences remained much the same. However from about the 1840s things changed. Criminal cases were brought before the Courts by police constables. The sentences passed were often fines with some imprisonments but no lashings, chain gangs or solitary confinement. These Courts also had many civil duties which their predecessors did not have. Such Courts still exist in Camden and Picton and are called Local Courts. They handle both criminal and civil cases.

....

Immediately on his arrival in Sydney in 1788 Governor Phillip established a Bench of Magistrates to administer justice in the new colony. The Judge Advocate presided over the Bench and he was assisted by Justices of the Peace appointed by the Governor. This Bench met in Sydney and, later, also in Windsor. It continued to function until the late 1810s.

Cawdor Bench of Magistrates: 1825 to 1828:

The nature of the Benches of Magistrates changed in 1821. When the Judge Advocate's Bench of Magistrates ceased to exist it was replaced by local Benches of Magistrates. These were made up by Justices of the Peace who were called Magistrates hence the name of the Benches. Justices of the Peace were appointed by the Governor.
Governor Brisbane published documents listing the names of persons who had been appointed Justices of the Peace. Some of the local men named in the 1821 list were: Henry Colden Antill (Stonequarry), Henry Grattan Douglass

(Stonequarry) and John Oxley (Kirkham). In 1825 the names of James and William Macarthur (Camden) were added to the lists. Over the years other men were appointed as Justices.

In addition to the names of Justices these documents also outlined the duties and responsibilities of Justices of the Peace. These were given in detail and were summarised in the opening paragraph

> ... and to keep, and cause to be kept, all Ordinances and Statutes for the Preservation of the Peace, and for the quiet Government of our People ... and to punish all persons offending against the said Ordinances and Statutes [1]

On 15 March 1825 the Cawdor Bench of Magistrates was established and this was the first court in the Camden region.

In 1825 John Wild, junior, was appointed as Clerk to the Bench [2] and he kept detailed records of the functioning of the Bench which met regularly. The Justices sitting on the Bench varied at different times and included H.C. Antill, James Macarthur, William Macarthur, John Oxley, T.C. Harrington and John Coghill most of whom were land owners with assigned convicts.

Records still exist for Cawdor between 1825 and 1828.[3] These included details of the alleged offences, written and signed evidence of witness and the sentences imposed. Most of those charged were convicts and those bringing the charges were often the overseers of convicts for their masters. Typical examples were: Mr White, overseer for Mr de Arrietta, charging Richard Robinson with 'running away from the service of his master' sentenced to fifty lashes and David Paton, overseer for Mr Murdock, laying a charge of 'neglecting duties' – fifty lashes. Other punishments were severe for example: absence without leave – up to six months in chain road gangs, [4] neglect of duties – seven days solitary confinement, insolence and neglect of duties – fifty lashes.[5] Women found guilty were sent to the 'Parramatta Factory'.[6]

Stonequarry Bench of Magistrates: 1828 to 1832

Stonequarry was the earlier name for Picton. For some unstated reason the Cawdor Bench closed and Governor Darling wrote in 1829
> The establishment of a Board of Magistrates at that place [Stonequarry] had become necessary, the Bench at Cawdor, which is seven miles from the above station [Stonequarry], having been discontinued...[7]

Major Henry Colden Antill played a major role in the Cawdor and Stonequarry Benches of Magistrates. He was appointed a Justice of the Peace by Governor Macquarie in 1821. In 1825 Antill moved to his property 'Jarvisfield' a land grant of 2000 acres he received in 1822. Antill was appointed a Resident Magistrate on 1 July 1825 and he remained a magistrate until his death in 1852.[8]

Often cases were heard in Antill's own house on 'Jarvisfield'. This was inconvenient and Antill arranged for a Court House to be erected on Jarvisfield at his expense. This Court House was used for the Bench of Magistrates up to 1832 and continued to be used for the succeeding Court of Petty Sessions up to 1864.

The cases brought before the Stonequarry Bench and the sentences handed down were generally similar to those at the previous Cawdor Bench. Some charges were unusual. In one case Macarthur's overseer said he had 'asked the prisoner to go with a flock of sheep and he refused. He said he would not be a shepherd. That he would sooner have his bloody back cut in two than be a shepherd.' His wish was granted – fifty lashes. Seven days in solitary confinement was the sentence to another convict who was 'slow in coming out of his hut after the horn blew'. In another case a prisoner in the Number 5 Chain Gang was alleged to have lost his blanket. As he 'is cook to the gang and is consequently not Ironed – is now ordered to be a Worker in Chains until he finds his blanket'. The sentence was effective as 'the prisoner produced his blanket two days after his sentence' Religion also came before the bench. A man charged with travelling sheep on a road on the Sabbath was 'admonished' and warned against repeating the offence.

Court of Petty Sessions at Stonequarry (Picton) : From 1832

Benches of Magistrates and their Clerks ceased to exist under these names in 1832 when they were renamed Courts of Petty Sessions and Clerks of Petty Sessions.[9] Stonequarry was proclaimed a Court of Petty Sessions in September 1832 and this was the first such Court in this area.[10] While there was a change in name, in practice, the Court continued to function in much the same way as had the previous Bench of Magistrates. The same Justices of the Peace continued to preside and the charges and sentences were much the same as in days of the Stonequarry Bench of Magistrates.[11] This Court still exists in Picton but its functions have changed as have those in the Camden Court of Petty Sessions (see below).

Court of Petty Sessions at Cawdor: 1833 to 1841

The Cawdor Court was not proclaimed until December 1833, a year after the Stonequarry Court. It lasted only a few years in Cawdor before it was transferred to the new village of Camden in August 1841. No records now exist giving details of its workings but these were probably like those of the Stonequarry Court of Petty Sessions in the 1830s.

Court of Petty Sessions at Camden: From 1841:

The Court of Petty Sessions was officially moved from Cawdor to Camden on 26 July 1841. Court sessions continued to be presided over by Justices of the Peace and among these were Charles Cowper, John Oxley (junior), James Macarthur, Jas. J Riley and George McLeay. At some time after the 1870s professional magistrates were appointed and they took over the duties previously performed by Justices of the Peace.

The only court records still available cover the periods 1847 to 1850, 1851 to 1854 and 1863 to 1865. [12] The functions of this Court differed greatly from those of earlier courts. No cases of complaints about convict behaviour were found and no physical punishments such as flogging, sending to chain gangs or solitary confinement were found.

However there were criminal cases and these were brought before the Court by police constables. An example was the stealing of clothing which resulted in two months imprisonment at Parramatta Gaol. Vagrancy also resulted in two months imprisonment while a woman found guilty of prostitution was sentenced to a month's hard labour at the Parramatta Factory. In some instances cases were referred to a higher Court. An example was of a man charged with the theft of potatoes who was 'to take his trial at such Court as Her Majesty's Attorney General shall approve... and accordingly [be] forwarded under warranty to Parramatta Gaol'. By this time people had money and many persons committing lesser offences were fined as the only punishment. Thus drunk and disorderly could incur a fine of ten shillings with four shillings and six pence costs.

Unlike previous courts this court had many civil duties which occupied much of its time. Among these were the issuing of slaughtering and timber licences, revision of electoral rolls, investigating and issuing annual hotel licences, issuing blankets to Aboriginals, appointment of Pound Keepers and conducting Coroner's Courts.

The Court of Petty Sessions has continued to function in Camden but at some time in the past professional, full time, magistrates took over the duties previously performed by Justices of the Peace. In 1985 the name of the court was changed to Local Court.

References

1 Government and General Orders, Sydney Gazette 3 December 1821, 3 June 1825, 17 November 1825.
2 Sydney Gazette 21 April 1825.
3 State Records microfilms 665-667. Liz Vincent in her book *Cawdor Bench Books 1825-1828* (1996) gives information on some aspects of the cases.
4 These were gangs of prisoners constructing roads. 'Chain' referred to the leggings of shackles around the ankles joined by a length of chain which they wore for all the time they were in the gang.
5 At this time men were appointed as 'scrougers'. A 'scourage' was a whip and a 'scrouger' was the man who applied the lashes, in other words a flogger (Shorter Oxford Dictionary).
6 In 1821 the 'Parramatta Factory' was a three storey building used to house women who had committed local crimes.
7 HRA, vol. 15, p. 189.
8 J.M. Antill *Journal Royal Australian Historical Society* 1947 vol 32 pp. 187-195.
9 Offenders Punishment and Justices Summary Jurisdiction Act, 1832.
10 Sydney Gazette 9 October 1832.
11 State Records microfilm reel 672. Records for some of the years 1853 to 1874 are on reels 673-676.
12 State Records reels 665, 666 and 1259.

CAMDEN HISTORY

Journal of the Camden Historical Society

March 2013 Volume 3 Number 5

CAMDEN HISTORY
Journal of the Camden Historical Society Inc.
ISSN 1445-1549
Editor: Dr Ian Willis

Management Committee
President: Bob Lester
Vice Presidents: Cathey Shepherd, Dr Ian Willis
Secretary: Doug Barrett
Assistant Secretary: Julie Wrigley
Treasurer: Ray Herbert
Assistant Treasurer:
Immediate Past President: John Wrigley OAM
General Committee: Sharon Greene   Janice Johnson
                     Peter Hayward OAM   Rene Rem
                     Julie Wrigley   Robert Wheeler

Honorary Auditor: Jim Hunter
Honorary Solicitors: Bowring, Macaulay and Barrett

Society contact:
P.O. Box 566, Camden, NSW 2570.   Online <http://www.camdenhistory.org.au>

Meetings
Meetings are held at 7.30 p.m. on the second Wednesday of the month except in January. They are held in the Museum. Visitors are always welcome.

Museum
The Museum is located at 40 John Street, Camden, phone 4655 3400 or 46559210. It is open Thursday to Sunday 11 a.m. to 4 p.m., except at Christmas. Visits by schools and groups are encouraged. Please contact the Museum to make arrangements. Entry is free.

Camden History, Journal of the Camden Historical Society Inc
The journal is published in March and September each year. The editor would be pleased to receive articles broadly covering the history of the Camden district . Correspondence can be sent to the Society's postal address. The views expressed in the articles are solely those of the authors and not necessarily endorsed by the society.

Donations
Donations made to the Society are tax deductible. The accredited value of objects donated to the Society are eligible for tax deduction.

Cover: Mary Ifould (1938) from the papers of Annette Macarthur Onslow

CAMDEN HISTORY
Journal of the Camden Historical Society Inc.

March 2013 Volume 2 Number 5

Contents

From the Editor	147
Macquarie Grove to Camden Aerodrome	148
From the Author	149
Maquarie Grove	
1. Behold where master Edward flies.........	150
2. The 'Broken Man of Camden'	153
3. The Pioneer Farm	155
4. The race-course that featured in "Silks & Saddles"	158
5. First Flights	161
6. Starting the Flying School	164
7. The arrival of the Air Force	167
8. Time in Exile	171
9. War ends and the show goes on	175
Camden Aerodrome	
From the Horse's Mouth -	179
Macquarie Grove Flying Notes	183
Films and Fun at Macquarie Grove	186
Now for a little light instruction	190
Pre-War and Post-War	194
The author	198

From the Editor

This is a special edition of Camden History drawn from a collection of articles about Camden Airfield written by Annette Macarthur Onslow. An earlier versions of most of the articles were published in the District Reporter in 2009 and 2011. The articles have been revised and additional material has been added by the author.

Camden Airfield is an important heritage item in the story of Camden and the site has changed little in over 65 years. The foundation of the airfield is intimately connected to the story of one of Australia's pioneering families, the Macarthurs of Camden Park. Edward Macarthur Onslow established the Macquarie Grove Flying School during the Inter-war years on the family pastoral property of Macquarie Grove.

The airfield is a tangible illustration of the forces of modernism that shaped early aviation in Australia. These forces emerged during the Inter-war period and have had a critical role in the progress and development of the modern nation of Australia and the country town of Camden. The beginnings of the Macquarie Grove Flying School parallel the foundation of major airfields elsewhere in Australia including Mascot, New South Wales.

The airfield was part of the story of the defence of Australia during the Second World War. It has a number of items of military airfield infrastructure that are intact and have retained their integrity from the war period, including the Bellman hangars. There is also one intact RAAF accommodation hut, that has undergone recent restoration and conservation, still located on the airfield. The hut was typical of those used by airmen between 1939-1946.

This complete series of articles provides an invaluable narrative on the early foundation of one of the country's important regional aviation facilities. The first nine articles relate to the Macquarie Grove Flying School, while the section on Camden Aerodrome is a mixture of wartime and post-war stories of the aerodrome. The Camden Historical Society thanks the author for providing the opportunity to publish them and for the use of images from her collections of photographs.

Ian Willis, Editor, *Camden History*, March 2013.

Macquarie Grove to Camden Aerodrome

Annette Macarthur Onslow

From the Author

To introduce these reprints I have added some details of the life we knew before, during and just after WWII when everything changed. I have also borrowed by kind permission from his descendants part of 'A Nostalgic Whimsey' by poet Hugh McRae, describing himself as 'The Broken Man of Camden'.

I believe that all who knew those times will share the sentiment, and I hope that I may arouse in all hearts a wish to share in the fun.

This brief sketch is told from our family point of view. The years of air force occupation of the aerodrome have already been well covered by Dr Ian Willis, and more recent developments have been recorded by Miro Viteck, John Laming, Keith Colyer, AL (Bert) Watson and others.

I am particularly grateful to Cecil Smith who corrected errors in the original articles and to the late Doug Baglin for his support over the years and to my sister Phoebe Atkinson who has done all the typing and donkey work for me.

Macquarie Grove Flying School 1939, showing the office and back gate to the house and one of the school's fleet of planes, a Gypsy Moth belonging to Flying Doctor Clyde Fenton. (photo late Mary Ifould)

Macquarie Grove
1. Behold where master Edward flies………

The Camden we knew in our Public School days had plenty of hitching-posts and horse troughs and wide, unsealed road verges which eased our riding to town.

Two stout draught-horses, a Clydesdale and a Shire, took turns at patrolling the streets with the dust cart, collecting the endless supply of horse manure. In the heat of summer this also attracted flies, and like many of the school children we were prey to conjunctivitis.

The cart was driven by an old Light Horseman, Bill Lysaght who also handled any plough-horse which might be working at Macquarie Grove. To my great embarrassment Bill, who was a great tippler, might come rolling out of the Plough & Harrow as I was passing, saying "I used to hold you in my arms when you was a baby!"

When we rode our ponies to school, we tethered them in the Davies' paddock, a paddock which was shared with school games, Basketball and Hopscotch and with Arbor Day plantings which never survived the heat of summer.

When the High School was built, Llewella Davies continued to exercise a proprietary right to that paddock by walking through the school buildings to town. Llewella, known to us all as Biddie, worked in the Camden News stationary shop. She had a rather sharp tongue and scared us children with her "What are you looking for now, Snookie?"

Home from school we might be greeted by hot pikelets baking on the slab of our old fuel stove. Food was rationed and we were always hungry, but Mum fed us well. It was however a break to have an after church, Sunday lunch at the Camden Inn and roast chicken was a luxury.

On school days we sneaked our pocket money to Scoles Café-cum-fruit shop to buy battered savs and soft drinks until Mum found out and stopped us. The tables were decorated with Iceland poppies and gum leaves and streamers of fly paper hung from the ceiling.

One knew Christmas was coming when the shop windows filled with red-net stockings packed with crackers and trinkets, and colourful beach buckets held tinsel-tied toys and wooden spades.

At Ernie Britton's chemist shop there were penny scales to weigh oneself and a particular product, unique to Britton's – Dr. Crookston's shampoo – a greenish liquid not unlike the herbal shampoo one buys today.

At Clifton's general store, biscuits came fresh from large tins to be wrapped in paper bags. There was a dignity about placing an order. Mum would sit on a highchair beside the counter while whoever served her, wearing a white apron, would take a pencil from behind his ear to record the list, while an assistant would box the goods to be carried to the car.

Many shops, like Maloneys and Whitemans, were wired for cash with a central control and a system of containers which, at the tug of a cord would whizz on a wire to the cashier for inspection and sorting of change to return to the counter by the same manner.

Buying shoes, one's feet were measured by an x-ray machine until that system was withdrawn. To overcome the slipperyness of leather soles, one bought thin strips of "Kromhyde" rubber to paste on.

Food supplies were simple. Bread which remained basically plain brown or white, could be varied with a fruit loaf, or a round, flour-dusted cottage loaf delivered by Stuckey Bros. Vegetables in season might come by horse and cart from the Chinese gardens – or be grown at home. Meat came from Boardmans, Dunks or Stewarts.

Petrol, as I remember from the time of my father's first car, came from a hand-pump bowser at Poole's garage opposite the showground, then from Harold Crick's corner. Cars could be serviced at the Main Southern garage across the road, where seated in the family car, I could watch an old horse circling the pug-mill at the neighbouring brick-works.

On certain days at the north-eastern end of town there would a confusion of sounds from the rattle of cans at the Milk Depot, to the clopping of hooves as teams delivered logs to Rideouts Sawmill. The melancholy whine of the saw-mill itself vying with murmurs and cries from the Sale Yards and the crack of whips and barking dogs driving cattle along the Stock Route.

Overall there might be whistle and rumble of "Pansy" the Camden train or tram. "Pansy" was distinguished by its own little dead-end Station Street and a notice at the buffer end of the line bordering Mitchell Street listing animals forbidden to stray on the line.

Pansy's route between Camden & Campbelltown had an extra station at Narellan and half a dozen halts or sidings along the way.

Close to the station was the Carrier Archie Tippet's yard. I best remember his truck with Camden Vale fruit boxes piled high. Further along was Burford the farrier where our horses were shod, and beyond his forge, a small paddock where a visiting circus could raise its Big Top.

We saw many circuses. The most popular was Cracknell's – a tiny circus with a clever Timor pony which inspired us to start our own circus.

A busy part of the station was the Parcels Office where all manner of small goods were delivered, from machines to caged birds and plants.

Mum, redesigning our post-war garden, ordered plants from Sorensen's Nursery. Chinese Gooseberries (Kiwi fruit) were a new attraction which to our amusement, arrived in two packages each labelled according to their gender – one pink and one blue.

I have said that we knew the train as "Pansy", but to poet Hugh McRae who wrote so lovingly of the town characters and happenings, it was "Black Maggie".

Hugh McCrae lived for many years at Elderslie. As a child I was taken to play with his nieces, Lorne and Robin Adams. The view from the train McCrae described in his farewell to Camden, was a poignant piece from 1939, the year of his departure.

The Onslow Circus - Pam on Tommy

2. The 'Broken Man of Camden' A Nostalgic Whimsy

By Hugh McCrae

We have come to live in town, after years in an outer suburb – by courtesy, named the country – a nice place, made of roly-poly hills, with English trees among pioneer ironbarks who had blackfellow friends even before James Ruse, at Parramatta, had "sowed the first graines." Before that …. Before 1788.

When we left, we felt sorry and emancipated a the same time. The needed change couldn't alter our affections; but it wasn't until the branch-line engine, called Black Maggie, had hoisted us to the top of Kenny's Hill that we began to regret. Here we saw for the last occasion, St. John's spire, lifted through the bushes, like Parson Paul's umbrella – unopen – in the beneficent air. Village-houses elbowed each other to be near; only the Plough & Harrow, under its private cover of pigeons, settled and aloof.

The distance is too great to pick out mine host; yet "wherever you are, Paddy King, it's good deeds you'll be doin', this day" Old-age pensioners bless him. Boys and girls, in the children's ward at the hospital, are forever his friends. In his prime, a public fighting-man – a hero of the ring – with three championships to his belt, he still keeps a farm where younkers are hardened to the game. On a summer's day at The Plough, in the created half-dark, he has often handed us a drink unimaginably cool.

Such brown beer remembrance! Re-creating in our ears the clip-clop of horse-shoes, straining of harness, whirring of wheels; venomous blistering whips.

The Big Show

There were giants in those days. The show days. Giants and pigmies, and snakes. Fat boys and pin-headed elfs. Boxers galore! All the paddocks about empty of man and beast. Even fruit and vegetables had come in.

The grazier, the farmer, the doctor, the banker, and the solicitors were there; their wives and families. Their cars, too, blunt-nosed and glittering, encompassed the ring. The air wrinkled with music of brass bands, blurred by race-dust, giddied by roundabouts, pounded by swings, inspired the necessary thirst.

And here's Joe Heffernan; voted a sorcerer because he has capacity; reads philosophy hanging to the tail of a cow ambulant over a ditch. Further away, but close against Mr. Downes's pocket, we can see the local scoundrel-of-all-trades – suspected of arson and jay-walking – "A bad lot," says the sergeant "not fit to be buried with Kelly!"

Now a plane swoops down; almost on top of us. Somebody in it everyone knows. The local satirist unafraid of being misunderstood improvises.
    Ecod! Ecod!

Then, without impediment:
Behold, where Master Edward flies. To place an Onslow in the skies. Despite of God!

But that last show, epitome of all Camden shows, has sunk into the void; belongs, now, to Once-upon-a-time.

(extract; *The Sydney Morning Herald,* Saturday 17 June 1939, p.13. Emphasis by author)

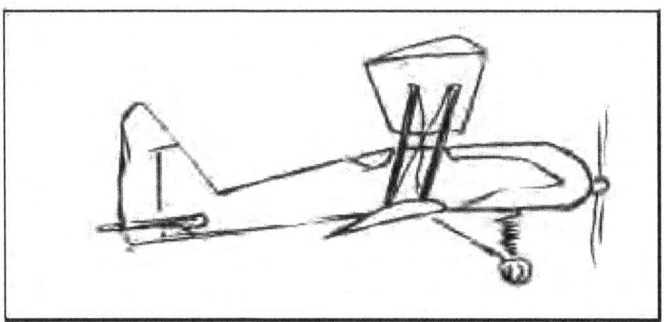

Drawn by Edward 1930

3. The Pioneer Farm

Sydney's urban spread is re-writing history. Old names disappear, or are left dangling, unattached to their source and without explanation.

Such an example is Macquarie Grove Road running north from Camden, across the flood-plain to Macquarie Grove Bridge at the river crossing once known as Hassall's Ford.

Who were the Hassalls and where is Macquarie Grove?

After the bridge, a sharp turn left takes you to Aerodrome Road. This is the old Macquarie Grove driveway, circuitous and narrow, passing through farm and homestead grounds on its way to the airport.

Much has been written lately about the wartime role of Camden Airport. We read about the Air Force and the huts, but Macquarie Grove property is not mentioned. Nor is its offspring, the Macquarie Grove Flying School which preceded the wartime takeover.

Macquarie Grove was the 400 acre grant made by Governor Macquarie in 1812 to the missionary sheepbreeder, Rowland Hassall.

Macquarie admired Mr. Hassall's handling of cattle and made him superintendent of the Cowpastures.

Macquarie Grove Farmhouse

The property has the rare distinction of being the place where the Governor and his entourage camped during the 1815 inspection tour and where he dined in Mr. Hassall's farmhouse and held Sunday service on its verandah.

Macquarie wrote with affection of "Mr. Hassall's finely situated and beautiful farm". He also wrote of the sad death of his own favourite greyhound, 'Oscar', mortally wounded in a kangaroo hunt and buried there on the farm.

No stone marks Oscar's grave, but many remnants of the farm still exist - early buildings and grand old trees, the original farmhouse and the later homestead.

The property, cradled in a wide loop of the Nepean River, comprises a hill where remains of the farm still stand, and a sandy flood plain with a selvage of rich alluvium where in 1916 Ferguson's Nursery leased ten acres of No.3 river paddock. A broken fence and an ancient peach tree used to mark the spot until river banks were mined for sand in the 1980s.

The Hassall family were prodigious settlers in the Cobbitty region. Best known is Rowland's eldest son Thomas, "the galloping parson" who lived at Denbigh and established the Heber Chapel and later St. Paul's Church on his grant, "Pomare Grove."

The second son, Samuel Otoo inherited Macquarie Grove, but died young, leaving all to his wife, Lucy Mileham provided that she did not remarry. She did remarry, and obedient to the law, she went to live with her new husband, James Howell at Boorowa, leaving Macquarie Grove to the care of tenants.

One of the tenants was the poet Charles Tompson, Camden's Clerk of Petty sessions, who wrote descriptive letters to the Herald about country life at Camden.

It is not clear when the Macquarie Grove homestead was built. There is no plan or document to tell the tale. The quality of the building material suggests 1840s or 50s.

By comparison Macquarie Grove farmhouse with its sandstock bricks and pre-lime mortar was under construction by 1813, and was the centre of a sizeable complex by 1815.

It was to this cottage that Lucy returned sometime after the death of her second husband in 1847. The cottage was renamed *Lucyville* to avoid confusion with Macquarie Grove homestead, which was now home to her second son, James Mileham Hassall and his family.

Lucy's dower of five acres included a vineyard and cellar established by Lewis Kowald, a German vigneron who had worked for the Macarthurs.

Peace was short lived. The floods of the 1860s cast Camden's farming community into gloom.

"I have been a great sufferer having lost all my crops," wrote James Mileham Hassall.

James took his family up country and for almost seven years Macquarie Grove homestead was leased to schoolmaster William Gordon for use as a boys' school. The virtues of such a school were extolled by the fact that it was "out of the way of the Ten Thousand Temptations that would exist in a town".

Hassall fortunes continued to dwindle, and in 1877 James Mileham Hassall was forced to sell Macquarie Grove.

The buyer was his old friend, Henry Carey Dangar.

Macquarie Grove Homestead

Filming 'Silks and Saddles' circa. 1919-1921. FA Macarthur Onslow starting the race

4. The race-course that featured in "Silks & Saddles"

After the sale of Macquarie Grove in 1877, great changes took place.

The new owner, H.C.Dangar M.L.C., pastoralist and property owner, was senior partner in the engineering firm of Dangar Gedye.

Dangar was a great racing man and breeder of thoroughbred stock. He owned "Gibraltar", a Melbourne Cup winner and sire of many famous horses.

Macquarie Grove became the family's summer retreat. A provider of garden produce and eggs, butter and cream for their Sydney home.

Frank Jessup, born there in 1884 was the son of Mr. Dangar's manager. He left a telling account of life as it was - the sort of relaxed and idyllic life which had inspired the tenant, Charles Tompson to wax poetic in his letters to the Herald.

Through Jessup we catch a glimpse of the river well stocked with blackfish, perch, mullet and big eels, and of its banks, the haunt of platypus and koala. The river which in a sudden "fresh" or flood might change its shape or activate the quicksands of Hassall's Ford, the usual river crossing before the bridge was built.

We see the pastures full of cattle branded with the crooked cross. Cattle whose unscheduled purpose was to clear the ford by being driven to and fro through the water to settle the sands.

Mr. Dangar was a keen supporter of rifle clubs. He sent the N.S.W. team to compete in Philadelphia and he established the rifle range at the southern end of the property. The cable footbridge used by the Camden Rifle Club, which Frank Jessup describes as downstream from the ford, has now disappeared, but the range itself, or Rifle Butts, a little sandy hill, remains more or less unchanged.

Mr. Dangar enlarged and improved the house and may have built the billiard room which, together with the kitchen wing, was demolished in the 1968 Heritage reconstruction of the house.

It is my guess that the race-course at Macquarie Grove, still extant when I was a child, also dates from Mr. Dangar's time.

The race-course was no more than a training track, such as was seen on many properties, but being close to the town, it became the popular gathering ground for horse events and picnic races.

Among the district enthusiasts were the Whites of Kirkham, Mrs.White, widow of James White MLC. MLA of racing fame, bought Macquarie Grove in 1894 and had it later conveyed to Henry Mackellar, her Kirkham Stud manager.

The grave of Kirkham's famous cup winner, "Chester", can be seen from the road, but his most prominent memorial is the grand Kirkham homestead, now called Camelot, built from "Chester's" winnings.

Kirkham's drawback was its easily flooded flat land which allowed no scope for a training track. No doubt the record floods of the 1890s prompted the move to the marginally safer ground of Macquarie Grove.

The restless land sales continued. In 1900 Macquarie Grove was bought by David Maxwell and, seven years later was sold to Percy Crossing, mortgaged and reconveyed in 1913 to James Pritchard who sold it in 1916 to my grandfather Arthur Macarthur-Onslow.

Arthur who had been manager at Camden Park's out-station - Richlands at Taralga, was now joint manager at Camden Park itself.

He had been looking for a sheep property in a warmer climate to carry out breeding experiments. Flocks were grazed on agistment and cows were milked at the old dairy, but no doubt at Camden, horses were his main interest.

In 1920 there was new excitement when a racing film "Silks & Saddles" was made - a film in which splendid horses were featured and, above all - a 'flying machine' which landed on the race-course.

My grandfather is seen in the photograph starting the race, but the big moment was to come when Edgar Percival landed his Avro 504K on Macquarie Grove race-course and flew the heroine to Randwick to win the day.

The film was released in 1921, but later it was lost and forgotten. Many years later a negative was rediscovered in cut fragments with tinting instructions (the method for indicating mood in silent films). It had no script, but the story was cleverly stitched together with captions and shown at the Sydney Film Festival.

I believe this was the first of many films which would be made in this district. The Avro 504K certainly staged the first landing at Macquarie Grove.

Footbridge to Macquarie Grove over Nepean River. C Athur Poole holding his Winchester Rifle on way to rifle range. 1900 (CHS1576)

5. First Flights

The 1920 landing of the Avro 504K on Macquarie Grove Race Course opened a new door to the world.

The pilot, Edgar Percival, became a great friend of the Onslow family. With his help, and that of aircraft designer Harry Broadsmith in 1924 a new 'plane was created. It was known as the B-4 or "the Onslow".

Arthur's eldest son, Denzil, aged nineteen and working with his father at Camden Park Estate, claimed to have financed it, but I think it more likely that the B-4 was a family effort. Even grandmother Sylvia ("Tim" to us all) was reported to have stitched the fabric for wings and fuselage on her sewing machine.

Edward and the B-4 circa 1927

The B-4 became the star of a light aircraft competition in Richmond where, out of eight entries, it was the overall winner. Flown by Edgar Percival, it won a great deal of prize money, but came to a sticky end when it crashed on take-off in 1927.

1927 marked a decline in fortunes generally. The amalgamation of the Camden Vale Co-op Milk Co. with the Dairy Farmers, led to disputes and strained relations. Arthur and Sylvia separated, but for most of their young family it seemed that the future was in the air.

Arthur's sons all became keen aviators, but it was the second son, Edward, my father, who would eventually take over the property and run a flying school.

Andrew, the youngest son, the only one of the three to join the Air Force, died in a training exercise in 1943.

Denzil had married in England in 1927. His wife Elinor did not like Australia, so Denzil bought a house in Scotland where his family settled while he led a divided life with frequent trips to Australia. He kept his connection with Camden and during the 30s he established two companies - Light Aircraft Pty. Ltd. (making parachutes) and Air Travel & Survey Ltd. which brought the DH Dragon (DH84) survey 'plane to Australia.

Edward gained his pilot's licence in 1930. He was deemed a natural flyer, and sometime later had the thrill of thirty minutes flying Kingsford Smith's Southern Cross. His instructor, the not so lucky, George Littlejohn was to accompany Smithy and Ulm on the last, ill-fated flight. Such were the joys and perils of aviation.

Meanwhile, Edward had married my mother Winifred and through borrowing and gifts had spent a fortune restoring Macquarie Grove's farmhouse ("Lucyville") which they made their home.

Both the cottage and the stables beside it were derelict and would have been demolished but for the for skill of architect Ken McConnel using bricks from the stables to save the cottage. The roof-line was altered and the building was partly re-modelled. My mother re-named it "April Cottage" for the month they went to live there.

My parents had barely one year there before it was suggested that they might need a bigger home. The family was expanding and grandmother "Tim" was now living alone in the large homestead. Her daughter Margaret had also married and was now living in India.

It had been "Tim's" express wish to swap houses. She held title to the property, so my father, who had already paid off her existing mortgage, devised a plan whereby she could have his newly restored cottage for a nominal rent while he would become owner of the rest of the property and deal with her mounting expenses.

Thus a legal agreement was drawn up making settlements with the rest of the family and thus we went to live at the run-down old homestead while Tim moved into "April Cottage" and re-named it "Hassall Cottage".

Edward now had a full time job as assistant manager at Camden Park Estate. His efforts to farm Macquarie Grove as his father had done, only ended in disappointment.

He was also captain of the Camden branch of the Light Horse Regiment which used the Macquarie Grove race-course for training. The importance of the race-course can be seen on this 1934 Ordnance Survey (Military) map.

Much of the sandy flood-plain was covered with tussock grass so the cleared area of the race-course made good space for troops to train or a light 'plane to land.

Edward set his sights on the latter.

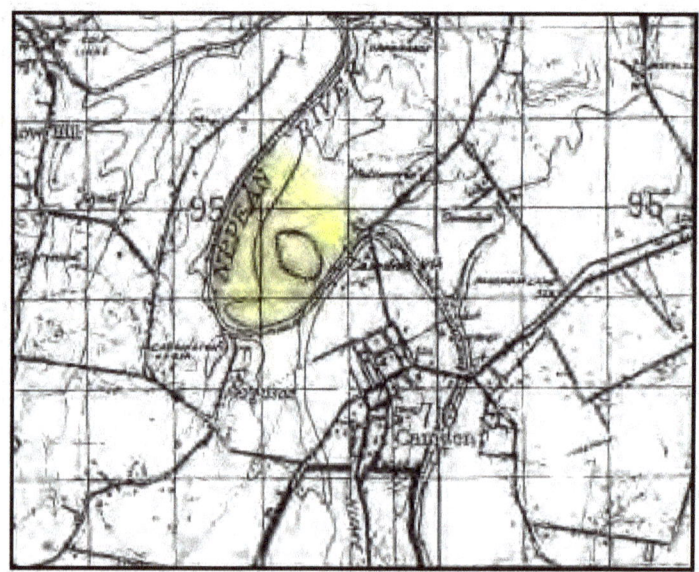

Macquarie Grove 1934, Ordnance Survey showing the race course where early planes landed.

Edward's Taper-winged Hornet and the shed in which two aircraft were housed. 1935

6. Starting the Flying School

In 1935 Edward bought his first aircraft - a taper-winged Hornet Moth (DH 87A), the ideal machine for primary instruction, but not for aerobatics. For that, when he gained his instructor's ticket, he would hire a Gipsy Moth (DH 60) from the Aero Club.

The 'plane was housed in the old tin shed – a rambling building housing garage, workshop, feed-shed and stable. Here, behind double doors which opened to the paddock, were two little 'planes - Denzil's Comper Swift and Edward's Hornet with folded wings.

The Hornet seems to have been a real Boy's Own Adventure 'plane. It won Edward his first race in 1936 - the Vyner Memorial Trophy. Later in the same year it featured in dare-devil flights fire-spotting over Burragorang and Yerranderie. It helped him to produce evidence against a road speeding fine, and at Narooma, where his mother had a cottage, it could land on the beach or the golf course, giving rides to the locals - and then, with folded wings, it could be driven like any car, down the main street.

The growing popularity of flying was starting to cause problems.
parachute. It almost went awry when winds blew the parachutist off course to land

In 1937, the year Edward had hoped to start his flying school, his 'plane was damaged on the ground where it was parked at Mascot.

Two aircraft, busily avoiding each other, caused one to crash into the stationary Hornet, severing the rudder. It took some time to repair.

Meanwhile preparations were made for Macquarie Grove's airfield. The race-course fence was removed, more ground was cleared and the sheep which had kept the grass well mown, were sold.

The Hornet was flying again by 1938, taking part in competitions and coming second in the handicap section of the Aerial Derby. Winifred flew with Edward and acted as time-keeper.

Events moved swiftly that year. Arthur Onslow died in March. His sons were here for the funeral, then Denzil left for England, accompanied by Andrew, to study aerial surveying and photography.

The first of two hangars was built and the flying school became fully established after a year of initial training. The Press applauded the general enthusiasm and the boost to employment. It was sunshine after the gloom of the Depression.

In August the aerodrome received its official registration from the Federal Government. It also received its first emergency visitor - an Ansett Lockheed Hudson airliner from Melbourne, unable to land in fog-bound Sydney.

In August the aerodrome received its official registration from the Federal Government. It also received its first emergency visitor - an Ansett Lockheed Hudson airliner from Melbourne, unable to land in fog-bound Sydney.

In September the first of the aerial pageants was staged in a picnic atmosphere. 'Planes from the Royal Aero Club of NSW, and Newcastle Aero Club combining forces with the newly formed Macquarie Grove Aero Club. There was competitive flying and joy rides for visitors.
Joy rides were a novelty. Visitors could now be seated in an Australian made, two passenger Genairco (VH-UOD). I am told that this old 'plane has since been restored and is today operating in Queensland.

Gliding was another attraction which eventually became part of the training course. Pioneers of the sport gathered here - Doc Heydon, Martin Warner, Sel Owen and Mervyn Waghorn among the greats. The pseudonym 'Kite' was given to these graceful sailplanes which were towed aloft from ground level, first by car, later by winch. Today a Pawnee tug-'plane is used.

A highlight of the first pageant had been the first descent by an Australian made parachute. It almost went awry when winds blew the parachutist off course to land over the river in the grounds of the Carrington Hospital.

Planes of the Macquarie Grove Flying School

over the river in the grounds of the Carrington Hospital.

In October there was more excitement when Denzil and Andrew returned from England with the DH Dragon - Australia's first Robot 'plane, equipped for aerial surveying and photography.

In November, Denzil's parachute manufacturing company featured again with another Australian first - a triple parachute drop staged by Brian Monk, Ben Turner and George Coleman.

Close to Christmas the scene changed again as pilots camped by their 'planes and kerosene flares were lit for the first of Camden's night flying exercises.

All told, Edward's Flying School was a success. Students were flocking to Macquarie Grove. Even trainee RAAF pilots from Richmond spent their spare time at Camden, "getting their hours up".

The second hangar was ready in May 1939. Both hangars had been extended with workshops equipped to make spare parts for wooden 'planes. Construction of propellers is reputed to have been an Australian first. There was a wireless telegraphy school, and accommodation for students was planned.

Edward and his fellow instructor, Les Ray, ran the course. Close to the hangars a little gabled hut served as the office, and with a fleet of nine 'planes it was reported to be "the finest show of its kind in Australia".

7. The arrival of the Air Force

The Macquarie Grove Flying and Glider School was officially opened by the Minister for Civil Aviation, Geoffrey Fairbairn on 30 September 1939.

A large crowd gathered and twenty-five visiting 'planes performed aerobatics or competed in air races, making a spectacular occasion.

The Sydney Morning Herald's Aviation Correspondent wrote:

> An inspection of hangars, workshops and other special arrangements revealed evidence of orderliness and efficiency not possessed by larger aerodromes in Australia.
>
> Messrs E., A and D Macarthur-Onslow have assembled a competent staff of engineers, aircraftsmen and groundsmen, and a wide variety of aircraft for training purposes including an Avian, two Pragas, a twin-engined Dragon, two Genaircos, a B.A. Swallow and a Comper Swift.
>
> The engine shop has been neatly and competently fitted out and the aircraft division includes woodwork machinery and full equipment for the making of propellers. [*The Sydney Morning Herald* 2 October 1939, p9]

The aerodrome 1939

Europe had been at war for almost a month and the rush was on to prepare our fighting forces.

The Minister's speech was full of desperation to train enough instructors to meet the demands of the RAAF training scheme. He himself had trained pilots (including test pilots) in WW1 before **he** had completed 100 hours flying. To those who did not want to be grounded by such non-combatant roles, he promised active service as soon as they had trained others to take over their jobs. He even reduced the age limit of applicants from 32 to 25 years.

So it was surprising that a week later the Minister expressed regrets that the RAAF "had not gained the services of Edward Macarthur-Onslow".

Edward, who had just turned 30, had 1100 flying hours to his credit and had already trained many pilots who had joined the force and would become 'big time'.

RAAF rules prevailed. He would have to enlist at a low rank and work his way up. Meanwhile what would happen to the Flying School? It was going to be a tough task to close it down and there were expenses to pay. He offered it to the Air Force to use 'for the duration of the war'.

At first it was refused. The property was not large enough to accommodate the necessary length of runway. Edward prepared to re-join his Army Unit leaving the next step to his old friend Dan Cleary.

Dan was a Camden man whom Edward had taught to fly. The company, Cleary Bros. were earth moving contractors. Dan was to negotiate an agreement with the sisters of the Mater Dei Orphanage next door. The object was to obtain some of the neighbouring land (Wivenhoe) to extend the unsealed runway which had been partly prepared.

This was achieved and, for a while the landscape resounded to the clamour of Caterpillar tractors and graders at work. (There were no bulldozers then). Acres of bushland were removed including the tall white gums of the river bank and the last of the apple-box trees centrefield. Flight-paths were cleared for a new breed of 'planes and by May 1940 the first of the incoming force arrived.

Huts had been built mostly in Macquarie Grove horse paddock, while we, the resident family, moved with our animals to a small cottage on the 15 acres still owned by the family. Our old haunt - now RAAF Central Flying School, was strictly out of bounds.

Our usual driveway had been closed off and a sentry was posted at the lower gate. We were obliged to use a farm track up a very steep hill, past the same check-point. Our old Ford car could only negotiate this hill at speed. As we made our run, we children thought it was great fun to wave to the sentry, until one day a new guard on gate duty, alarmed that mother did not 'Halt' on command, aimed his rifle at the tyres and we slid back to a muddy stop.

Our privations were not to last. We were moving to Sydney where my sister Pam and I would go to school. Our youngest sister, Phoebe, was a baby.

Our old house, Macquarie Grove, was now the officers' quarters. As a gesture of goodwill, mother had offered them some of our poultry for their Christmas dinner. Grandmother "Tim" was still based at Hassall Cottage and our chickens now shared her chook yard. The Air Force scoffed the lot!

Much would happen in our two and a half years of exile. "Tim" held court for a while, entertaining small groups of airmen with sing-songs and tea. However when Andrew, the only one of the brothers to join the RAAF, was killed in a training accident, she moved to the relative peace of Mt Gilead, the home she had bought for him, leaving Hassall Cottage to the care of a garrison of NCO Light Horsemen who patrolled the aerodrome.

This was the situation we found when we were allowed to return, towards the end of 1942.

The home paddock was full of rafts of timber from felled trees which had been salvaged from the river banks.

The tide of war had turned, and the American 5th Air Force had been given a mandate "to do whatever was necessary for military purposes" at Macquarie Grove.

This almost involved us when, by mistake they cut **our** fences in an effort to park 'planes under our garden trees.

The aerodrome had ceased to be Central Flying School. It was now No. 13 OBU (Operational Base Unit.)

The sentry box had been moved to a point beside our garden fence and my young sisters did deals with the guards, for American chewing-gum.

Macquarie Grove House and hangers. 1939

8. Time in Exile

Our schooldays in Sydney in (1940-42) at a delightful Prep-school run by Harold and Eula Broinowski had been rudely interrupted by the Japanese invasion of Sydney Harbour in 1942.

Though it was only a scratch on the surface of Sydney, no one knew what would follow, and many children were evacuated to country places.

In Sydney, peeping from the seclusion of brownout curtains, we had witnessed searchlights tracing night skies – now we were heading countrywards again to stay with Aunt and cousins at Denham Court beside the Ingleburn army camp. Here we had ponies and could ride, or drive a sulky for supplies, to Ingleburn village. With petrol rationing horses became our chief form of transport.

The best thing about Ingleburn was the pony club run by Teddy and Margot Hirst – the inventors of polo-crosse. We were too young to play the game yet but the contact was made – and later back at Camden, riding across to Ingleburn by what were then still unsealed roads, for shows and gymkhanas was no trouble.

Riding to school. Pam on Patsy and Annette on Bluey. 1942

Time at Denham Court was always a holiday – we moved to Campbelltown where we would go to school. The wonderful Mrs. Pentland who had formerly run St. Helen's Park as a holiday guest house, allowed us to stay as long term paying guests. The grand old two storey house, St. Helen's Park, had no mains water or electricity.

In daylight hours, power was supplied by a noisy generator, supplemented at night by blue glass oil lamps which we carried up to bed. A collection of rainwater tanks and an artesian bore supplied the water.

From St. Helen's we could ride by back roads to our school in Campbelltown. We had the choice of Public School or Convent and we chose the latter because it had the best paddock for our ponies.

Saint Patrick's Convent was on a picturesque site near the top of the hill, dominated by the tall white chapel – (all that remains of that school today).

We had to wear uniforms –dark tunics, black stockings, navy blouses buttoned at the wrist and navy hats with the school badge. Thus clad, Pam and I rode to school with sandwich lunch in our saddle bags.

We were among the very few protestants there and were constantly reminded of our shortcomings for lack of "the true faith". Nonetheless we persisted with some of the best and most vigorous teaching which stood us in good stead in later schools.

Those relatively carefree days still harboured the underlying menace of war. At St. Helen's we overheard the adults talking – "where would we hide if Jap Bombers came over?" At the eastern edge of the property a bush track followed the watercourse to Wedderburn bridge. Somewhere along there we might find a cave?

The Pentlands were selling their horses. The mare Bonnie and her colt had gone to the Sedgewicks at Mr. Annan. I coveted and won the dashing white Bluey, while Pam, in the custom of sisterly hand-me-downs took on my old pony, Patsy.
I pause here for a moment of enchantment.

Back in the early 1930s, Tommy a Shetland pony, and his little governess cart, had been raffled to aid the Childrens' Hospital. For sixpenny tickets, our friends the Martin family at Merrylands, had done a swap with the winners who had no paddock. Now, ten years on, they were seeking a home for this treasure.

Thus it became ours, and one more extraordinary wartime conveyance which took us to school in Campbelltown and later to Camden Public School.

It had been a strange arrival at Campbelltown station – the pony and cart and the unexpected bonus of the old man, Austin, who accompanied the turnout in the guard's van and who drove it the miles to St. Helen's Park along the Appin Road. Just back from school, we were greeted by the

tinkling bell on the pony's bridle as he was driven up the long driveway.

Austin, who had worked for the Martins, stayed with us for many years, congenial, indispensible handyman and groom, he remained our mother's 'right hand' throughout the '40s.

Our time at St. Helen's was to be short-lived. The property was sold and we were homeless again. It would take time and much negotiation before we could return to Camden, so Mum looked around for something to tide us over. Two small farmhouses were on offer – charming, but run down. One was at Ambarvale beside the two tub silos, the other on the hill now occupied at TAFE. The possibility was remote and Mum's intention vague, so instead she took baby Phoebe to stay with our grandparents at Wollongong, while Pam and I went to stay with the Brooker family who ran a dairy farm, conveniently on our back road to school.

We had our ponies, but from there it was easier to walk across the paddocks than to saddle up and ride to school. Taking this short cut, we experienced another animal adventure.

Crossing a paddock one morning, we were followed by a small black dog – a dog who appeared to know us and which we eventually recognised as our old black bitser Toby from pre-war days. Toby had been given away when we moved to Sydney in 1940.

What a joyful reunion we had. We had no idea where he'd come from. He was obviously very hungry as was evidenced that night when he helped himself to Les Brooker's dinner kept warm in the half open oven. That he broke the plate as well did not endear him to the Brookers.

Such dear kind people, they put up with our foibles and gave us "home from home" while we hogged their wireless listening to 'The Children's Hour' or 'First Light Frazer', 'Mrs Obbs' and 'The Search for the Golden Boomerang'. I imagine they were very relieved when news came that we could return to Camden.

The old Ford car which carried us home to Camden, was no triumphal chariot. It still bore the scars of a 1940 crash while taking father to his military camp on the muddy Wallgrove Road.

Unsealed roads, which were kinder to horses's hooves, could be treacherous for cars, and civil crash repairs were the last consideration of the war.

Austin followed with the horses, our three hitched behind the sulky drawn by his 30 year old mare, Topsy. The journey had to be timed to avoid meeting the Camden Tram (Pansy) whose line ran parallel to Narellan Road.

There was no mud to contend with. Ironically the saving grace for roads, in the war years, was lack of rain.

1943 Dog Toby, Phoebe on Tommy, Annette on borrowed pony, Bunty, and Pam on Patsy.

9. War ends and the show goes on

War ended in August 1945, but a relative peace was slow to follow. In Camden's farming community there were problems on the home front where there had been the devil of a drought.

In the hot, westerly winds of the previous summer, construction of a cross-runway on the aerodrome, had covered us with red dust. It nipped a corner of land which Dan Cleary had acquired from Wivenhoe to lengthen the main runway. The Cleary family peacefully farming there eventually solved the problem by constructing a dam.

Their neighbour Tom Donohue, farm manager at the Mater Dei orphanage bemoaned lack of compensation for lost land. He asked if he might graze his cattle on the aerodrome during the day and remove them at night, adding, "You can see tons of good grazing there."

Edward had had a long and arduous war in command of the 9th Division's 2/2 Machine Gun Battalion. He had fought at El Alamein and been awarded a DSO. He had been in New Guinea where he was mentioned in Despatches now, from Morotai he was granted early release to deal with a home problems.

The family company. Camden Park Estate Pty. Ltd., supplied a large percentage of Sydney's milk (*Camden Vale the Milk with the Golden Cap*). The manager, J.S. Haddin had had a heart attack and there was no one to take his place or even to make decisions. Edward, who had been assistant manager before the war, felt it was his duty to return.

It took a few years to iron out the future of Camden Park. Meanwhile there was his aerodrome to sort out as well.

Air Force contingents remained at Camden for some time after the cease-fire. There was a new and very welcome freedom, but for most of the servicemen awaiting repatriation, there was an age old longing to be home for Christmas. Many of these men, far from home, shared our table and our fun.

Our first peacetime Christmas dinner was enlivened by two RAF officers blindfolded and trying to feed each other green peas balanced on forks.

We were still sending food parcels to Britain particularly at Christmas time. Food rationing would continue there for several years, so Edward's brother Denzil devised a means of avoiding duty on imported Christmas cake by separately packaging the raw materials – suet, flour, sugar, egg powder and dried fruit to be made up on arrival.

During the Xmas period a large number of children

Edward failed in his attempt to buy back his property. The wartime agreement had been verbal and his friend the Minister had died in an air crash.

1946 was a year of long deliberation. The Government having at first agreed to Edward's request to reclaim the aerodrome quite suddenly changed in favour of Civil Aviation - "not for present, but for future use" whatever that should mean.
Edward then applied for a lease and was granted five years from the end of 1946 during which time he re-opened the Macquarie Grove Flying School. His fellow instructors were George Coleman and Geoff Hoskins.

Many of his pre-war colleagues drifted back. Many newcomers joined. The flying and engineering fraternity were grateful for post war jobs.

From mid November 1946 until May 1947, "The Camden News" ran a weekly column, "Flying Notes" discussing the doings of the Flying School. These entertaining and often educational notes were embellished with remarks from a mythical being known as "The Old Roan Cow."

Here is a sample from Christmas 1946.

> During the week proceeding Xmas there were many demands for air transportation by a V.I.P. (Very Important Person). This V.I.P. was always in a hurry and was most insistent that he be delivered to his destination on the split second. His journeys were always a top secret but we can reveal his identity by reproducing one extract from Macquarie Grove's flight log.
>   Aircraft: VH-ASQ
>   Time in Air: 30 min.
>   Flight: Local
>   Pilot: F. Xmas.
> The school's design staff is now fully occupied in producing a flying machine capable of lowering the Old Gentleman down the chimney. It is hoped that this aircraft will be available for Xmas 1947.

Christmas Party, 1945. Diedre McEwan (sixth from left), Jennifer Johnson, Barbara Starr, Father Christmas (Geoff Hoskins), Pam Macarthur Onslow, Anjeanette Coleman

were received at the main hangar in the time honoured style. The V.I.P. was escorted to the aerodrome by a formation from the Flying School and he departed later in his own aircraft and in an exhausted condition. Just before taking off he thoughtfully delved deep into his bag and made small presentations to some of the staff. The Chief Engineer received a diamond studded spanner inlaid with mother-of-pearl and equipped with a special device making it impossible to fit any nut. The Chief Pilot received a book entitled "How to fly an aeroplane".

Flying operations were maintained throughout the holidays, though interrupted at times by weather and festivities. Despite the somewhat bumpy conditions those who had their first flight as a Xmas Treat thoroughly enjoyed themselves.

The Old Roan Cow is on holidays.

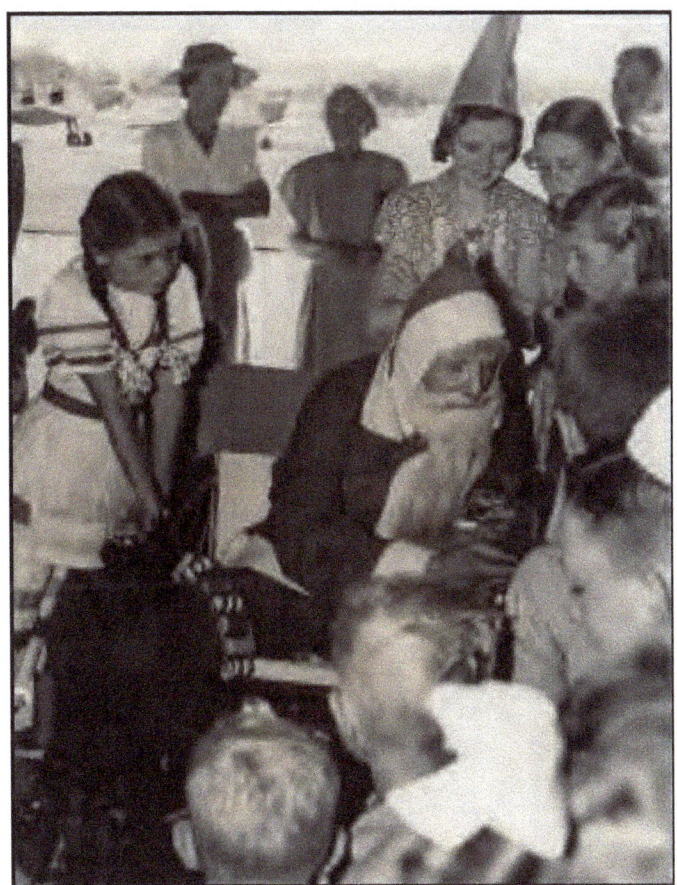

Christmas Party 1945. (LtoR) Mona Osborne, Sylvia (Tim) Macarthur Onslow, Anjeanette Coleman, Father Christmas (Geoff Hoskins), Diedre McEwan, Pam Macarthur Onslow.

Camden Aerodrome
From the Horse's Mouth -

An eminent politician once said: "There is a mistaken belief that things will go better with Government."

He might have been referring to Camden Airport, which is in the news again.

Forget any mention of Sydney's need for a second International Airport – Camden is too small, and if such an airport were established nearby, Camden Airport would be closed and we should become victims of even greater noise and pollution.

We cop Sydney's pollution anyway. Every cooling summer nor-easter brings the brown haze closer to us and, trapped by mountain ranges to south and west, Camden gets the highest reading in the Sydney Basin.

I doubt that any of this has been considered in the race to develop this once fine rural area.

In a series of articles in The District Reporter (Nov/Dec 2009) I told the story of the beginnings of Camden Airport.. The pivotal point of the story was the friendly agreement

Edward Macarthur Onslow

between my father, Edward Macarthur-Onslow and his friend, the Minister for Air who arranged that the government might buy the property for Air Force **use** for the duration of WWII and allow our family to reclaim it after the war. This agreement was never fulfilled due to the death of the Minister and an unsympathetic change of government.

Edward's aerodrome had been small and relatively unobtrusive – "moderately ambitious but by no means extravagantly so" - according to "Air Log" (an aviation journal). "The onset of war struck it just when it was moving ahead."

Snap decisions were made and every fighting man wanted to be where the action was. Edward, then a Captain in the army, enlisted with his troop and spent the next five years in the Middle East and Pacific Islands, where he commanded a Machine Gun Battalion.

After years of wandering in exile, we, his family, had returned to our home on the sub-divided edge of the old property where it was hoped that the greater property might be pieced together again and the pre-war flying school re-established.

There had been changes in the intervening years. The USAF had been given free-rein to develop the place. Edward, un-fazed by this, offered to buy it all back. His aim was to scale down the wartime enterprise to fit the peacetime community. He was, after all, a farmer at heart. The aerodrome flat land was flood land and the rough, river paddocks could agist stock again.

"The Air Log" in 1947 took up the story.
    "The government vacated the place. The RAAF no longer needed it, nor did they want to maintain it. The Dept. of Civil Aviation had no use for it, but somebody or other just did not want to let it revert to private ownership."
So the government kept the aerodrome "**not** for present but the future use." Edward was allowed a temporary lease without guarantee and the rest of the over-large hangars were hired out piecemeal to firms such as the Sydney Morning Herald.

For a very short time Edward's "Macquarie Grove Flying School" was back in its old hangars. "The Air Log" was impressed. They found the place a tonic –
    "Every member of the staff, even the girl secretary, was an ex-servicee. There were twenty on the construction and maintenance – All ex-RAAF and most of them local lads."

One of the eight remaining Air Force huts became a canteen where staff could have three course meals. This, together with delightful surroundings and, as a rule then, crystal clear air, made it all very attractive for flying people.

It did not last long. The 'Rift in the Lute' was Sydney's plan to spread itself into rural areas. Edward had returned to the management of the family company farm, (Camden Park Estate) where he pioneered Australia's first Rotolactor -–but that's another story.

In his old age he was smitten with a hand defect, so I typed some of his letters –– mostly about aircraft noise. The government wanted to resume some more of our land in order to construct a new access road to the aerodrome. I wondered what he would say?

His answer was a flat **"NO** – this is a heritage property."

There at last was the underlying truth about Camden Airport. This was no ordinary place, but a place of historic significance, well recorded in the history books.

Along with next-door Wivenhoe (formerly Macquarie Gift) Macquarie Grove had been named in honour of Governor Macquarie and was the farm he most admired. It was where he stayed and dined and where his favourite dog died and was buried.

Macquarie Grove is thirty years older than the town of Camden and in 2012 it will celebrate is bi-centenary.

Authorities who have sanctioned the Airport Master Plan 2010, appear to have turned a blind eye to its past. The recent imposition of a revised Australian Noise Exposure Forecast (ANEF) contour covering a region of schools, conference centre, retirement village and many heritage buildings – a region which generously lent itself to the WWII war effort, is now having to forbear with further restrictions.

We see here a classic case of government having refused a return of property to the rightful, and responsible owners in 1945, letting the generations go by and handing its problem sixty-five years later to yet another private enterprise.

[Across top] AVRO "ANSON" belonging to Agricultural Aviation Services Pty., Ltd, of Brisbane, in the process of receiving a complete C of A overhaul at the delightfully rural establishment of Macquarie Grove Flying School Pty., Camden (N.S.W.) One of the boys is chewing some lunch on a bench in the sun.
[Left centre] EDWARD MACARTHUR-ONSLOW, General Manager of Macquarie Grove Flying School, and secretary RHODA VANCE. The pen and paper at hand with Mr. Onslow were not in the picture for effect. He had dashed in, just before we packed up to leave, and was signing some mail and other what-nots when we fitted the flash-bulb and said: "Hi, there!"
[Right centre] JOHN S. McCONNELL, Works Manager, who after 20 years with de Haviland's, became attracted to rural aviation earlier this year and now thinks the whole set-up has metropolitan counterparts 'licked to a cinder'.
[Bottom left] The SYDNEY MORNING HERALD'S first Dakota, of two which were 'rehabbed' for their C's of A at Macquarie Grove. (Note the registration letters). Figure in the vicinity of the wing-fuselage fairing is that of Works Manager McConnell.
[Bottom right] Glimpse through part of one of the 3 hangars of Macquarie Grove Flying School.

Macquarie Grove Flying Notes

World War II ended on the 15th August 1945. Three months later Edward Macarthur-Onslow anticipating a return to his pre-war business, but no longer backed by his two brothers, registered "The Macquarie Grove Flying and Gliding School Pty. Ltd." as a company. Committee members included two particular friends, his fellow instructor Les Ray, and contractor Dan Cleary who had helped to engineer the aerodrome.

The Air Force lingered on for a while. It would be another six months before the school could operate, and then only with a limited leasehold. They had to make the most of their time.

Flying had lost much of its novelty so Edward began a campaign of "Flying Notes" in the Camden News. These entertaining snippets covered everything from latest technology to local gossip under the watchful eye of "The Old Roan Cow" who grazed on the boundary.

The school's fleet of 'planes was predominantly D.H. Tiger Moths. The Flying Notes ran weekly from 14 November 1946 until 20 May 1947. Here are some samples:

> 14.11.1946
> *An innocent bystander recently asked Aubrey (Titus) Oates whether he had enjoyed his flight in one of the School's Moths. The enquirer was somewhat startled when he received the grave reply that it had been found very restful. "Titus" is the de Haviland Mosquito Test Pilot and that job entails flying each day at speeds in the vicinity of 400 miles an hour. Yes, a Tiger Moth is restful and so Mr. Oates spends his busman's holidays flying at Macquarie Grove.*

It should be added that Bankstown's de Haviland test pilots when they weren't "tearing holes in the sky", quite often came to lend a hand instructing on the gentler aircraft at Macquarie Grove Flying School.

> 9.1.1947
> *The de Haviland Chief Test Pilot (Brian) "Black-Jack" Walker, paid a call to Macquarie Grove during the week. Black-Jack arrived in an Australian built D.H. Mosquito and saw to it that his arrival was not overlooked. After stopping one engine in the air he showed that his machine can still*

whiz round at a very high speed with only one "donk" operating. In the last war the word "donk" became Air Force parlance for an aeroplane engine. How it originated can never be proved but it is fairly safe to assume that it arose from some disillusioned pilot accusing his engines of producing so many donkey power instead of horses. Incidently the modern British technical reference to an engine of a multi-engined aircraft is – power egg.

When Black-Jack stopped one of his two engines, (or motors or power units, or power eggs, or donks) in the air, he did so by first stopping its fuel supply. That alone will not stop the engine turning over because the air pressure on the propeller blades will keep them rotating. He then pressed a button and each propeller blade turned until edge on to the air-flow. With the blades in that position they were unaffected by air pressure and so the engine was stopped.

To restart his engine he simply pressed another button and the blades returned to the original position at which the pressure of air caused them to turn the engine over again. The edge on position of the blades is known as "the feather" because of its similarity to the manner in which a racing rower turns his oars when returning to the dip position. There are many reasons for this feathering operation but perhaps we have been technical enough already.

It is not generally known that flying from Macquarie Grove began as far back as 1920 when the great aircraft designer, Edgar Percival, frequently flew from the field. His activities so impressed the Macarthur-Onslow brothers that, after learning to fly themselves, they eventually formed a Flying School in 1937.

This story has been told in The District Reporter "Back Then" articles Nov-Dec 2009.

In 1920, Percival flew an Avro 504K, a World War I trainer which can be seen in action in the classic film "Silks & Saddles" available in DVD from the National Film Archive.

Many Camden scenes feature in the film – the Macquarie Grove Racecourse (training track), Camelot and 'Belgenny' farmyard and stables.

Camden was a Mecca for many early films.

AVRO 504K First World War Trainer. The first aircraft to land at Macquarie Grove aerodrome in 1920

Films and Fun at Macquarie Grove

Camden's pleasant countryside attracted film makers, but in several cases it was the access to an aerodrome for flying scenes which occasioned a film, or it might be a film director merely booking a flight to seek out locations.

> "Camden News" '***Flying Notes***' 16 January 1947
> Among those who made charter flights during the week was Mr. Harry Watt, producer of "The Overlanders." Mr. Watt who is scouring the country in search of a suitable location for "Eureka Stockade," is a most experienced air traveller. During the production of "The Overlanders" alone he covered 13000 miles by air.

Films, as new to the world as flying itself, were part of our lives.

It was, after all, the making of the film "Silks & Saddles" in 1920 which inspired the creation of Camden Aerodrome and, as War approached in 1939, we were expecting another flying film, "The Power & the Glory" to be staged at Macquarie Grove.

It was finally made during Air Force occupation in 1941 starring a very young Peter Finch. For authentic background it showed a rare image of the old Control Tower.

A frequent visitor in the 1930s was Ken Hall, Director of the 'Dad & Dave' series of films. My father, Edward Onslow flew him around to look for locations here, but the site of the Rudd family 'Selection' had already been settled at Castlereagh where most of those hilarious films were shot. Some scenes however were filmed in this region.

One day I was told: "Quick, get on your pony and go down to the river flats" – There was no time to put a saddle on – I joined the line up of riders, horse drawn vehicles and old jalopy cars about to be filmed for the crazy rush scene in "Dad Rudd MP." My pony was excited and restless. When a gun was fired to start the action, she bolted and, riding bareback I had little control; ruined three takes and was finally removed from the set. So much for a budding movie career in 1939.

A second film involved the Air Force towards the end of the war. In 1944 the incumbent 21 Squadron was about to convert from Vultee Vengeance bombers to Liberators (B24s) and the obsolescent Vultees were given the unusual role of doubling as Stukas (German dive bombers) in Charles Chauvel's film "The Rats of Tobruk."

Chauvel had had much success with his film "Forty Thousand Horsemen". A WWI story. Now he was tackling a recent and more newsworthy subject, bravely in the face of the newly returned 9th Division, victims of the Tobruk siege. He made a few mistakes.

Looking for locations for *Dad and Dave* films at Camden Park. Ken Hall, director, Edward Macarthur Onslow and Bert Bailey, Dad Rudd character. (left to right)

For some time, we school children had watched with interest the building of a grotesque pile of ruins on a hillside, in full view, but out of bounds, south of Narellan road. The property was part of Glenlee, hilly and treeless, stretching all the way from Menangle Park.

This was to be the film-set of Tobruk, marked today on the map by Tobruk road. While the structures remained unpainted, rough mud bricks, the bare ground was covered with sand to look like desert. No one had mentioned that Tobruk's desert was rocky.

I am told that no allied bomber could dive like a Stuka, but by folding back the canopy, and exposing the flight crew, the Vultee could execute a feasible vertical dive.

Bomb targets in the film were faked by ground explosives. Here a strange accident befell a member of 21 Squadron, a certain Corporal Clark who was wounded and taken to Camden Hospital.

It was a minor head wound. Its cause remained a mystery until a bloodied cow-pat was found in the aircraft itself and it transpired that the ground explosion had shaken up the contents of one of Camden's peaceful cow paddocks.

Corporal Clark celebrated his survival by gilding the cow-pat and having it mounted and placed on his home mantelpiece.

Chauvel's film however had little to celebrate.

I believe that if the men of the 9th Division, who attended the preview could have thrown cow-pats at the film, they would have.

Their criticisms ranged from its precious language to details of uniform such as the sergeants' stripes being on the wrong arm, and anachronisms in equipment, such as use of jeeps which were never at that time in Tobruk, or the 'planes intended to represent Stukas, not dive-bombing as intended, but flying at low level.

They gave credit to some episodes and while the reconstruction of the town was considered excellent - so much else was incorrect that it was generally dismissed. In other words it was a bit of a joke.

So what would the 'Old Roan Cow' the guardian mascot of the "*Flying Notes*" have thought of missile cow-pats?

"Camden News" 19 December 1946, The "Old Roan Cow" said:
> *"I'm going to take the bull by the horns"* at which point she had rushed out of the hangar and was later reported to be undergoing repairs in the school's workshops.

Now for a little light instruction
Macquarie Grove Flying School

My father, Edward was a great teacher. In the fragmented two years before the Air Force took over his aerodrome, he and his fellow instructor, Les Ray, had trained 42 pilots.

Now in the post war years, he had taken his degree in aircraft engineering and more of his time was devoted to maintenance and the restoration of salvaged aircraft.

At the flying school, instruction remained paramount and one of Edward's pre-war companions, former RAAF Squadron Leader George Coleman AFC, was appointed Chief Pilot.

> Camden News '*Flying Notes*' 21 11.1946
> Well known in Camden, George had been flying since 1927 and had held the position of Chief Instructor to the Royal Aero Club of N.S.W., the Kingsford Smith Air Service, No. 4 Flying Training School and Central Flying School R.A.A.F. He also served with the R.A.F. abroad and as Test Pilot to de Havilands. His flying instructor's licence was endorsed for instruction on single, twin and three engined land planes, sea planes and autogyros.

George's training methods may have seemed unorthodox to some, but in fact he drew on very ancient logic.

> '*Flying Notes*' 5.1.1946
> When in the year 1542 a Mr. Ascham published a book called "Toxophilus or the Schole of Shootings" he really meant "Archery or the School of Shooting." He was not to know that exactly 400 years later his basic principles of shootings were to be practised by members of His Majesty's Air Forces in order to prosecute a war in which they happened to be involved. It is a fact that this ancient sport was revived in a big way by the R.A.F. when it was discovered that the co-ordination of eye and muscle required in shootinge the arrowes was much akin to that necessary for flyinge the aeroplane."

For a post war aerodrome which had become over-run with rabbits, plenty was said

George Coleman, chief pilot of the Macquarie Grove Flying School at Camden, instructing Margaret Norman in archery, because he believed that the bow and arrow develop the same eye muscles used in landing an aeroplane.

about potential target practice, not least by our local doctor.

> **'Flying Notes'** 30.2.1947
> **THE DOCTOR INVESTIGATES:**
> Dr. R.M. Crookston was intrigued by the Chief Pilot's claims that Archery is beneficial to flyers as well as being unpleasant for rabbits. He therefore tried it for himself on one of his recent visits to Macquarie Grove. The damage inflicted on the colourful archery target by his first quiver of arrows was rather slight but the Doctor came back for more and is now on the threshold of becoming an accomplished archer. It is not true that he intends to dispose of his guns.

The technicalities of flying constantly referred to Nature.

> **'Flying Notes'** 28 11.1946
> The wild duck is an interesting bird, both with and without his feathers. He is reputed to have the highest wing-loading of all birds that fly. All small boys know what wing-loading is, but for grown-ups we should explain that a high wing-loading simply means a very heavy bird (or aeroplane) with very small wings.
> Together with others of his family the same wild duck has always presented an interesting problem. When flying in company they

choose to fly in Vee formation and the burning question is – how do they appoint the leader?

(See later for Macquarie Grove's answer.)

'Flying Notes' 12.12.1946
The easiest way to understand the terms head-wind and tail-wind is to bear in mind that when an aircraft becomes airborne it assumes the speed of the wind which bears it. Then, apart from that speed, it has the speed obtained from its propeller. Therefore if a propeller pulls an aeroplane along at 60 m.p.h., then the machine will remain stationary as far as the earth is concerned.
Having absorbed that lesson in theory of flight you will, no doubt, be able to tell us the approximate speed of the wind when three of Macquarie Grove Flying School Tiger Moths returned from a charter flight on Friday last. A Tiger Moth lands at 45 m.p.h. and when these three "sat down" they did not roll forward more than a few feet.

'Flying Notes' 16.1.1947
Recently one of the school's lady pupils was asked by her instructor to fly towards the aerodrome. After a while she allowed the aeroplane to wander off course and eventually steadied up with the aerodrome dead astern. The instructor decided to let her correct the mistake without his assistance, but the aerodrome continued to recede. "We don't seem to be getting any closer," said the pupil. "Don't worry," replied the instructor, "you hold your course and we'll get there, even if it does mean flying round the world."

……and Macquarie Grove's answer to formation flying; appointment of a leader.

It happened thus – with the day's labours finished, the routine Sunday evening instructor's formation was taxying out for take off. However, in the bustle it had been forgotten to appoint a leader and formations do look bad when everyone tries to lead at once. Well everyone did try and the race went to the swift Geoff Hoskins, who said later that it was reminiscent of the scrambles of the dark days of war. Geoff maintained his leadership and was accepted without question. So now we know how the ducks do it - or do we?

That old roan cow was concerned in an unpleasant incident yesterday. It appears that she wandered onto the aerodrome and was asked to leave by one of the ground staff. She then stamped off shouting "If you had four legs you would be a heeler but with only two you are just a heel."

Edward Macarthur Onslow and George Littlejohn (instructor), 1930.

Pre-War and Post-War
Macquarie Grove Flying School

The parachute, like the aeroplane, had long lived in man's imagination before it materialised.

Among his famous designs for flying machines, the 15th century Leonardo da Vinci had envisaged "a tent of linen by means of which a man might throw himself down from a great height without sustaining injury."

The first experimental parachute drop took place in France in 1783. It was from a high tower. In the same year Joseph and Etienne Montgolfier discovered that a fabric bag filled with hot air could rise and fly.

Their first hot-air balloon passengers were a sheep, a duck and a rooster. When eventually time came for human passengers, experiments could be made with parachute descents.

Fast forward 155 years to Camden NSW and the trial of the first Australian made parachute. The manufacturer was "Light Aircraft Pty. Ltd." a company run by Denzil Macarthur-Onslow, Edward's elder brother. Trials at Macquarie Grove aerodrome included the very first Australian triple parachute drop.

War brought advances in all techniques. Parachutes became commonplace, but there were still real and imagined dangers.

> *"Flying Notes" 19.12.1946*
> *The story was told by Group Captain Pelly-Fry, D.S.O. R.A.F., and its truth is vouched for. During the war in the Middle East it was decided to drop a party of Gurkha troops in the rear of the enemy. In planning this operation the Gurkha Officer was flown over the area by the R.A.F. at 1000 ft. On return to base he was asked by the pilot if the arrangements were satisfactory. "The height" said the Gurkha, "is too great. From a thousand feet my men may be hurt." "Very well," said the pilot, "what height do you suggest?" "We shall drop from 200ft" announced the Gurkha." The R.A.A.F. Officer then explained that 200ft was insufficient height to permit the safe opening of the parachutes. "My men and I." insisted the Gurkha, "will leap upon the enemy from 200ft and no more. Of these parachutes we know nothing and care less. Such strange equipment is unnecessary."*

In the pre-war period the Macquarie Grove Flying School held several Inter Club competitions and flying displays. In December 1938 there was a grand Aerial Pageant with the first of the War Games – "Storming the Fort."
In this a "Strong Post" occupied by "the Enemy" had to be cleared by "Mechanised Cavalry" supported by aircraft and "a Demolition Squad of Engineers."

This promised much excitement and increased sabre rattling.

Some time after this my cousin Sue King and I were on our ponies at Campbelltown Show when an announcement came to clear the ring because we were about to be bombed.

THE ROYAL AERO CLUB OF NEW SOUTH WALES

Aerial Pageant

CIRCULAR.

Enclosed please find Member's Ticket and Car Sticker for admission to the Club's Aerial Pageant to be held at Macquarie Grove Aerodrome, Camden, on Sunday, December 4th, commencing at 2 p.m.

Tickets for admission to Members' Enclosure for members' guests may be obtained at this office:

Adults — — — — — — 2/-
Children under 12, Free
Car Sticker — — — — — 6d.

TRIPLE PARACHUTE DESCENT

For the first time in the history of Australian Aviation a Triple Parachute Descent will be made by

BEN TURNER   GEORGE COLEMAN
BRYAN MONK

On the same programme will be

THE AERIAL DERBY FOR THE "SUN" CUP

and a Spectacular Finale—
"STORMING THE FORT"

We want to make this Pageant a real success, so roll up every one of you, and bring all your friends.

**REMEMBER THE DATE: SUNDAY, DECEMBER 4th.
PLACE: MACQUARIE GROVE AERODROME, CAMDEN.**

STANLEY C. BRIDGLAND,
Manager.

We scattered and watched as two little Tiger Moths from Macquarie Grove dropped flour bombs, bags of four which left a veil of "Self Raising" dust in the ring. I wonder how many people remember that incident today?

Beyond that moment the world was to undergo such changes. The simplicity of those innocent years would be lost forever. Post war we might be grateful that aeronautics could turn to practical use in agriculture and industry, in peaceful transport and tourism, in space exploration and science.

> *"Camden Advertiser" 30 January 1947*
> *Making Snow Clouds Provide Irrigation.*
>
> *Ordinary sky clouds can be turned into snow by dropping dry ice pellets into them from aeroplanes, according to the General Electric Company.*
>
> *Details were recently given in a newspaper cable from New York.*
>
> *The company, which has just completed tests says that clouds drifting towards cities can be turned into snow on the way, thus providing water for irrigation.*
>
> *In five hours, it is estimated, one aeroplane could sprinkle enough dry ice pellets to make hundreds of millions of tons of snow over a wide area.*
>
> *This sounded a lot, added a company spokesman to a newspaper reporter, but it would probably mean only a few inches of snow actually on the ground.*
>
> *(Here's a chance for local farmers to engage Camden Macquarie Grove Flying Club [sic] 'planes to test this theory with the object of eliminating drought periods. We, in the township would appreciate a cooling snow storm or two during the hot summer months, particularly in our waiting period for the construction of a local swimming pool.)*

Cloud seeding continues today by different means. No problem has been solved yet, but at least we can say that at last, at last, Camden has its swimming pool.

...and so we say good bye.

The author

Annette Macarthur Onslow

(1933–) Annette worked as a freelance commercial artist and illustrator in Australia, France and England.
She was production assistant to a London publisher, associate editor with an Arts Journal and, as a puppeteer she worked with Norman Hetherington on early shows and featured on opening night of ABC television.
Her books range from a brief history of the family property *Camden Park Estate (1958)* to *Uhu* the story of a little owl, which won The Australian Children's Book of the Year in 1970.

CAMDEN HISTORY

Journal of the Camden Historical Society

September 2013 Volume 3 Number 6

CAMDEN HISTORY
Journal of the Camden Historical Society Inc.
ISSN 1445-1549
Editor: Dr Ian Willis

Management Committee
President: Bob Lester
Vice Presidents: Dr Ian Willis, Rene Rem
Secretary: Janice Johnson
Assistant Secretary: Julie Wrigley
Treasurer:
Assistant Treasurer:
Immediate Past President: John Wrigley OAM
General Committee: Cathey Shepherd   Sharon Greene
                    Roslyn Tildsley   Julie Wrigley
                    Robert Wheeler   Lee Stratton

Honorary Auditor:
Honorary Solicitors: Bowring, Macaulay and Barrett

Society contact:
P.O. Box 566, Camden, NSW 2570.   Online <http://www.camdenhistory.org.au>

Meetings
Meetings are held at 7.30 p.m. on the second Wednesday of the month except in January. They are held in the Museum. Visitors are always welcome.

Museum
The Museum is located at 40 John Street, Camden, phone 4655 3400 or 46559210. It is open Thursday to Sunday 11 a.m. to 4 p.m., except at Christmas. Visits by schools and groups are encouraged. Please contact the Museum to make arrangements. Entry is free.

Camden History, Journal of the Camden Historical Society Inc
The Journal is published in March and September each year. The Editor would be pleased to receive articles broadly covering the history of the Camden district . Correspondence can be sent to the Society's postal address. The views expressed in the articles are solely those of the authors and not necessarily endorsed by the society.

Donations
Donations made to the Society are tax deductible. The accredited value of objects donated to the Society are eligible for tax deduction.

Cover: Camelot 1983 (J Wrigley)

CAMDEN HISTORY
Journal of the Camden Historical Society Inc.

September 2013 Volume 3 Number 6

Contents

Kirkham to Camelot Sharon Greene	199
President's Report 2012-2013 Bob Lester	212
The CIFA Story Noreen Newton	218
Tank or Bank? Janice Johnson	220
Clarissa Whiteman, First World War Nurse Julie Wrigley	223
Crown Land and the Wild Cattle of the Cowpasture Plains Peter Mylrea	224
The Gallipoli Evacuation Janice Johnson	231
Extract Camden News 1895	236
Camelot Ian Willis	239

Kirkham to Camelot

Sharon Greene

A brief history of the creation of a local icon and the Faithfull Anderson family.

Any motorists wending their way along Camden Valley Way who care to look to the north west may be rewarded, however fleetingly, with a glimpse of a rather remarkable structure. If it is summer, one might see only a collection of turrets thrusting themselves defiantly above the leafy tree line. In winter however, with the trees naked, keen-eyed motorists are given more of a view, with perhaps parts of the roofline being discernible under those turrets and their accompanying chimneys. What these motorists are seeing is of course Macarthur district's very own Camelot. Located on Kirkham Lane, less than a kilometre from Camden's main thoroughfare is one of the area's best-known and enigmatic houses. If one were to dare a closer inspection of what was fleetingly glimpsed through the car window from Camden Valley Way, one's eye, would truly be delighted with the romantically styled array of turrets, gables, chimneys, broad windows and arched verandahs. Just as remarkable as the architecture of this building is the story of its inhabitants, most notably one family, who resided there during the turn of the twentieth century, the Faithfull Andersons. This article shall aim to briefly examine the history of this fabulous piece of local architecture and how that history intersected with the lives of one of the region's historic families.

The red-brick homestead which was to be eventually known as Camelot was originally built in 1888 for parliamentarian and race horse owner James White(1) who gave it the rather less ostentatious name of Kirkham(2). The house had been designed by Canadian-born architect John Horbury Hunt, the same architect who is believed to have built several years earlier, the two-storey cottage located nearby (3). Hunt built many homes for the White family throughout NSW, his work for them being seen in the far north at Armidale where he was the architect of the house Booloominbah(4) this being in similar style to Camelot however on a much smaller scale.

Aside from the homestead, White built a large double storey stable block, that still remains today, located across the road from the Kirkham homestead and today it is known as Kirkham. In those early days Kirkham Lane did not exist, now however it divides the area with Camelot on the left and the double storey stables Kirkham on the right. White died in 1890 and the property was then subdivided, the Kirkham homestead and its stables with two cottages remained together on the greatly reduced estate.

Family Grave at Springfield NSW of Frances Lilian Faithfull Anderson, William Hugh Anderson and Clarice Faithfull Anderson who lived at Camelot (S Greene)

The homestead was to acquire its more glamorous name from its next owners. Miss Frances Lilian Faithfull; her first name was Frances however she preferred her second name Lilian and was known thus during her lifetime. This anomaly appears to be a trend in the Faithfull family with a preference to use their second Christian name. Lilian Faithfull was born into a prominent, wealthy and well-respected family which has links back to the Second Fleet. Her ancestor William Faithful (1774-1847), soldier and settler, arrived in New South Wales as a private in Captain Joseph Foveaux's company in the New South Wales Corps on the *Pitt* in February 1792.

Lilian was born in 1859, the youngest child of William Pitt Faithfull (the son) and Mary Deane. Lilian was born and raised on her parents' large property known as Springfield, near Goulburn in New South Wales(5). Lilian and her two older sisters were well educated and well read. As was the custom at that time for the landed gentry where they were tutored at home by a governess. Her five brothers however were university educated with each taking up a professional career. The family could boast: to have a barrister-at-law, a solicitor; a company director; a licensed surveyor and a medical doctor.(6) Lilian did not marry until later in life (by the standards of the day) finally walking down the aisle in 1898 in her thirty-eighth year. Her husband was William Hugh Anderson, son of the local bank manager; he was also the station manager at Springfield. They were married at Saint Saviour's Cathedral, Goulburn(7) on 16 February 1898. The parents of both the bride and the groom had passed away(8) by the time of their marriage. Some within the family believe there were 'a number of reports' circulated that Lilian had married against her family's wishes. Whatever the sentiments of her family were, a photograph taken on their wedding day shows there were well over one hundred well-wishers, with the entire Springfield population assembled outside the homestead and the main entrance to the big house decorated with wreaths of flowers and adorned with banners and flags(9).

It would appear Lilian and William were given the portion of James White's estate which held Kirkham Homestead and the two cottages. It is said that when Mrs William Hugh Anderson saw the property for the first time she was reminded of one of Lord Alfred Tennyson's verses in the poem 'The Lady of Shalott' which reads:

> *On either side the river lie*
> *Long fields of barley and of rye,*
> *That clothe the wold and meet the sky,*
> *And thro' the field the road runs by*

Camelot, c1910s (Campbelltown City Library Collection)

To many tower'd Camelot.

Thereafter *Kirkham* was known as *Camelot*(10)

When the Andersons arrived at Camelot the newlywed couple settled easily into life in the Camden area. Having already resided in country Goulburn the transition to another country estate was relatively effortless. Two years after their arrival they celebrated the birth of their first and only child, a daughter named Clarice Vivien Faithfull Anderson. At this time William's occupation was listed as a grazier(11). The change in circumstances and responsibility from running a large property with many thousands of acres at Springfield to the much smaller property of Camelot, meant that he was considered a man of leisure. However with time on his hands this possibly led him to develop some anxieties. As was expected of the landed gentry, William became involved with and gave support to the local community, a move which was supported by his wife.

Camden like most country towns at the turn of the century was undergoing many changes: a new fully-fenced cemetery was dedicated in 1898, reticulated water arrived in 1899, and a new bridge over the Nepean River was officially opened in 1901. This bridge linked Narellan and Camden, finally providing a crossing for the railway, with a width of 20ft clear for all other traffic(12). There was much celebrating on the day the bridge was declared open as the road between Narellan and Camden was often cut off by flood waters. As a tribute to all the hard work done by the workmen and on the day of the bridge's official opening, Mrs Anderson left a five-pound note with the men to celebrate the occasion(13).

Such acts of benevolence to the community remained a reoccurring feature of Lilian Anderson's life. During the Great Depression Mrs Anderson would give food and blankets to the homeless who often lived under the Camden Bridge, and also offered to construct a shelter-shed, complete with fireplace, water and conveniences for the travelling unemployed on the camping ground as the southern edge of the town. This was agreed to and Mrs Anderson met the full expense of its erection(14). Her staff would report acts of kindness where she would regularly have food delivered to local poor families (15). Later in her life she donated money for the foundation of the local Red Cross Society becoming one of its founding members. She was also benevolently involved with the Temperance Society, the Country Women's Association and Camden District Hospital(16).

William was likewise community-minded and became a member of the board for the Camden Show Society; he annually entered and won horse events at the show. He was briefly elected as an alderman to Camden Council in June 1903, however he later resigned in October of the same year due to ill-health (17). This was the first public manifestation of William's ill-health and provides historians with some initial outward hint of his personal struggles with depression and constant melancholia which seemed to plague him.

Aside from his work in the community, William Anderson was reported as being a great horseman both for riding and driving. The Sydney Hunt Club used to conduct drag-hunts on Camelot and neighbouring properties, all of which were organised by William. He drove tandem, unicorn and four-in-hand. Unicorn was a three horse team, one horse leading while it was also harnessed in the middle of a pair, side-by-side(18).

His enthusiasm for horses saw them housed splendidly in the stables at Camelot, which are as regal as the homestead itself; no doubt they had been built by James White, Camelot's original owner who was well-known in the horse racing and breeding world(19). White's horse Chester was the 1877 Melbourne Cup winner, and it has been suggested that the money from Chester's win that year is what enabled White to build the homestead in the first place.

The initial shadows of depression and declining mental health which contributed to his resignation as town alderman in 1903 had unfortunately consumed Anderson and on Thursday 16 May 1912 he committed suicide at the family property. Behind the stables at Camelot stood a large hayshed and in the early hours of the morning William set the hayshed on fire and once it was alight he shot himself with a rifle he had removed from his study. Both he and the rifle were consumed by the fire which was first noticed by other Camelot residents at 5.30 am. Sadly by 7.00 am all efforts made to extinguish the fire were considered impossible. Dr Allen arrived about 9.00 am as several employees were still attempting to extinguish the flames by removing the iron sheeting and hosing the smouldering hay with water. Dr Allen later found the rifle and large bone pieces in the middle of the remains of the hayshed. Dr West, the Anderson's family doctor, was later called to the scene where he formed the opinion that the human remains, clothing and gold-capped tooth all recovered from the scene were those of William Hugh Anderson(20).

An inquest was held into Mr Anderson's death where a variety of witnesses reported of Anderson's personal struggles with depression and alcohol. Thomas Teasdale, one of Camelot's gardeners, reported at the inquest that he had seen Mr Anderson the day before his death and knew he had been ill towards the end of his life, variously suffering from the cumulative effects of alcohol and depression(21). Similarly Camden Police Sergeant William Schwarer reported at the inquest that he had known Mr Anderson for four years, stating that he also believed him to be addicted to drink and of rather eccentric habits and no doubt at times he appeared to be temporarily insane; describing him as the kind of person that at any time might be expected to commit suicide.(22). Dr West, the family's doctor, was unable to state whether William died as the result of the fire or the gun-shot(23). Whatever the direct cause of his death, the final findings of the inquest found that his death was by suicide and was brought about by a combination of Mr Anderson suffering mental health and alcoholism.

His death was shocking and very dramatic, however his suicide appears to have been forgiven by the community as there were no words of condemnation appearing in the local press, in fact quite the contrary can be found. The local paper the *Camden News* described Anderson 'an ex-alderman and a useful citizen who had won the esteem of the residents'(24). Thankfully during this period the churches had begun to relax their attitude towards those who committed suicide and Anderson's remains were allowed to be buried in consecrated grounds.

In February of 1913 Mrs Anderson made an offer to Camden Council to provide and erect a drinking fountain in memory of her late husband. Council accepted the offer and selected the location for the fountain at the junction of Argyle and John Streets in the township of Camden(25). The Andersons had been residents of the Camden/Narellan area for only fourteen years when William died. The honour of having a memorial placed in such a prominent position in the town was an indication of the high esteem in which the family was held.

The monument was constructed of circular Pyrmont freestone fashioned along smooth flowing lines, standing nine feet in height and fixed on octagon Bowral Trachyte base, with two feet of solid concrete foundation. It featured two nickel taps, which were spring loaded and operated by pushing the tap down. Each tap was accompanied by two plain metallic copper mugs attached to the fountain by chains (26). The taps, mugs and trough (bowl) were in accordance with the Health Department's regulations of the day(27). The fountain was supplied with fresh water from the relatively new reticulated town water [connected in 1899](28) and also featured underground drainage to remove surplus water. There was also a small trough at the base to provide water for dogs. At the top was an ornamental gas-lamp [gas lighting became available in 1912](29) which provided illumination and therefore the fountain was available twenty-four hours per day(30). The original design had two gas-lit lamps; however the Council decided one would be sufficient(31) perhaps to be consistent in style with the other gas lamps along Argyle Street. It was constructed and erected by Walter F Peters, Camden's monumental mason, timber merchant and undertaker (who later become an alderman and Mayor). The total costs of the fountain, for both the construction and erection were met by Lilian Anderson.

When the fountain was completed she wrote officially to Camden Council and formally presented to the Council the gift of the memorial drinking fountain. Correspondence received from Mrs. Anderson was later reported in the *Camden News* of 24 July 1913 stating:

> I now understand the Memorial Fountain is completed and I desire to present the same to the Municipality for the benefit of the Camden public. May I express a hope that this fountain may prove a blessing to many a thirsty soul, and so be a fitting memento of the sympathy which the late Mr. W H Anderson had for all fellow creatures(32).

Anderson Fountain, Camden. CE Coleman, 1920s. (Camden Historical Society collection)

The Mayor acknowledged the very fine gift and it was accepted unanimously by Council(33). The *Camden News* reported the council's reception and appreciation of the gift, highlighting that the Council regarded the fountain as 'an ornamental and useful gift which cost the donor a good deal of money and it will be deeply appreciated'(34).

The fountain was inscribed with two verses chosen by Mrs. Anderson. The inscription on the lower section under the trough of the fountain says:

> *Memoria in aeterna*
> W. H. ANDERSON
> *'CAMELOT'*
> 16TH MAY 1912

> SO WE'LL DRINK TO HIM IN SILENCE HERE
> HE'S FOLLOWED UP THE TRACK
> WHERE MANY A GOOD MAN'S GONE BEFORE

BUT NE'ER A ONE CAME BACK

And then on the other side it reads:

> IN MEN WHOM MEN CONDEMN AS ILL
> I FIND SO MUCH OF GOODNESS STILL,
> IN MEN WHOM MEN PRONOUNCE DIVINE
> I FIND SO MUCH OF SIN AND BLOT;
> I HESITATE TO DRAW A LINE
> BETWEEN THE TWO WHERE GOD HAS NOT.
>
> ---------
>
> *GOD SLEEPS IN THE STONE,*
> *DREAMS IN THE ANIMAL,*
> *AND WAKES IN THE MAN.*
> *EXCELSIOR*

And on the base, near the dog drinking trough it read:

> PRESENTED BY MRS W. H. ANDERSON
> R.E.R. YOUNG. MAYOR 1913

The main inscription, *We'll drink to him in silence...* is from the poem by A B "Banjo" Paterson called 'Tommy Corrigan'. Tommy was an Irishman and a favorite jockey who died on 13 August 1894, two days after a fall from a horse while steeple-chasing at Flemington(35). The poem was first published in *The Bulletin*, 18 August 1894 and these words are from two lines in the fifth verse(36).

The second inscription, *In men whom men condemn as ill* . . . is taken from the poem, *Byron* which was penned by American writer Joaquin Miller (1837-1913). Miller had been successful in London and was sometimes referred to as the 'Byron of the Rockies'.

The fountain now stands in Macarthur Park near the park's main gazebo. It had to be moved from its original location in the main street when it came in danger of being destroyed by the increased traffic running through Camden. It was moved to one corner and finally to Macarthur Park when the main street became part of the Hume Highway. It has been said that behind the stables at Camelot and where the hayshed once stood, there stands a similar memorial, smaller in size and inscribed – 'A silent memory to William, who once lived at Camelot'.

On 1 August 1932 Mrs Anderson and her daughter Clarice changed their name by deed-poll from Anderson to Faithfull Anderson, Faithfull being Mrs Anderson's maiden name(37). Frances Lilian Faithfull Anderson died on 19 June 1948 and her daughter Clarice Vivien Faithfull Faithfull Anderson died on 16 March 1979. Clarice was unmarried and childless, thus bringing to a close the Faithfull Anderson line. They are buried together with William in the private family cemetery at Springfield, near Goulburn(38).

Their respective Wills were to cause some confusion; Lilian requested the property be used as a convalescence hospital and Clarice, aware of the changing of society's attitudes and the urge at the time to demolish anything that was old, gifted it to the State of New South Wales, therefore preserving Camelot. After a protracted legal dispute as to which will was legally binding, the judgment was that Lilian's will, would be final. Unfortunately the design of Camelot with its narrow corridors and stairways made the costs involved in converting it into a functional hospital or convalescing home too immense.

A decision to sell the property was made and Camelot was put on the market; it was sold to a private individual in the early 1980s. However finance and various plans saw it change ownership several times. During this period it was opened for public inspection on some occasions. Fortunately the current owners have restored much of the house as a home, maintaining most of the original designs and features. The gardens unfortunately no longer embrace their former grandeur, however attempts have been made to restore them to some extent and the gardens have been able to recapture a small measure of their former splendor.

Wedding at Camelot, 2010 (www.cavallonerofriensians.com)

Note
In September 2010 I visited Springfield near Goulburn, the birthplace of Lilian Faithfull and where she married William Hugh Anderson on 16 February 1898. Following a tour of the beautiful gardens and grounds of *Springfield* homestead and farm, we visited the family cemetery and I had the opportunity to pay my respects to Lilian, William Hugh and Clarice at their final resting place on the hilltop overlooking Springfield.

This article was originally submitted to the Narellan Writer's Competition in 2008

by **Anderson Memorial fountain, Macarthur Park, 1998 (Camden Historical Society collection)**

Sharon Greene and updated May 2013

1. Brochure, *Camelot Kirkham*, Camden Open Weekend, 9-10 June 1991.
2. The Kirkham estate was part of an earlier land grant to John Oxley, Surveyor-General of NSW.
3. *Ibid.*
4. J.M. Freeland, *Architect extraordinary, the life and work of John Horbury Hunt: 1838-1904*, Cassell Australia, North Melbourne, 1970, p. 99.
5. NSW Registry births, death and marriages, *Frances Lilian Faithfull*, 28 June 1859, birth. NB: Springfield is still a working sheep farm and is occupied by descendants of this family.
6. Peter Taylor, *Springfield, the story of a sheep station*, Allen & Unwin, Sydney, 1987, p. 209.
7. *Ibid.*
8. NSW Registry births, death and marriages, *William Hugh Anderson & Frances Lilian Faithfull*, 16 February, 1898, marriage.
9. *Ibid*, p. 97.
10. Brochure, *Camelot Kirkham*, Camden Open Weekend, 9-10 June 1991.
11. NSW Registry births, death and marriages, *Clarice Vivian Faithfull Anderson*, 20 June 1900, birth.
12. G.V. Sidman, *The town of Camden*, p. 49.
13. *Ibid.*, p. 48.
14. *Ibid.*, p. 82.
15. Camden Historical Society, *Camelot files*.
16. Sidman, *The town of Camden*, p. 80.
17. *Ibid.*, p. 52.
18. Brochure, *Camelot Kirkham*, Camden Open Weekend, 9-10 June 1991.
19. Australian Biography Online, *James White (1828-1890)*, Copyright 2006, updated daily. http://www.adb.online.anu.edu.au/biogs/A060417b.htm?hilite=james%3Bwhite, accessed 29 May 2007.
20. *Camden News*, Inquest 23 May 1912, p. 3.
21. *Ibid.*
22. *Ibid.*
23. NSW Registry births, death and marriages, *William Hugh Anderson*, 16 May 1912, death.
24. *Camden News*, 24 July 1913, p. 5.
25. Sidman, *The town of Camden, A Facsimile with Index* Compiled by Liz Vincent, Picton, 1995 (1939). P. 62
26. *Camden News*, 24 July 1913, p. 5.
27. *Ibid.*, 24 July 1913, p. 5.
28. Sidman, *The town of Camden*, p. 46.

29. *Ibid.*, p. 59.
30. *Camden News*, 24 July 1913, p. 5.
31. *Ibid.*, 29 May 1913, p. 3.
32. *Camden News*, 24 July 1913, p. 2.
33. *Ibid.*, 24 July 1913, p. 2.
34. *Ibid.*, 24 July 1913, p. 5.
35. Dictionary of Biography Online, *Tom (Tommy) Corrigan*, (1851-1894), Copyright 2006, updated daily. http://www.adb.online.anu.edu.au/biogs/A030435b.htm, accessed 25 May 2007.
36. University of Queensland, *A.B. (Banjo) Paterson*, poetry search, http://www.google.com/search?q=cache:DwW4BZLz3LoJ:www.qu.edu.au/~mlwham/ba..., accessed 22 may 2007.
37. *Camden News*, 4 August 1932, p. 6.
38. *Camden News*, 19 March 1979, p. 16.

President's Report 2012-2013

Bob Lester

It is with great pleasure that I present my first president's report for the Camden Historical Society. The past twelve months have afforded me an insight into all areas of the society's operations and the opportunity to work along side a dedicated group of members to continue the work the organisation undertakes for its members and the community at large.

The year saw the Society continued to play an important role within the local community, providing information, awareness and opportunities for local residents and visitors to see and hear about the many stories associated with Camden's past.

Through the increased number of Museum visitors, the wide range of requests for information, hits on our webpage, visits from local schools and increased attendance at its monthly meetings, it would seem that the Society is doing something right.

Strategic Plan review

To maintain our focus the Society's committee undertook a review of its strategic plan formulating a new one that covers the period 2013 to 2018. Whilst maintaining the society's main objectives the plan will enable it to focus on good management of the museum and on a range of community activities advocating for the area's historical environment. The plan has been placed on to the society's website and will be used to assist us in advocating to government and funding bodies. I encourage people to have a read of it and play their role in maintaining the society's focus.

One of the plan's strategies is to maintain a strong partnership with the Camden Library and the Camden Family History Society. Committee members have attended regular meetings to coordinate activities during History Week and Heritage Month. Also the availability online of the society's photographic collection occurs through the partnership with the library whose resources enable easy access and the capability of people to obtain good quality prints.

The value of this partnership to council was reinforced during the new general manager, Ron Moore's visit to the museum to have a walk through and discuss issues with committee members. We hope to see more of Ron at the museum and thank him and other council staff for their ongoing support.
Museum

The management of the Camden Museum remained a major focus of the Society during the year with a number of exciting exhibitions and events undertaken. Through a Camden Council grant two museum quality cabinets were purchased in which we can now store and display a number of items from our textile collection. Along with a storyboard and interpretive signage they tell a wonderful story about Camden's past with most museum visitors taking the opportunity to pull open a drawer for a peek inside.

The development of this display enabled a number of society members to be involved in working bees that have become a feature of most exhibitions these days. Work has been progressing in the development of the Red Cross exhibition and book through a grant from the Australian Government. This grant required the Society to undertake work in kind through exhibition development, book research and its promotion and launch.

I am sure many of you have read items in *The District Reporter* published about the activities of the Red Cross in Camden and seen the displays of items the museum has in its collection. The exhibition area in the research room has been renovated in preparation for the installation of the main exhibition which will be launch in mid September leading up to the main launch in 2014.

A great deal of work behind the scenes has occurred by many Society members and great interest from the Camden community through donations and information.

The year also saw the celebration of the 50th Anniversary of the closure of the Camden line. Closures of most things are seldom celebrated but just like that day back on the 1 January 1963 the significant role the line played in Camden's history was acknowledged and remembered by many people.

The display of photographs and newspaper articles was well read by visitors a presentation was given on the line at one of our meetings, articles were written, new publications were released and new stories unearthed about the many journeys of Pansy. The Society would like to thank the New South Wales Rail Museum for the loan of the header board that was displayed on the front of the last train to leave Camden and which is included in our display upstairs in the museum.

Visitor numbers for 2012-2013 have reached an all time high with 6,825 (5,442 in 2011/2012) people coming through the doors to view the displays, as part of a school or group visit or attend a society meeting or function. These numbers shows that the museum is being well used and is an important tourist destination for Camden visitors.

The museum volunteers continued to play an essential role in making these visitors feel welcome, able to access our research files and leave with a bit more knowledge and understanding of Camden's past.

Our volunteer coordinator Rene Rem has ensured the front desk has been staffed on all shifts, enticing more people to become volunteers and facilitating a volunteers training day during the year.

Society meetings

Whilst our monthly meetings enable us to properly manage the society's affairs, they are more important as a means to maintain members' interest, increasing their knowledge, tell stories about our collective histories and bringing new members and visitors to the museum. This year saw the first time I have seen the main area of the museum overflowing with people for the talk by David Funnell on his memories of Argyle Street.

This was nearly matched by the numbers that came along to hear our speakers on Harrington Park, Camelot, cricket in Camden and Alan Baker and his paintings. One of our meetings saw the whole place rearranged to form a catwalk area where 'local models' provided the audience with a glamorous presentation of dresses and fashion from the past. Well done for a memorable evening.

Communication

The society maintains a number of avenues through which it can communicate with its members and inform the community about our activities.

The website has been revamped by our webmaster Stephen Robinson even though he has spent much of his time touring Australia or setting up a new home in Tasmania. The web is important to enable younger generations and the not so young to research our records and keep in touch.

Regular newsletters have been developed by Ian Willis and printed by our Federal member's office. Ian has also been the editor of our much valued journal which is well read by all concerned and reflects the variety of research undertaken by our members.

Attendance at the Camden Show and Camden Antique Fair each year remains a valuable way of communicating with the public with our display of publications gaining great interest. Thank you to all who have volunteered to be part of these displays and to the people who have organised them.

New publications have regularly hit our sales area with books on a variety of subjects and interests. They provide a source of income for the society and a way of communicating stories on aspects of life in Camden. By reading these books and the weekly articles that appear in 'Back Then' in *The District Reporter* no Camden resident should be unaware of a our rich local history.

Our committee

Like most community organisations nothing gets done without the efforts of people who dedicate much of their time and energy in the many tasks that need to be performed to make things work effectively and meet the expectations of our members.

I wish to thank all members of the committee for their efforts, know-how and time in making the society tick. Everyone had a role to play in our successes this year and I look forward to working with them again in the year ahead.

Unfortunately the year saw the stepping down of Doug Barrett as Secretary after many years in the role. He said he only started as a favour to Colin Mills (a familiar story for many of us) but this ended up being a lot longer than he thought. Through Doug's skills and dedication many of the Society's systems were updated and brought into the modern way of doing things. He worked tirelessly for the benefit of the Society, doing many things we are only just now finding out and fully appreciating.

On behalf of all Society members I wish to thank Doug and wish him and his partner Cheryl all the best for their future. We do hope to see him back around the Museum in the not too distant future.

August 2013

The CIFA Story

Noreen Newton

Camden International Friendship Association (CIFA) is a s.355 committee of Camden Council and is the volunteer group who operate, on Council's behalf, the various activities associated with the Friendship Agreement between Camden and Shonan Councils which was signed in 1997. This was the result of a number of visits and discussions between interested parties over four years. The initiative to establish a friendship with a town in Japan came from Mrs Theresa Testoni, a former mayor of Camden, who drove the initial negotiations and was the inaugural President of CIFA. The formalities took place in Shonan in 1997 while Councillor Frank Brooking was Mayor.

In 2002, the town of Shonan became part of nearby Kashiwa City and the name Shonan disappeared. The Camden-Shonan relationship became the fourth international friendship association supported by Kashiwa City Council and it has gone from strength to strength.

About 270 Camden district students and 70 adults have benefited from the CIFA exchange program by visiting and homestaying with Japanese families. There has been a similar number of Japanese people involved in the program in the Camden district. For all of these people it has been a life changing experience.

Over the past eighteen years CIFA has organised:

- A 16 day visit by the Camden High School concert band in 1994
- The annual exchange of Camden and Kashiwa student groups led by local high school teachers
- Three soccer team exchanges involving Camden Tigers Soccer Club
- Homestay for 30 university students while studying English for three weeks at UWS
- A nine month exchange for two Camden students and a three month exchange for two Kashiwa students
- Four adult groups on Cherry Blossom Tours, with homestay in Kashiwa on three occasions
- The construction of a Japanese garden designed by a member of Kashiwa Council's staff. He spent one month in Camden, homestayed by CIFA members.
- Teacher exchanges between the two towns
- Regular displays of Japanese cultural items in Camden Council

office and Camden and Narellan libraries
- The Anime and Cultural Club formed to meet the needs of our younger members
- Reciprocal visits to celebrate the signing of the Friendship Agreement and the 5th, 10th and 15th anniversaries of the Agreement.

At the time of writing (October 2012), the President of CIFA is Mr Richard Leemen. Contact with CIFA can be made through Camden Council by contacting Nicola Barnes, Executive Officer.

Tank or Bank?

Janice Johnson

On the afternoon of Monday April 15, 1918 Camden was abuzz at the unusual visitor at the corner of Oxley and Argyle Streets Camden. A British WWI tank had arrived in town; or to be more correct a mock-up of a tank. The mock-up was built from wood and canvas and mounted on a truck chassis.

It is believed that the mock-ups which toured Sydney during Tank Week April 3 to 10, 1918 were then deployed to regional areas. The truck would transport the kit to transform it from truck to tank, and the transformation would take place not far from where it was displayed. The Camden tank was possibly transformed inside the showground area. It did not rumble as it trundled into town but nevertheless horses would have shied and shoppers startled when it appeared. Fortunately, as a mock-up, there were no tank treads to tear up the street.

In November 1917 two tanks had taken part in London's Lord Mayor's Show and proved very popular with spectators there. Britain's Nation War Savings Committee used the tanks to sell war bonds and war savings certificates, with great success.

The Australian Government realised that for their sixth War Loan campaign to be a resounding success they needed to do something that would fire the public's imagination. There was every reason to hope that a campaign, similar to the one that had taken place in Britain, would be equally successful in Australia. The tank mock-ups became a travelling Tank Banks.

Small towns such as Camden were also visited. In each locality school children were marched from their school to the tank, the national anthem sung, and cheers given for the King and the Australian army.

The Lord Mayor of Sydney, Alderman Boynton Smith, and two returned soldiers accompanied the tank and were officially welcomed to the municipality by the Mayor of Camden, Alderman George Frederick (Curly) Furner. Mayor Furner introduced the visitors to the large crowd that had gathered to see the tank and add their contribution to the war loan. Appeals on behalf of the war loan were made by the lord mayor and two returned soldiers.

As the war dragged on recruitment figures were falling. The government, through the returned soldiers, pointed out the patriotism of Australia was

Tank Bank in Camden. Mayor Furner right, Sydney Lord Mayor to the centre (CHS)

"now being tested at the point of the bayonet, and at the edge of the sword." The fierce foe they were fighting was trying to strangle democracy in Europe.

The defeat of the Allies would mean the end of Australia as a land of freedom. The soldiers challenged the men in the crowd – "Did those eligible men who are holding back realise that it was the aim of Germany to get control of the Pacific, and take possession of Australia? If Australians failed in their duty now they would lose everything worth having as a self-governing country."

Britain was continually pointing out to the Australian government the need of the hour was more men for the front. The men of Camden needed to unite in a determined effort to help in winning the war.

The war could not be carried on without money. Money was needed for food, clothing and to care for the soldiers who were fighting for them. The Mayors pointed out that not all may fight but all could help. "Every man must do his part; every woman must do her part. If you can't enlist you can do your share by loaning your money to the Government."

The appeal by the two Mayors for the people of Camden to contribute to the War Loan was a resounding success. Men and women entered the tank one by one and two young ladies would sell war bonds from a table set up inside.

Once the transaction was completed the customers would exit on the other side. Business was brisk but owing to the late hour many applications for bonds had to be refused, these people however were asked to call on the local banks the following morning.

Just prior to the tank leaving for Picton the Lord Mayor announced that the Camden subscriptions to the Tank Bank received that evening totalled £8,620. This total was increased the following day to £10,040. Total Subscriptions by the people of Camden to the Sixth War Loan by the end of the week totalled over £40,000.

Clarissa Whiteman, First World War Nurse

Julie Wrigley

Recently two photos have been donated to the Camden Museum of Clarissa Muriel Whiteman who served in France in World War One. Clarissa was the daughter of Charles Thomas Whiteman (1849-1903) and Ann Whiteman, nee Bensley (1850-1930). The Whitemans and Bensleys were part of a strong Methodist community in Cobbitty Paddock and Cawdor at the end of the nineteenth century.

Charles and Anne married in 1872 and had twelve children: Annie, Amy, Frederick, George, Alice, Hubert, Henry, Clarissa, Jessie, Ida, Ruth and Elsie. Clarissa was born on 10 June 1885 (with her name registered as Muriel Clarissa) and she grew up in Camden, at that time a small country town. The family lived at "Melrose" at 69 John Street (which unfortunately burnt down in 1977; and is now the site of Melrose Retirement Units).

Clarissa's father, Charles Thomas Whiteman (1849-1903), had founded Whitemans in 1878 as a farm produce store, and a general store was built in 1900. Charles was a prominent figure in Camden. He was a foundation alderman in 1889 and was elected Mayor in 1892 and 1893.

Clarissa grew up in a large secure family with examples of community work and service.

In April 1903 Clarissa and five of her sisters were bridesmaids for their eldest sister Olive Whiteman who was married at Camden Wesleyan Church. Sadly their father Charles Whiteman died a month later. He left his estate to his widow Ann, who lived for another 27 years. She left the running of the store to her sons and by 1913 Ann had moved to a stately home, "Craig-y-Nos", Cheltenham Road, Burwood.

Clarissa Whiteman trained as a General and Obstetrics nurse, passing her final examinations in December 1913. Her hospital training included working at Manly Cottage Hospital and the Royal Hospital for Women in Sydney. She had gained experience as a ward sister and a night superintendent in various hospitals, and then in 1914 war broke out. At the age of 29 years Clarissa enlisted on 26 April 1915, and was appointed as a staff nurse as part of special reinforcements sent to in France. She embarked on 15 May in 1915 from Sydney on the *RMS Mooltan*.

Clarissa's war records can be read on the National Archives of Australia, which provides digital copies of World War One soldiers' and nurses' service records. She was sent to the First Australian General Hospital at Rouen in France, where she worked until she was given two weeks' leave in England in July 1917, appointed a sister in September 1917, and given a week's leave in Paris in February 1918. On 6 July 1918 she was transferred to England 'for Marriage' and on 26 July 1918 she resigned her appointment 'on account of Marriage' and was discharged. In the records there is a copy of the letter that the matron-in-chief in Rouen Hospital wrote to AIF Admin-

Sister Whiteman (3rd row, 2nd from left) at Heliopolis, No 1 Australian General Hospital. (AWM)

istration Headquarters, "*I beg to inform you that Sister Clarissa Muriel Whiteman was married on the 18th instant and vacated her position in the Service on that day.*" It was only women who were discharged "on Account of Marriage"!

There is also a copy of a Release by Discharged Member of the Australian Imperial Force in England, stating that "*such discharge having been granted to me in England at my own request and all arrears of pay having been received by me, DO HEREBY DECLARE that I have no further claim upon the Commonwealth Government for or in respect of a free passage from England to Australia now or an any time hereafter. . .*" This formal Release is signed by her as both "Clarissa Muriel Whiteman" and "Clarissa Muriel Stephen". Apparently Clarissa's return to Australia was now her husband's responsibility!

Clarissa Whiteman married Major Edgar Horatio Milner Stephen on 18 July 1918 in London. He had been born in 1878 at Petersham, Sydney, graduating from Sydney University in medicine in 1902, and Master of Surgery in 1904. He had embarked on the *RMS Mooltan* in 1915 and had served with the Australian Amy Medical Corps from 29 April 1915, including periods with the Field Ambulance; dealing with casualties from Gallipoli at the Australian General Hospital in Cairo, Egypt; and serving in the hospital at Rouen, France. Romantically both Clarissa and Edgar managed to have two weeks' leave in England in July 1917. The records show that Edgar was serving at A.I.F. Headquarters in London, a year later, when he married Clarissa Whiteman at St Paul's Church of England, Hampstead. He completed his war service in October 1919.

It seems that Clarissa and Edgar Stephen met in France, though they may have met earlier as both enlisted on 26 April 1915 and embarked on 15 May 1915 on the *Mooltan*. After the war they returned to Sydney and lived in the eastern suburbs. In the 1930 electoral records they lived at 131 Queen Street, Woollhara. They did not have children but Edgar had a distinguished career as physician to the Royal Alexandra Hospital for Children, and was one of the first consultant physicians to restrict his work to children. Edgar died in February 1954, and Clarissa died at Darling Point in April 1960. The Camden Museum is pleased to hold the photos of Clarissa, who was such an interesting member of a prominent Camden family, and to remember her time of service in the First World War.

Crown Land and the Wild Cattle of the Cowpasture Plains

Peter Mylrea

To explain the title of this article three historical facts are relevant.

First, at the time of the settlement of Sydney in 1788 all the land in the new colony was considered to be owned by the British Monarch, King George the Third, and was called Crown Land. In the first years of the settlement the Governors had the right to make free grants of Crown Land to individuals.

Second, in the cargo on the First Fleet there were cattle imported from South Africa. Soon after their arrival in the settlement they escaped, moved west and multiplied. They were considered to be lost until they were discovered seven years later in 1795. Early attempts to control them were unsuccessful hence they were referred to as the 'Wild Cattle'.

Third, Governor Hunter gave the name Cowpasture Plains to this district in 1795 and this is the origin of this name.[1] While the area of the Cowpasture Plains has never been clearly defined it was all west of the Nepean River and approximately south of the Razorback Range, west beyond Mount Hunter and north past Brownlow Hill.

Arthur Phillip was the first governor of the colony of New South Wales and he was succeeded by Lieutenant Governors Francis Grose and William Paterson until 1795. During the terms of these men there was no knowledge of the Cowpastures or the Wild Cattle.

In contrast, the six governors who succeeded Phillip were involved, to varying extents, with both the Cowpasture land and the cattle. Their contributions are discussed in the following notes.

John Hunter: Governor 11 September 1795 to 27 September 1800

Hunter played a major role in discovering and protecting the Wild Cattle of the Cowpastures.

By 1795 there were rumours of cattle to the south west of Sydney and Hunter sent Henry Hacking to investigate. He reported to Hunter that he had found cattle and Hunter decided to investigate the matter for himself. To this end he led an exploratory expedition in 1795 to what is now called the Razorback Range.[2] There he found mobs of cattle and was 'attacked most furiously by a large and very fierce Bull'. He was 'now satisfied that they were of the Cape of Good Hope Breed, and no doubt the offspring of those we had lost in 1788'. He considered the cattle were a valuable asset to the colony and as a consequence in December 1795 he issued a proclamation 'that any person whatever shall use any means to destroy or otherwise annoy the cattle they will be prosecuted with the utmost severity of the law'.[3]

In regard to Crown Lands, Hunter did not make any land grants west of the Nepean River so all the Cowpastures remained as government Crown Land.

Philip Gidley King: Governor 28 September 1800 to 12 August 1806

The governorship of King was an important period for both Wild Cattle and Crown Land and for the development of the wool industry.

On the 14 September 1801 an important event occured which was to have significant ramifications. On that day Lieutenant John Macarthur fought a duel with his commanding officer Major Paterson. As a consequence Macarthur was sent to England to face a court martial. He departed for London in November 1801. The court martial did not take place and he returned to Sydney in June 1805.

In July 1803 King made a trip to the Cowpastures to confirm 'the Adventatious Reports I had heard of it'. At that time meat was preserved by rubbing salt into it ('salted beef') and during this visit 'a small Hut was built and a Cask of Salt placed in it'.[4] On 1 March 1804 King reported that six stray bulls had been killed and salted for public use.[5]

King concluded that the cattle, which were running on government (Crown) land, were a valuable assets for the colony. He considered that they should be protected so he issued a proclamation forbidding persons to cross the Nepean River to enter the Cowpastures without a government permit.[6] This was, in effect, a continuation of the ban on unauthorised entry made by Governor Hunter in December 1795.

While this was going on Macarthur did not waste his five year stay in England. He promoted the idea that Australia could produce fine wool for the English wool industry. He also sought a personal land grant of ten thousand acres to allow him to expand his sheep farming activities.

On 1 March 1804 King wrote to Lord Hobart, Secretary of State[7], recommending that the cattle should be left undisturbed and that 'no ground whatever ought to be granted or leased to individuals on the other [western] side of the Nepean.'[8]

Perhaps King had heard of Macarthur's advocacy for he wrote in a dispatch to Lord Hobart, Secretary of State, dated 14 August 1804 'I am not unaware that applications may be made for ground being granted at the Cow Pastures on the other side of the Nepean.'[9]

However Macarthur's advocacy in London was successful as indicated in the following dispatch from Earl Camden, Secretary of State, to Governor King.

> Downing Street, 31st October 1804.
> The Committee of His Majesty's Privy Council for matters respecting trade and plantations having taken into consideration the advantages which may accrue to this country from the growth of fine wool in New South Wales, have recommended to me to take measures for the encouragement thereof;

and they having further represented that, from the pains which have been taken by John Macarthur, Esquire, in increasing and improving the breed of sheep in New South Wales, it would be expedient to promote his views by such a grant of lands as would enable him to extend his flocks in such a degree as may promise to supply a sufficiency of animal food for the colony as well as a lucrative article for export for the support of our manufacturers at Home, - I am Commanded by His Majesty to desire that you will have a proper grant of lands, fit for the pasture for sheep, conveyed to the said John Macarthur, Esq., in perpetuity, with the usual reserve of quit rent to the Crown, containing not less than five thousand acres. [10]

John Macarthur requested land in the Cowpastures. This lead to disagreements with Governor King who wanted to follow his policy of not granting land in that area. King suggested other possible sites but this was of no avail and on 1 November 1805 King wrote to Macarthur 'I do not consider myself at liberty to decline or defer granting You the Accommodation prescribed by his Lordship'. [11]Macarthur received two grants of Crown land on 18 December 1805, one he called 'Camden Park' (2250 acres) and the other 'Upper Camden' of 2750 acres. [12] (See map)

Concurrently with the grants to Macarthur another grant of Crown Land was given to Walter Davidson which he called 'Belmont'. In a dispatch on 31 October 1804[14] Earl Camden instructed Governor King to give Mr Walter Davidson a grant of 2000 acres next to Macarthur's grants together with an appropriate number of convicts. Davidson was a nephew of Sir Walter Farquhar and 'it is extremely desirable to encourage gentlemen of such connexions to establish themselves in the colony.' [15] Davidson arrived in the colony with John Macarthur in June 1805. He did not establish himself in the colony as he left permanently in March 1809! Davidson allowed the Macarthurs to make use of his property ('Belmont') until he sold his free grant to them in 1837 for four thousand pounds.[16]

Thus by the end of 1805 John Macarthur owned or had the use of 7000 acres of land while the rest of the Cowpastures remained as government Crown Land. It was not until 1822, seventeen years later, that John Macarthur and his sons, James and William, were to receive further grants of land.

William Bligh: Governor 13 August 1806 to 26 January 1808

Bligh was Governor from August 1806 until he was deposed in January 1808 by the coup known as the Rum Rebellion. In these two years he maintained the status quo by not making any land grants. With regard to the cattle he wrote in 1807 that 'As the Plans of some individuals [not named] appear to me to be so self interested that no ultimate good would attend them.... I think it best that the government should for some time longer keep the concern [Wild Cattle] in their own hands'.[17]

Lieutenant George Johnston, Major Joseph Foveaux and Colonel William Patterson. These officers served in succession, between 26 January 1808 and 31 De-

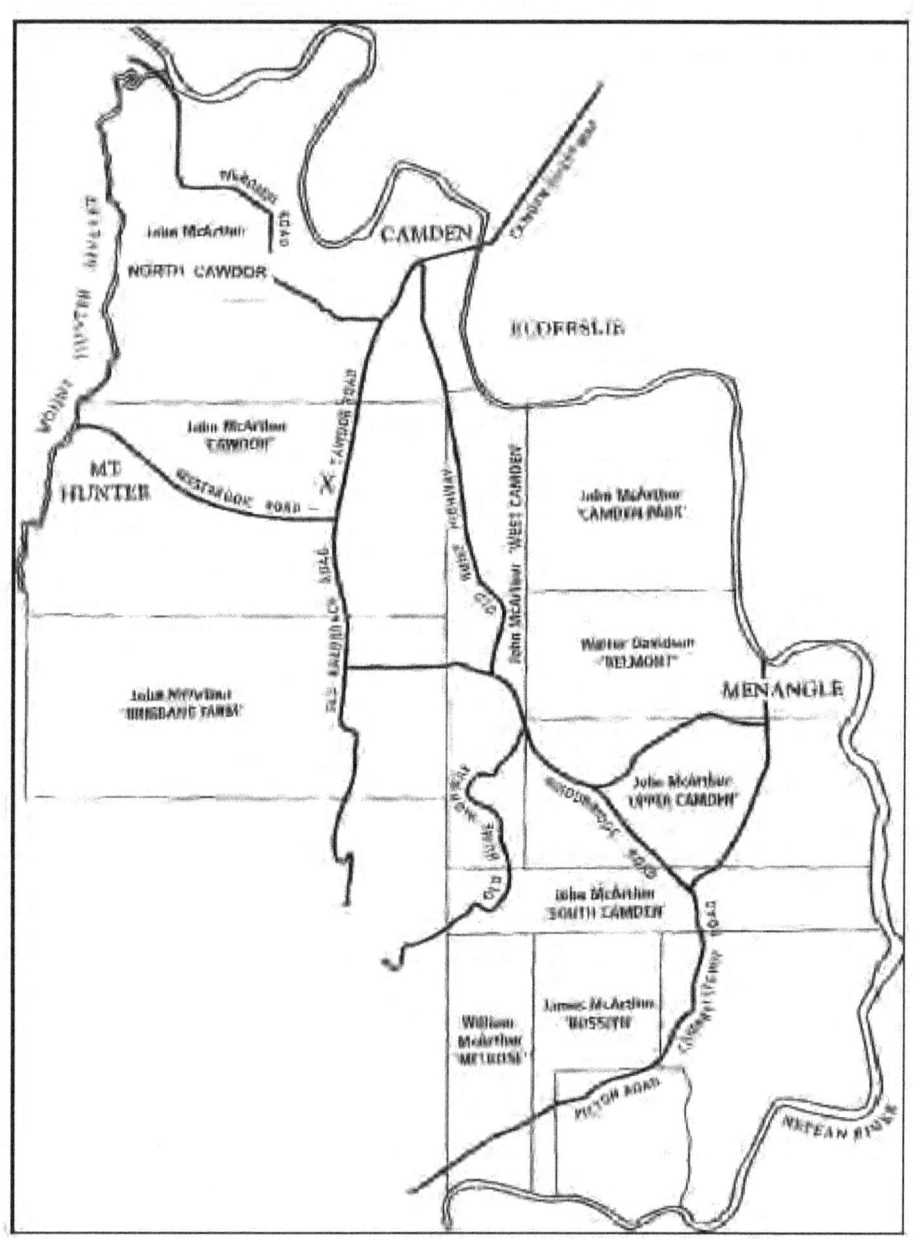

A map showing the properties owned by the Macarthur family at the end of 1825. The X (near the name of Cawdor Road) was the location of the Government Stock Yards.[13]

cember 1809, as administrators of the colony after Governor Bligh had been deposed and until Governor Macquarie arrived.

They made few comments on the Wild Cattle and they made no grants in the Cowpastures.

Lachlan Macquarie: Governor 1 January 1810 to 1 December 1821.

Macquarie did not give any land grants to John Macarthur during his governorship but he did pay attention to the Wild Cattle.

In November 1810 Macquarie made his first tour of the colony. In the Cowpastures he saw numerous herds of Wild Cattle. He came to the same conclusion as his predecessors, King and Bligh, that the cattle were a valuable asset to the colony, that they should be protected and that no more grants of land should be made in the Cowpastures. [18]

However Macquarie wished to utilise the cattle for the benefit of the colony and in June 1813 he issued instructions for the erection of 'Substantial Strong Stock Yards' throughout the Cowpastures.[19] However, it seems that these had not been constructed by October 1815 when Macquarie toured the Cowpastures because he made no mention of stock yards in his journal.

By 1822 the stock yards had become the centre of the government activities in the Cow Pastures. By then there were four large paddocks each of one hundred acres with strong fences, some other stock yards and a tanning house. There was a brick house for the Superintendent of Government Stock and the Overseer and a weatherboarded house for the stockmen.[20] There were also stock yards at Stonequary Creek [Picton] and at Brownlow Hill. These were all inspected by Macquarie in his tour in 1822.[21] During this tour Macquarie gave the name of Cawdor to the settlement in honour of his wife's birthplace in Scotland.

Thomas Brisbane: Governor 1 December 1821 to 19 December 1825.

Sir Thomas Brisbane became familiar with the Cowpastures soon after he arrived in the colony when he accompanied Macquarie on his tour of the Cowpastures in January 1822.

During the four years of his governorship Brisbane gave seven land grants to the Macarthurs. All were in the Cowpastures.

On 9 July 1822 he gave grants of land to the sons of John Macarthur. Both were for 1150 acres; the grant to James Macarthur was called 'Roslyn' and that to William Macarthur was called 'Melrose'.[22]

The next three grants were to John Macarthur but they were not straight out Grants. The first was on 27 May 1823 and 'was given and granted in payment for three hundred rams purchased by His Majesty's government from this grantee.' [These rams went to Tasmania.] The name of this grant was not named in the title deed but was probably 'Brisbane Farm'. The next two grants were 'given in lieu of land in the District of Toongabbie surrendered by this grantee to the Crown'. These were 'West Camden' which had an area of 2065 acres and 'South Camden' of 1565 acres. The final two grants to John Macarthur were made on 5 October 1825. One was 'Cawdor' which had an area of 5000 acres and the second was 'North Cawdor' with an area of 5400 acres.

These were the last grants the Macarthurs received in the Cowpastures. Thus by the end of 1825 the Macarthurs were the owners or occupiers of 27,700 acres of land.

Ralph Darling: Governor 19 December 1825 to 3 December 1831.

It was during Darling's governorship that the story of the Wild Cattle came to an end. In accordance with instructions from Earl Bathurst, Home Secretary in London Darling arranged for the sale of the Cowpastures cattle. This took place at Parramatta on 30 March 1826 [23] and on 5 April l the convict stockmen at Cawdor were ordered to return immediately to the Hyde Park Barracks in Sydney, presumably because there were now no government cattle in the Cowpastures.[24] These were the concluding actions in the story of the Wild Cattle which had begun in 1788.

References
HRA = Historical records of Australia
ADB = Australian Dictionary of Biography
1 Mylrea ,PJ *Journal of the Camden Historical Society* vol 3 March 2012 p. 94.
2 HRA vol 1 pp.550-1.
3 HRA vol 1 p.683.
4 HRA vol. 5, p.581; vol. 4 p. 462.
5 HRA vol 5, p.461.
6 HRA vol. 4, p. 334.
7 The men holding the position of Secretary of State changed frequently. Lord Hobart held the position from   17 March 1801 to May 12 1804 and was succeeded by Earl Camden from 14 May 1894 to 10 July 1805.
8 HRA vol. 4 p. 463.
9 HRA vol. 5 p. 7.
10 HRA vol 5, p. 161.
11 HRA vol 5, p. 579.
12 Land Titles Office Old System Titles, Grants and L eases Vol 3.
13 Site of stock yards as shown on State Library map M Ser 4 00/1 A3004 map 20.
14 HRA vol 5, p.162.
15 HRA vol. 5 p. 162.
16 ADB vol 1, p.290; LTO Book 10, Number 277.
17 HRA vol 6 P. 154.
18 HRA vol. 7, pp. 379-80.
19 HRA vol. 7, p. 743.
20 HRA vol. 10, p.694-5.
21 Lachlan Macquarie *Journal of His Tours in New South Wales,* Library of Australian History pp. 142,236.

22 The information about all these grants is given in Grants of Land volume 10, Old System Titles, Land Titles Office.
23 Sydney Gazette 11 March 1826; 22 March 1826.
24 State Records of New South Wales, 4/3528, reel 2915 p. 140.

The Gallipoli Evacuation

Janice Johnson

One little known story of the Gallipoli campaign in World War 1 is how the evacuation of the peninsula was successfully accomplished. The battle for the Dardanelles continued for eight long months until December 7, 1915 when the British Government finally agreed to the need for a withdrawal. Due to adverse weather conditions this was postponed until December 10 when the evacuation commenced undercover of night and continued until December 20, 1915. For the evacuation to succeed without heavy losses being sustained it was essential that the Turkish command be kept unaware of the gradual withdrawal of the troops and equipment.

It was essential not to raise the suspicions of the Turkish military. The plan to convince them that nothing suspicious was happening began in late November. The Allied troops maintained a strictly enforced silence over a three day period. On the third day the Turks sent a reconnaissance plane to attempt to find out the reason for the silence. However the troops had been told to stay in their dugouts and not look up.

The Turkish command then sent a ground party to check what was going on. Whilst the Allied troops had been told to hold their fire until ordered to shoot, finally someone got nervous and opened fire and then the Turks then realized they had been tricked. That exercise helped to lull the enemy's suspicions during the actual evacuation.

As part of the secret evacuation of the Anzac and Suvla Bay sectors on December 17, 1915, two days before the final evacuation of Anzac Cove, Major George Macleay Macarthur Onslow organized the famous cricket match at Shell Green. The cricket match was played whilst shells passed overhead and was used to distract the Turkish troops from what was happening near the beach.

By the morning of December 18 half the troops had been evacuated, including the official historian, Charles Bean, who was then only able to view the final stages from on-board ship. Each morning the beaches looked normal and everything seemed as it had previously. The last 40,000 men were then evacuated over the next two nights.

Williams Pier, North Beach, Gallipoli, December 1915, with the Sphinx in the background during the evacuation preparations (Australian War Memorial C01621)

Picton soldier Private William Henry Hooker wrote home from Zeitoun, Egypt giving an eyewitness account of the final stages of the evacuation.

Picton Post
Wednesday, May 17, 1916

Letter from a Soldier

Private W. Hooker writes from Zeitoun on 18th February as follows:-
The most thrilling experience I have had yet was the evacuation of the Peninsular. It was a marvellous feat; scores of thousands of men were moved from under the enemy's nose and shipped away without Jonnie knowing it. The first intimation we had of shifting was when the officers' baggage began to get under way then speculation was rife as to who was going to relieve us, for none of us, at least only one in a thousand, thought of evacuation. The thought that we were giving our friend the enemy the

boot, was the last thing in the world to think.

However as things developed we could not do anything but take notice of the rumours of evacuation. Nothing was doing for a couple of days and then we got definite word of evacuation. I can tell you it gave us a queer feeling to know it, for the Turks only wanted a hint and the landing would have been nothing to the evacuation. All arrangements were made to fight a big rear guard action.

All hospitals in Egypt, Lemnos, etc., were cleared to make room for the thousands of casualties expected. How glad we are to think that all this preparation was unnecessary.

Things were humming at this time: you can't imagine the feeling of excitement prevailing everyone. The air seemed charged with electricity. I suppose it was just the same feeling which our first division had before the landing. Everything was being moved which would be of value to the Turks. Our artillery was sadly depleted. My word we missed it, and many a one wondered how the enemy didn't notice the dearth of artillery fire from us.

At last the news came – first batch to move off 5 p.m. Saturday. Who was to be the first? About half of each battalion was to go. This lot would be fairly safe except from artillery fire. They were picked out and as they moved off with muffled boots, to time, we watched them leave. You can guess our thoughts: we wondered if we would see them again. We still had about one third our strength left, and all good men. The feeling was very acute, it was suspense: still we all wanted to be the last to leave. That's if there was to be any last. The next lot was to leave at 5 p.m. next evening; this would leave 32 men holding a post which in the first place was held by 1,000 men. We all thought it would be an honour to be one of the 32. We got the names that day: I was lucky enough to be one of them.

I said goodbye to my best mate at 5 p.m. that day. He was terribly disappointed and so was I. If our officers had known him as I did he would have remained to the last. I was his nearest companion the eighteen and a half weeks we were at Gallipoli and in my opinion he was the best soldier I have had the pleasure of meeting. He was one of those fellows who do everything they are asked without a word, excepting it's a cheerful word, and he was a grand mate. He had a temper but it was all good. I felt like letting him stay in my place that day but of course it would have looked as though I was shirking.

Well they left and there we were 32, with no chance in life if Johnnie had come. We were there to bluff them by our fire and you can rest assured it was bluff, as it was 32 against perhaps 2,000 men. I kept my eyes skinned that night. We did 7 hours watch at night off without being able to leave the fire steps, and Johnnie was very annoying with his bombs. That seven hours seemed seventeen, for by then we felt that the operation couldn't have gone on unseen. We had bombs all primed and ready to give them a go for their money, and many a time I had a look to see if my bomb striker was in position. There was no one to talk to, for each man had to hold a parapet for two on his own; it was quite nerve racking but it had to be done. One of the 32 got hit with a piece of bomb, but only retired to have his wounds dressed and came back again. I had a narrow shave at about 11 p.m. being spattered with stones and pieces of bullets for a machine gun, but only got an ear barked and a couple of bruises. I was cheering for our bomb mortar at the time, and as it was perfectly moonlight Johnnie must have seen me. Anyhow a miss is as good as a mile.

We moved off at midnight our boots muffled with sacks blanket, leaving 7 behind for 2½ hours; our thoughts were with those seven fellows still bluffing the Turks for our safety. They were admired and envied. We were very glad to hear the next morning that we had all got safely off including the last seven. I would have like to have been one of them.

This is my evacuation experience in brief. Of course that duty lies with our battalion. When you realise that this was done with scores of battalions you get some idea of the thing, and you must remember that at places we were within 15 yards of the Turks.

By 11 p.m. on the night of December 19 there were less than 2,000 men still on Gallipoli. The remaining men set self-firing rifles. According to Les Carlyon's "Gallipoli" – *"a kerosene oil tin was filled with water. Underneath it was an empty tin with a string attached to the rifle trigger. On the night of December 19-20 holes would be punched in the bottom of the upper tin. After about 20 minutes the lower tin would fill with water, over-balance and fire the rifle."*

Fuses were also set to go off after an hour to wreck tunnels and destroy any equipment that could not be removed. *"the beach engineers fired a huge pile of explosives planted in tunnels under the Turkish frontline..."*

Camden Tram Station
Extract Camden News
Thursday 31 October 1895, page 1, Columns 1-2 (Vol 16 – No. 828)

Notes

It is not many months since that the Railway Commissioners paid a visit – we were going to say to the township of Camden, but, that would not be technically correct – to the Camden tram station, and remained inspecting their property for the period of half an hour, and then returned; after promising that the requirements demanded on behalf of the residents of Camden by the late Mayor, should received their careful attention. The only *requirements* that we know that have been effected is the repair to the crane at Camden, and, to give credit, we must not omit to add, that the existing lamps of the footbridge at Campbelltown are, or have to be, lighted when considered necessary. Now that does not amount to much considering the many important requirements named to the Commissioners, and which have been either shelved, or, are still having the mature and deliberate consideration at the hands of these gentlemen in Sydney. Take the question regarding the station accommodation, surely to goodness, in all common fairness, we are entitled to better treatment. Camden as a centre, is one of the richest and most prosperous of any town or district outside the metropolis within a radius of 50 to 60 miles; and this the Commissioners know fully well; certainly, we are not on the main line, or else we should be blessed with a substantially built station with all modern conveniences, in the shape of waiting rooms for passengers, and no doubt had Camden been on the main line the building would have been of an imposing appearance; that in our case is not required. What we want, and what we must have, is a railway station, where conveniences can be obtained, not only for the travelling public, but also for produce. Look at the present structure; there is not one atom of comfort for the public, not a room or shed, nor even a veranda, where shelter can be had; the passage way through the weatherboard station leading to, what we were going to term a platform – is always packed full with passengers luggage, boxes of fruit, boxes with fowls, boxes with eggs, boxes with butter and boxes of everything conceivable, bags of seed etc., and in addition, the weighing machine stands prominently forward in the passage way, and is a great source of danger to anyone who knocks up against it. The room to the left intended as a "waiting room" has neither chair nor table, and is consigned to the mysteries of, unclaimed boxes, and boxes and parcels waiting to be called for; the fact is, there is scar[c]e room for even the ever attentive station master, and his also ever attentive assistants, to carry on their work. And we venture to affirm that a more miserable overcrowded railway station does not exist in Australia. Menangle railway station is a palace to it. Why! Because it is on the main line! not because it has a greater population, or a greater amount of goods traffic. We incidentally mentioned the word "platform," our readers will kindly forgive us for using such a designation to such a structure, we, however, regret that we cannot find a word to express our meaning more explicitly. Well, the so called platform to use an Australian expression is a "perfect beauty". We all know perfectly well the state of this structure, especially after the milk tins have been carted away; this platform *sic* is not only faulty in construction, but is not by yards long enough, and many feet lower than it should be. It must be understood, that this district is a food producing one, and in what direction do the Commissioners foster the industry! Is there a covering to keep the rays of the sun off the milk – fresh from the cow? No! our dairymen after bringing their milk to the station, after using all modern appliances in cooling their milk prior to leaving their respective dairies, have to keep their milk cool during transit to the station by adopting the best means available and on arrival at the station have to stand in the glare of the sun waiting their turn, before the milk cans can be unloaded from the carts into the milk van. This is not as it should be, and we enter our protest to this condition of matters being continued any longer. Not only should the dairymen's milk vans be placed under cover, but the van itself should have more protection from the burning heat of the sun. These words apply equally to Summer and Winter supply, for in the winter the milk leaves by the afternoon tram, at near the hottest part of the day, and in the summer at near 9a.m., and we all full well known in Camden, that the sun at that hour is not conducive to the well keeping of milk. We have referred to the accommodation at present existing at the Camden station for passenger and goods traffic and we unhesitatingly say that steps should immediately be taken by the Railway Commissioners, and call for tenders for at least "reasonable accommodation" in the direction pointed out. Unless some of our citizens move and look after their own requirements in the interests of themselves, and the general public, so long shall we have to "grin and bide" the existing wretched accommodation. " Those who ask shall receive". We have , only last week, been honored with a visit of the Lieutenant-Governor of New South Wales, and Lady Darley, together with several titled gentlemen; it would be interesting to know the impressions formed by the highest in our land , as to our tramway – it is not a railway – accommodation, we *did* observe that the *one* wooden steps, at other times laying uselessly on the platform or near it, was made use of for the benefit of our vice-regal visitors; we *wonder* whether the same convenience would be offered to the "toilers of the soil" in the second, nay even in the first class carriage; we say first class, we mean the compartment which opens out into that portion of the carriage devoted to the carriage of dairy produce and articles coming under the designation of general goods, and which is used by first and second class passengers alike as a smoking compartment; this is not a nice sentiment ; nor is it right, that a compartment containing produce, milk, butter, fruit, and other perishable articles, together with the postal mails should be converted into a smoking compartment; what with tobacco smoke and expectoration of smokers, we should not consider such would add to the good keeping of these perishable goods. We point these facts out in order that the Railway Commissioners may not say "That, what the eye does not see, the heart never grieves for." It must , however, be stated that Mr Eddy the Chief Commissioner did not pay Camden a visit at the interview herein mentioned. We have in another instance pointed out in this journal the importance of being placed in telephonic communication with Campbelltown from the Camden station, and if we remember correctly, this also was placed before the notice of the Railway Commissioners by the late Mayor at their visit to – again we were going to say to the township of Camden – Camden tram station. What has been done in this matter? Nothing that we know; in this instance, we must admit, that, the income likely to be derived by the use of the telephone would not exactly justify the expenditure, yet, on the other hand we think that the Commissioners might have, instead of dropping the subject altogether – approached those who are interested in the use of a telephone wire to Campbelltown on the matter of cost, and as a business transaction, endeavour so to minimise the cost by the monetary assistance of the township. As briefly pointed out in our last week's issue. Mr. Onslow Thompson has, at his own expense, brought Narellan and Cawdor into direct telephonic communication with Camden, it strikes us very forcibly that Mr. Thompson had better buy the township, erect a railway station, light the town with electricity, construct a water-works, and set up "shop" as a general public benefactor: or it is assuredly a fact, that we are devoid of public enthusiasm in our midst. Now is the time for the newly elected Mayor Alderman J.D. Rankin to arise and shine, for he has many brilliant opportunities at present existing in our midst.

Transcribed by Cathey Shepherd

Camelot
Reminiscences from the past
Bob Brookes, Fred Gibson, Sharon Greene, Brendan and Rachel Powers
Camden Historical Society, 8 May 2013

Ian Willis

The house

John Wrigley, who gave a short introductory talk on the history of the house, said, 'The house took five years to build and one Camden builder served his whole apprenticeship on the job'. The house has '365 windows - a view for every day of the year'. Mrs Anderson named the house Camelot in 1900 after a verse from Tennyson's poem "The Lady of Shalott".

Betty Yewen said, 'The Camden Tourist Committee organised an open day in the 1980s and 6000 people passed through'. Sharon Greene said, 'I queued up in the 1980s to look through the house. I have has always loved the house which is very romantic. I am captivated by the house.'

Julie Wrigley reported on articles from *Trove* that in 1904 William Anderson had won a wager that his ponies Pepper and Grisette could pull a sulky from Sydney to Camden in less than 3 hours. In 1906 there was a fancy dress party at the house. Local teams competed for the local polo trophy, the WH Anderson Memorial Cup at Cobbitty. One article in 1933 described the garden, 'in the full bloom of Spring'. Janice Johnson reported that there was a garden party for 'Jack's Day' on 25 October 1915.

Bob Brookes

Bob lived on the property as a child growing up with his foster-parents Ted and Margery Smith. They lived in the Rose Cottage near the Wivenhoe entrance of the property. Bob was fostered with the Smiths after his parents died.

Bob said, 'The White family owned Belltrees near Moonan in the Upper Hunter. 'In the 1950s the Camelot roof caught fire amongst the shingles.

'At that time the property had 5 full-time gardeners and there was a full hedge around the house. You could not see in. It was never opened to the public'.

Fred Gibson

Fred was an electrician who was part of a team that re-wired the house and did a host of other minor jobs in 1956-57. The job took 18 months.

Fred said, 'Clarice Anderson was a great lady and very generous. She lived in the house with her companion, Miss Isabel Cocks. Miss Anderson had a labrador as a pet and was very soft-hearted about animals. In the last few years of her life she lived with her companion at Bundeena.

Fred said 'There were lots of possums in the roof. I was given the job of trapping them and Miss Anderson escorted me down the paddock to make sure the possum was released unharmed.

'In the roof there were wooden boxes which were lead-lined for flushing the toilets.

'To work on the ceiling lights, floor boards occasionally had to be moved. They were held down with hand-made nails, which are square in shape, not like modern wire nails.

'The original lighting was supplied by acetylene gas lighting in the dining room and other rooms.

'The main dining room had a 5 candle chandelier and we converted it to electricity.

'The roof leaked onto the lathe and plaster ceilings. This contributed to the need to re-roof the house.

'In the music room there was both a grand piano and a baby grand piano.

'In the entrance there is a semi-circular staircase and there was a very imposing picture of Mrs Anderson.

'The servants' quarters at the back of the house were converted to a flat.

'There are 2 wrought iron gates which were sandblasted and repainted. Janice Pinkerton said, 'Dad did a lot of repairs. When the house was empty after Clarice's death, young louts broke in and did some damage.'

Sharon Greene

Sharon reported that in 1913 Mrs Lilian Anderson donated a drinking fountain for the main intersection in Camden between John and Argyle Streets, as a memorial to her husband who had died in 1912.

Correspondence received from Mrs. Anderson was reported in the *Camden News* of 24 July 1913 stating:
> May I express a hope that this fountain may prove a blessing to many a thirsty soul, and so be a fitting memento of the sympathy which the late Mr. W H Anderson had for all fellow creatures.

The Mayor acknowledged the very fine gift and it was accepted unanimously by Council. However the fountain was moved after a number of accidents including one with the Camden night cart. It was relocated to Macarthur Park.

Camelot 1983 (J Wrigley)

Brendan and Rachel Powers

Brendan and Rachel Powers, local business proprietors, are the current owners of the house.

Brendan said, 'We find the house both a joy and a heartache. We have tried to maintain the fabric of the building in the restoration and conservation. We are trying to keep as much of the original as we can manage, and we have done as much work as we can ourselves. We have tried to keep things original, but money gets soaked up and living in the house has its problems.'

He said, 'We have had a lot of help from local Camden builder, Andrew Wiggins'. Brendan said, 'I grew up at Harrington Park where my mother was the cook for Sir Warwick Fairfax. After buying the house, Rachel and I developed an interest in antiques.'

'Camelot came on the market while I owned L J Hooker and I purchased it from the Trust Bank who were the mortgagees who repossessed the house from Michael Howarth in 1999.

'We have had a number of heritage consultants look at the house. One was from the UK who was a stables expert.

'We have cleaned the roof. We have removed the ivy which was pulling the mortar from between the bricks and pulling down some walls. We have replaced gutters. There is little rising damp as we have changed the levels to get rid of water.

'We have restored the servant bell system. We have basically restored the house, but we have 4-5 rooms to go. We will leave the old kitchen where the old stove was used to run the heating system for the house'.

'We have one fellow painting the stables for about a year'.

'We have re-done 30km of fencing on the property'.

'As we removed the bamboo we found a glass house in the middle of it. We have removed the South African Olive. We have tried to source the old plants that were originally in the garden. When we arrived the garden was covered with grass. We have gradually uncovered the old garden with its hearts, spades, clubs and diamonds, which were the themes based around a pack of cards.

'We love the house and it is our main hobby, but it consumes a bottomless pit of money. We want the house to be here for our children it they want it. We want to preserve it for a better future.'

Acknowledgements
The author gratefully acknowledges the helpful comments and suggestions by John and Julie Wrigley and other presenters mentioned on drafts of this article

CAMDEN HISTORY

Journal of the Camden Historical Society

March 2014 Volume 3 Number 7

CAMDEN HISTORY
Journal of the Camden Historical Society Inc.

Contents

Joy Riley, Memories of John Street Ian Willis	243
The Hassall Family as Land Owners in Cobbitty Peter Mylrea	248
A Flood in Camden in 1819	254
Phillip Haylock, The Very Sociable Policeman John Wrigley	256
A Conversation with Joyce Thorn of Cobbitty With Cathey Shepherd Ian Willis	259
Cobbitty Water Supply (Brochure)	260
World War One Ray Herbert	269
Launch of Report *Managing The Future of Camden Park* Ian Willis	271
My Dearest Ellen John Wrigley	273

Joy Riley, Memories of John Street

Ian Willis

Joy Riley vividly recalls living in John Street as a child and growing up.
'I lived at 66 John Street for the first 40 years of my life before moving to Elderslie with my husband Bruce Riley. The two front rooms of 66 John Street were built by the first John Peat, Camden builder, to come to Camden. In the 1960s I had some carpet put down in my bedroom, the floor boards were so hard, as they only used tacks in those days to hold carpet, the tacks just kept curling up.'

She says, 'The back of the house was built by my grandfather, William Dunk. They lived next door at 64 John Street. He also built the Methodist Church at Orangeville or Werombi.

Joy recalls, 'My parents Jack and Laura Dunk (nee Rix) married in 1929 and lived at 66 John Street. My sister Doreen (Shepard) was born in our dining room in 1931.

Nurse Taplin and Annie Lysaght delivered her. I was born at Nurse Taplin's hospital.

66 John Street, Joy Riley's mother on verandah in early 1960s. (Joy Riley)

64 John Street, early 1900s. (Joy Riley)

66 John Street, early 1900s (Joy Riley)

Wellbourne, in Oxley Street in 1938.

'My father served in the Second World War and as a Rat of Tobruk. He passed away in 1962 aged 54 years. My mother died in 1976.

Camden was growing in the 1960s and 1970s and there was a need to expand car parking in the business centre of the town. Joy says, 'Camden Council resumed half of the backyard for a car park. The home was put up for sale around 1978 and sold to John Fahey. He demolished and rebuilt the present premises that are used by Chris Patterson MLA.'

Residents of upper John Street
Joy Riley's memories of John Street extend over 40 years and she recalls the following folk who lived along John Street between Argyle and Broughton Street.

No 58
This property was owned by Alan Boardman (butcher) and rented by Stan and Enid Rolfe, whose children were Phyllis, Kathey, Laurence and Mary. It is now Wandalite.

No 60
Mr & Mrs Dodge, who came from the Burragorang Valley, lived here and it is now the entrance to the carpark.

No 62
Mr & Mrs Colin Clarke (chemist), children Graeme, Robin and Bruce. It was later funeral parlour and a veterinary practice.

No 64
The original owners were William and Jemimma Dunk, and after their death sold to Albert and Ellen Rix. It was then rented to Stan and Gladys Richardson, whose children were Dawn (Garrel) and Jean (Lloyd) until Albert Rix retired from Camden Park who then returned and lived there until he died. After this it was rebuilt for business purposes.

No 66
The original residents were Dick and Ruby Hayter and the front two rooms built by the first John Peat to come to Camden. The back half of the house was built by William Dunk. From 1930 to 1977 Jack and Laura Dunk, whose children were Doreen (Shepard) and Joy (Riley). The house was sold to John Fahey in 1977 and demolished in 1978. It is now the office of Chris Patterson, MLA.

No 68
The house was owned by Dick and Ruby Hayter, local builder who had a motor bike and side care. There children were Phyllis, Dorothy and Agnes. It was then owned by

Bank of New South Wales, corner of John Street and Argyle Street, Camden, 1941 (J Dunk/Joy Riley)

RAAF 'Glamour Boys' from Camden Airfield marching down John Street after a service at St John's Church led by Jeff Bate in 1941 (Joy Riley)

Thelma Smith and now occupied by a beauty spa business.

No 70
This was occupied by Ernest and Nellie Willmington who came from Luddenham. Their children were Thelma (Smith) and Gladys (Richardson). It is now the medical rooms for Dr Grogan.

No 72
The house was occupied by Mr and Mrs Kanes, whose children were Dot (Smith) and husband Tom. Their granddaughter is Jan (Chanter). It is now a doctors surgery for Dr David Taylor, Dr Newman and others.

No 74
This property was owned by Ron and Agnes Smart, son Tony.

No 76
There were the two Miss Parker, who were spinsters, and then Ned and Joan Heington and their daughter Christine.

No 78
Mr and Mrs Coulter, whose children were Tony, Ray and Jacquiline lived here.

No 80
The house was occupied by Mr & Mrs Irwin Dowle whose children were Jack, Betty and Max. It was then owned by Mr and Mrs Betts, whose children were Colin, Bruce and Mrs Mitchell. It is now a doctor's surgery.

St John's Church, John Street view, 1941 (Joy Riley)

The Hassall Family as Land Owners in Cobbitty

Peter Mylrea

The Hassall family were the major land holders in Cobbitty from 1812 and their holdings were second in size only to those of the Macarthurs at Camden. Rowland Hassall was the first to own land in Cobbitty and he was followed by his sons, Thomas, Samuel, Jonathon and James.[1] They obtained their land by grants and purchases.

Rowland Hassall (born England 1768, died Parramatta 1820)
Rowland Hassall and his wife were devout Christians who arrived in Sydney in 1798. In the following years he became a successful business man and a wealthy property owner.

In 1812 Rowland received a land grant from Governor Macquarie of 400 acres on the Nepean River. This he called 'Macquarie Grove' and today it is the site of Camden Airport. A house must have been built on the property soon after this because in 1815 Governor Macquarie with a party of gentlemen, including Rowland Hassall toured the Cow Pastures.[2]

On Saturday 7 October 1815 the party

> crossed the Nepean River at a ford immediately below Mr Hassall's farm, and encamped ... at Macquarie Grove, which is the name Mr Hassall has been so good to give to this very finely situated and beautiful farm.
> and
> Sunday 8 Oct. Divine Service [was] performed in the veranda of Mr Hassall's house. [After touring during the day] we returned to our camp at Macquarie Grove ... and sat down to a very good dinner.

On the next day they left Macquarie Grove and travelled to Mr Bent's Farm which was at Bent's Basin.

In 1816 Governor Macquarie gave small grants of land in Cobbitty to a number of men (see Table). Later Rowland Hassall purchased those of Arkell, Aspey, Blackman, Core, Hearne and Ward. He also purchased the larger grant called 'Cubbady' from Gregory Blaxland. In his will Rowland bequeathed these properties to three of his sons, Thomas, Jonathon and James.[3] Samuel did not receive any of these because Rowland wrote in his will

> As whereas I have expended a Considerable sum of money in the Improvements of the Farm and Lands of Macquarie Grove in this my Will before devised [bequeathed] to my Son Samuel which renders it of more value than

248

of any of the Estates devised to any other Sons

At the time of his death Rowland owned 'a considerable stock of Horned cattle, sheep, horses and swine and which are of Considerable Value' and these he bequeathed equally to his wife and children.

The Rev. Thomas Hassall (born England 1794, died Denbigh 1868)
Thomas Hassall was the first son of Rowland. He had strong religious convictions and sailed to England for training and became a priest in 1821. He returned to Sydney in 1822 and held a number of church appointments until 1827 when he was appointed to the large parish of Narellan and made his home in Cobbitty. In the years which followed he played a prominent role in the district.[4]

He was the owner of a number of properties. The first was 'Pomari Grove' which he obtained as a grant in 1815. On the death of Rowland, his father, in 1820 Thomas inherited 'Stoke Farm', 'Arkell Farm' and 'Hearne Farm'.

An unrelated man, Charles Hook, had received a land grant of 1100 acres in 1812. He later sold the property to Thomas Hassall who called it 'Denbigh'. This was to be Thomas's home and the centre of the Narellan Parish until his death in 1868.

Thomas was active in the physical development of the Anglican church in Cobbitty. Soon after he arrived in Cobbitty he wrote, 'I have erected a neat Brick Building (35 feet long and 10 broad with a small room attached) in a convenient and eligible situation upon the Cobberry [sic] Road'. This building was erected on Hassall's land called Pomari Grove. The building is now called the Heber Chapel.

Thomas also sold land. In 1838 he sold forty acres of land opposite the Heber Chapel to Queen Victoria [the royal head of the colony at that time] as glebe land for the church. He received 75 pounds and on this land the church rectory would be built. A little later, in 1839, he sold another parcel of land to Queen Victoria. This was the land on which the Heber Chapel had been built. It was also the land on which the future St Paul's Church would be erected.

Samuel Otoo Hassall (born England 1796, died Macquarie Grove 1830)
Samuel owned two portions of land in the Cobbitty district. The first was a grant of 200 acres which he received in 1816 and which he called 'Bosworth Farm'. The second property was 'Macquarie Grove' which he inherited from his father in 1820. He fell on hard times in the 1820s and died at the early age of 34.

Jonathon Hassall (born Tahiti 1798, died Matavai 1834)
Jonathon received a land grant of 200 acres in 1815 which he called 'Matavai' and on his father's death he inherited 'Cubbady'. This had been a land grant to Gregory Blaxland in 1816 which Blaxland sold to Rowland Hassall. Jonathan was not a good business man and when he was in considerable financial debt he sold Matavai to his

brother James. He became mentally deranged and committed suicide at 36 years of age.

James Hassall (born Parramatta 1802, died in Victoria 1862)
James received a land grant in 1816 but the deed did not give a name to this property. He also inherited four small properties from his father. When his brother Jonathon got into financial difficulties James purchased 'Matavai' from him. On 'Matavai' he built a large two storey house complete with a ballroom. This was the scene of many grand functions, notably the annual Harvest Ball. James prospered and became a wealthy man. However he was harshly affected by the 1840s recession and became bankrupt.

Rowland Hassall's four daughters
Rowland Hassall had four daughters but he did not bequeath any Cobbitty land to them. He also owned farms and properties in other parts of the colony and it was these that formed the inheritance for his daughters.

Closing of the Hassall era
This review has covered the first two generations of the Hassalls in Cobbitty. The death of Thomas Hassall in 1868 marked the closure of the second generations of Hasssalls which generation bequeathed or sold their properties to others. This article does not follow the subsequent histories of these properties.

At the time of Rowland Hassall's death in 1820 the Hassalls owned 14 properties in the Cobbitty district containing about 3500 acres of land. This compares with the 5000 acres of land which had been granted to the Macarthurs by that time.[5]

References
1 For details on Rowland Hassall and his sons see *The Hassall Family 1798-1998* written by Jean Stewart & David J. Hassall.
2 Lachlan Macquarie *Journal of His ours in New South Wales and Van Diemem Land 1810-1822*, Library of Australian History 1979.
3 A copy of probate on Rowland Hassall's will is in the Supreme Court, Probate Division document No 81 Ser 1 dated 2 March 2002. Also see Appendix 1.
4 P.J.Mylrea *Camden District. A History to the 1840s.* Camden Historical Society 2002.
5 P.J.Mylrea Camden History Journal 2013, vol. 3 p. 224.
6 Information and dates on land grants are given chronically, by governors, in the Register of Land Grants, and Titles Office, Old Systems, Sydney

Appendices 1 and 2 on following pages

Appendix 1

Land owned by Rowland Hassall and his four sons Thomas, Samuel, Jonathon and James.[6]

ROWLAND HASSALL

Map No	Date	Original Grantee	Subsequent History	Acres
2	1812	Rowland Hassall 'Macquarie Gift'.	Bequeathed to Samuel Otoo Hassall.	400
40	1816	Rowland Hassall 'Stoke Farm'.	Bequeathed to Thomas Hassall	470
42	1816	Thomas Arkell	Bought by Rowland Hassall. Bequeathed to Thomas Hassall.	100
41	1816	John Aspey	Bought by Rowland Hassall. Bequeathed to Jonathon Hassall.	100
30	1812	James Blackman	Bought by Rowland Hassall. Bequeathed to Jonathon Hassall.	40
16	1816	Gregory Blaxland 'Cubbady'	Bought by Rowland Hassall. Bequeathed to Jonathan Hassall.	500
22	1816	George Core	Bought by Rowland Hassall. Bequeathed to Jonathon Hassall.	60
20	1816	Abraham Hearne	Bought by Rowland Hassall. Bequeathed to Thomas Hassall.	65
15	1816	JosephWard	Bought by Rowland Hassall. Bequeathed to Jonathon Hassall.	300

THOMAS HASSALL

39	1815	Thomas Hassall 'Pomari Grove'	[Now known as 'Pomare.']	150
44	1812	Charles Hook 'Denbigh'	Bought by Thomas Hassall in …	1100
		'Stoke Farm'	Inherited from Rowland	
		Arkell Farm	Inherited from Rowland Hassall.	
		Hearne	Inherited from Rowland Hassall.	

SAMUEL OTOO HASSAL

	1816	Samuel Hassall 'Bosworth'		200
		'Macquarie Grove'	Inherited from Rowland Hassall.	

NATHAN HASSALL

	1815	Jonathon Hassall 'Matavai'	Sold to James Hassall.	
		'Cubbady Farm'	Inherited from Rowland Hassall.	

JAMES HASSALL

	1816	James Hassall	In the title of grant there was no name given to this property.	230
		'Matavai'	Bought from Jonathan Hassall.	
		'Ward Farm'	Inherited from Rowland Hassall.	
		'Aspey Farm'	Inherited from Rowland Hassall.	
		'Blackman Farm'	Inherited from Rowland Hassall.	
		'Core Farm'	Inherited from Rowland Hassall.	

Appendix 2

Map of Cobbitty. The numbers correspond with those in Apendix 1 and show the original grantees of the land. The hatched area shows the land owned by the Hassalls. The cross (near 39) is the location of the Heber Chapel and St Pauls Church.

A Flood in Camden in 1819

Written by Rowland Hassall on 9 March 1819
Comments by Peter Mylrea (2014)

What follows is probably the first recorded account of a flood in Camden. It was written by Rowland Hassall, of Macquarie Grove [1], in a letter to Governor Macquarie dated 9 March 1819 and which was published in the Sydney Gazette on Saturday 13 March 1819.

Last Friday [4 March] the flood was considerably higher than it has been through the last month when, towards the evening, there were several guns of distress fired up the river, which caused my son Samuel to man the public boat with three of our own men, a stockman named Ratcliffe, and a Cow Pasture constable named Salter, with Samuel at the helm; and made the best of their way to the report of the guns, till they came to the flat near Mr. M'Arthur's wharf [2], where they found two men by their stacks of wheat (nearly up to their arm pits in water), whom they took into the boat, and then attempted to make the high land; but in crossing the gully which runs through the middle of the flat [3] they met with a most severe accident; the bow oar which the constable had in his hand made a false stroke, and instantly the force of the water which ran in torrents, struck the boat a-midships against a tree, and cut her right through the centre, when, in a moment, six of the eight persons sank to the bottom; but fortunately two who could not swim, had the presence of mind, one to grasp the tree and get into its branches for security, and the other the head of the boat, who went down the stream crying for mercy, and at length came in contact with a tree, upon which he climbed, and which has proved in the end, the means of saving them both. Salter the constable has never been seen since, and I have no doubt that the poor man is drowned, as every effort has been made to find him, but in vain.

My son and the other four, who all sank to the bottom after many narrow escapes, and great exertions to strip themselves of their clothes in the midst of the flood, and swam to high lands, being just saved in their bare skins, and some of them much bruised and hurt, and so weak that they were not able to stand being thus situated. I was thankful that so many lives were spared, and my dear son's [sic] in the numbers; yet I was very anxious for the welfare of the two poor men on the trees in the midst of the flood, and saw no way to accomplish my wishes, but by replacing the boat, and used every exertion to that end, and had just given up all hopes when Mr. Gregory Blaxland informed me that he had a boat which would fully answer my purpose at Brush Farm, which cost him £12, and I should have it for £11, which I agreed to purchase for public service. Mr Rouse was good enough to allow us a cart, which we dispatched instantly with the boat, and arrived at the Cowpastures safe on Sunday morning.

In a recent letter from my son, I find that the two men are safely bought from the trees, and that Salter the constable is not yet found, but that every search was made, and should be made to find him.

Sydney Gazette 13 March 1819.

Notes

1 Macquarie Grove is now the location of Camden Airport.

2 There are no other records of the Macarthurs having a wharf on the Nepean River. Perhaps it refers to the structure on the river where sheep were washed before being shorn.

3 This suggests that the flat was that which lies between the present day Belgenny Farm and Camden Park House and across which Navigation Creek flows.

Phillip Haylock, The Very Sociable Policeman

John Wrigley

Many readers will remember the fine singing voice of Phillip Haylock, who is now retired to Queanbeyan NSW. Phillip grew up in Camden as a son of the local policeman Constable Harry Haylock and Edith Haylock nee Miller.

Thanks to Phillip, the Camden Museum has a number of photos, mementoes and memoirs of the days in the 1930s-1940s when his family lived in one of the two residences which were part of the Camden Police Station. Constable Haylock served in Camden for eleven and a half years from 1932 until 1944. This photo shows Constable Haylock in the centre, standing in John Street in front of the police station together with four detectives from Sydney about 1937.

Harry Haylock threw himself into Camden activities while he was stationed here. When he was transferred to Redfern in 1944 a large farewell evening was held for him at the Camden Bowling Clubhouse. The Mayor, Alderman

Constable Haylock (centre) with four Sydney detectives at Camden Police Station, C1937 (Phillip Haylock)

Stan Kelloway, outlined the many local activities of the guest of honour who was then the treasurer of the Camden District Hospital Board; treasurer of the Camden Parents and Citizens Association; secretary/treasurer of the Camden District Cricket Association; and secretary/treasurer of the Wollondilly District Rugby Football League. He also captained the Camden Cricket Club for many seasons.

Constable Haylock had successfully organized many charitable and patriotic carnivals and dances and was joint organizer of the annual Hospital Ball for several years. He also organized the Children's Fancy Dress Party which took place the day after the Hospital Ball. The mayor said that his transfer to Redfern was a great loss to Camden as they fully appreciated everything he had done for the advancement of the town and district.

Alderman Whitford said, "Harry Haylock proved that a police officer could maintain the law and remain a friend to the people. He won the goodwill of the community and displayed exceptional ability as an organizer."

The Rev Wesley Stocks said, "Harry Haylock was not only a good police officer but was also a very fine man with a lovable personality." Sustained applause greeted the announcement by Mr. F.J. Sedgwick, chairman of the Camden District Hospital that his board would elect Mr Haylock as a life member of the hospital in recognition of his exceptional work as a director. Mr. Sedgwick said that Mr. Haylock was also held in high regard at Campbelltown and his departure would be a terrific loss to the sporting bodies and the district. Other speakers who spoke warmly about the guest included Councillor Edgar Downes, President of the Wollondilly Shire Council; Harry Willis, President of the Camden Bowling Club; and Arthur Gibson, publisher of the Camden Advertiser, representing the Press.

Harry's record of citizenship seemed to have no end He was also a member of the local Order of the Oddfellows Lodge and was very active in raising money for the Red Cross in an 'Air Race' competition.

Son Phillip has recalled, 'Mum and Dad came to Camden eager to fulfill their obligations. It was all new to Mum but she took to the challenge and fitted in well. In those early days of the Depression on many occasions the cells were used as accommodation for itinerant workers passing through. Mum cooked for whoever was in the cells and they received a portion of the same meals as us. I remember a prisoner, after being released, saying it was the best meal he'd ever had!'

'I have remembered an anecdote regarding the way Dad had with the locals. This was told to me by one of the participants. Six o'clock was the legal time for the closing of the hotels. The police used to walk Argyle Street and see that this was observed. This evening Dad came to a certain hotel around six-twenty and still quite a lot of noise was coming from the bar. Of course the front doors were closed, but there was always a side door to exit. At this time the Hospital Ball was due soon and Dad, being treasurer, took every opportunity to extract money from all for the occasion. He came in the side door and said, "Well, what have we got here?" The bar was still being used by quite a few young lads so he placed a full book of tickets on the bar and said, "When I come back, I want that book all taken and you out of here." Sure enough, all the tickets were sold!

'Dad was a very keen cricket player and one Saturday afternoon at the showground, on a very windy day, he hit a six and broke a car's windscreen. Arthur Gibson wrote in the Camden Advertiser of "Harry Haylock's Hurricane Hitting".

Phillip Haylock says of his father's involvement with community events, "After his day's police duty was over, Dad was involved in anything that moved."

I thank Phillip for his assistance in preparing this article.

A Conversation with Joyce Thorn of Cobbitty With Cathey Shepherd
Camden Historical Society 12 March 2014

Ian Willis

Joyce Thorn is a local identity in Cobbitty after living there most of her 90 years and she has seen many changes over the years.

Joyce owned the Cobbitty General Store from 1948 to 1971. 'In those days everyone knew everyone else and there was a real sense of community', she said. 'There were about 25 houses along Cobbitty Road and a population of about 200 people'.

Her life philosophy is refreshing. She says, 'I believe you're only as old as you feel, and if you're well, then age isn't a worry'. Joyce has worked for a host of community organisation in the village including the Red Cross and St James church.

In her conversation she recalled the 1959 Cobbitty Queen Competition to fund extensions to the church hall, New Year Sports Days which continued up to 1941 and the names of the rural properties in the Cobbitty area including Fresh Fields, Marchdale, Riverview, Westwood, Kathleen Haven, Sugarloaf and a host of others.

Joyce talked about the Cobbitty Progress Association which functioned from 1946 to 1955 and was formed by Wilfred Chittick. The members campaigned for the permanent water supply for the village after the Second World War. Before this time the village had to rely on tank water and water drawn from the Nepean River. The army had built tanks to supply the Narellan Army Camp with water. Officers at the camp told the villagers to write to government officials. Over 11 years the association wrote 69 letters to have water put onto the village. The project was forecast to cost £9,000 but by the time it was finished it had doubled from original estimates. The official opening was held in front of the St James church hall with all the local dignitaries attending including Jeff Bate the local state member.

The souvenir programme that follows for the opening of the Cobbitty Water Supply was kindly supplied by Joyce Thorn,

COBBITTY

WATER

SUPPLY

MEMBERS OF THE BOARD

President:
J. W. GOODSELL, Esq., C.M.G., F.A.S.A.

Vice-President:
S. HAVILAND, Esq.

First Constituency:
G. H. SMITH, Esq.

Second Constituency:
A. H. MOVERLY, Esq., J.P.

Third Constituency:
Ald. A. N. CAMPBELL, J.P., A.M.I.E. Aust., M.A.I.E.

Fourth Constituency:
T. H. M. de BURGH, Esq., B.E., M.I.C.E., L.G.E.

Fifth Constituency:
Ald. G. E. MAUNDER, J.P.

Secretary:
W. V. AIRD, Esq.

Engineer-in-Chief:
T. B. NICOL, Esq., B.E., M.I.C.E., M.I.E. Aust., M.ASCE.

COBBITTY WATER SUPPLY

Official Turning On

by

HON. J. J. CAHILL
Premier of New South Wales

on

FRIDAY, 16th SEPTEMBER, 1955

Issued by the Sydney Water Board, 1955.

Cobbitty is situated on the north side of the Nepean River about five miles north-west of Camden by road. It is in the centre of a very pleasant area to which holiday makers are attracted during the summer months.

The village is steeped in the early history of the Colony. There is an interesting entry in Governor Macquarie's diary in 1815 where it is recorded "early next morning we made a start and by 10 a.m. arrived at a remarkable prominence overlooking extensive flats they call "Kobady." In one of the aboriginal dialects there is a word "Cobah" meaning "the place of a hill." This prominence is now known as Paddy Clark's Hill from one of that name who once lived there. Settlement began about 1812 and numerous grants of land were made, many of which were to Mr. Rowland Hassall or

View along Cobbitty Road.

members of his family. One of these, Mocquarie Grove, of 400 acres was later acquired by the MacArthur-Onslow family and part of it is now used as an aerodrome.

In 1827 the Rev. Thomas Hassoll, the eldest son of Mr. Rowland Hassall, was appointed chaplain of the districts south of Liverpool—Cook, Mulgoa, South Creek, Cobramatta (now known as Rossmore), Camden, Goulburn Plains, Bong Bong and Inverary. The Heber Chapel which he built at his own expense, and which still stands beside the present church, was dedicated by the Rev. Samuel Morsden on 30th November, 1828. It remains to this day the only memorial to Bishop Heber, Bishop of Calcutta, in whose diocese Australia then was. The Church of St. Paul, a structure of Gothic architecture, was consecrated on 5th April, 1842.

Not very far from the church in a south-easterly direction stands the stately old Colonial house called "Wivenhae,"

St. Paul's Church.

Heber Chapel.

"Wivenhoe."

once the home of Sir Charles Cowper, for many years Premier of New South Wales. It is now part of the Mater Dei Orphanage.

During the war, the Board constructed for the Commonwealth Government a water supply from Kenny Hill Reservoir to a military camp that was established about two miles east of Cobbitty at Greens Corner at the junction of Bringelly and Cobbitty Roads. It consisted of two 50,000 gallon tanks constructed within the boundaries of "Harrington Park" and some 15,000 feet of water main. After the war the Board took over this work in anticipation of future development.

Following earlier representations, an agreement was concluded between the Board and Camden Council in April, 1950, providing for a water supply to be given to Cobbitty with financial assistance from the Government under the assistance plan whereby Governmental aid up to 50 per

Tanks at Harrington Park.

Machine excavating trench.

cent. of the total cost is granted in suitable cases, to enable service to be made available in outlying areas without imposing on local ratepayers an unduly heavy burden. Work commenced on 29th April, 1955, and was completed by the end of June. It required the laying of some 19,353 feet of 6in. and 4in. mains from the tanks at Bringelly Road along Cobbitty Road. Although some rock was encountered in sections of the work, the greater part of the excavation was carried out mechanically. The use of rubber rings for the joints enabled pipe laying to keep abreast of the machine excavation which was carried out where possible in the footway. A bulldozer was employed for back-filling the trenches. Good weather and the use of machines enabled the work to be completed for about £9,000 less than the estimated cost of £22,000.

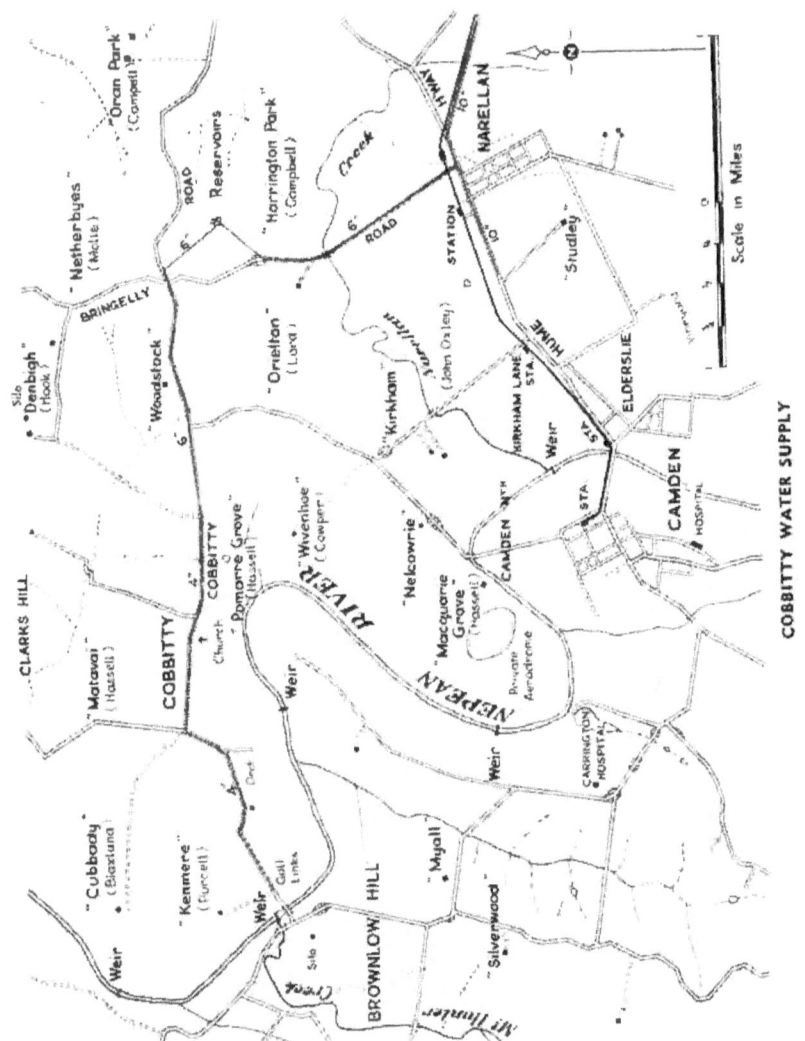

World War One

Ray Herbert

On the 4 August 1914 war was declared between England and Germany. Australia responded with naval forces sent to capture Bitapaka Wireless Station in New Britain on the 9 September 1914.

Australian Naval and Military Expeditionary Forces landed at Rabaul, New Guinea on the 11 September 1914, the Australian Submarine A.E. 1 was lost off New Guinea.

On the 24 September the Germans in New Guinea surrendered and the Australians occupied Madang.

While these events were occurring the Australian Imperial Force were completing training and preparing to depart. The Contingent sailed on the 1 November.

Among the earliest to enlist were Major Victor Horatio Butler Sampson from Bringelly who was killed in Action at Fromelles, Lt. Colonel Astley John Onslow Thompson the then Manager of Camden Park who was killed in action on the 26 April 1915 at Gallipoli.

The men from Camden fought at Gallipoli, Palestine, Syria and the Western Front, a number are buried in places like Jerusalem, Cairo, Alexandria, Gallipoli, French, Belgium and British Cemeteries.

As the anniversary of the commencement of the First World War is fast approaching it is time to hunt through the family photo album and try to find your ancestor who may have served.

Your help is required in the search for photos of the men and women from Camden to be added to the society's collection and to be displayed on the Camden Remembers website.

There are a number of photos we do not have the names of the men can you **HELP?**

Do you know these men?

Launch of Report *Managing The Future of Camden Park*
17 March 2014

Ian Willis

A number of society members attended the launch of a report *Managing The Future of Camden Park* by The Hon Robyn Parker MP Minister for the Environment and Minister for Heritage on Monday 17 March 2014 in the presence of around 70 people.

The launch proceedings were opened by the Chair of the Camden Park Preservation Committee Mark Webeck, who introduced the current owners and custodians of Camden Park, John and Edwina Macarthur-Stanham. John spoke briefly and was followed by Peter Watts AM, the retired director of the Historic Houses Trust of NSW. He outlined details of the comparative assessment evaluation used in the report, which included character, intactness, documentary collection, resources, age and quality, continuity of ownership and contribution to history. Camden Park had the highest ranking of 'exceptionally significant' on a national level when compared to other important historic houses across Australia.

Architect Howard Tanner stated that the commissioning of the report by the Camden Park Preservation Committee was attempting to ensure the quality and ambience of the current Arcadian view of the house into the future. The report states that Camden Park is the most important homestead in Australia. Howard Tanner explained that there was a need by those managing historic properties to review their heritage values every 30 to 40 years to ensure that it remains intact. He stated the current report was prompted by threats from power lines running across the property and coalmining under the house. He stated the biggest long term threats to the current setting of Camden Park are from mining, urban growth and new transport links adjacent to the property. The property sits across three local government areas and really does not fall into the consciousness of any of the local councils. The property needs more regional type planning, which is a state government responsibility. He concluded that the report raises alerts about the future control of the property, and that no-one in the future can claim that they did not understand the issues surrounding the conservation of the house and property.

Managing the Future of Camden Park

My Dearest Ellen

John Wrigley

The letters of 'Mrs Rolf Boldrewood' (Margaret Brown, nee Riley) to her older friend Mrs Ellen Foreman (nee Moore) were kept until recently undisturbed in a tin box on the sideboard of the dining room at 'Ellensville' Mount Hunter. The letters covered over fifty years from 1851 to 1905. Pacita Alexander has written an account of the letters and explained the lives of the two women and their families. The book "My Dearest Ellen" has been recently published by The Oaks Historical Society and is full of local and family history.

This article uses two extract from Pacita Alexander's book. In the first extract Pacita has quoted from Ellen Moore's diary written at the property Raby. In the second extract Pacita has quoted from the first letter that has survived from Margaret Riley, aged thirteen to Ellen Moore, aged thirty-two, while Margaret was living at Denham Court. Pacita explains the context of the letters:

Ellen's Diary at Raby, 1848
Ellen's first entry in her diary was *Went to Sydney with the young ladies.* The young ladies may have been Margaret Riley and her sister Sarah now well settled in life at school at 'Bella Retiro'. In 1848 Margaret was living at Denham Court (House) with all her young cousins, the Moore household at Raby included Edward, then twenty-five, Ellen's sister Elizabeth (known as Betsy) eighteen years old, with Robert, who was twenty-eight, coming and going... It was a life with lots of social interaction, especially for Ellen to DC, as she called Denham Court. In February, 1848 Ellen wrote *Very hot day I went to DC on horseback.* Then in October, on a fine day she went to DC on Friday, '*cut out dress and worked at it all day*', *stayed there on Saturday, went to Church on Sunday,* but because it rained she couldn't go home till Wednesday... There was a continuous stream of visitors to Raby, according to Ellen's diary. Her father was continually on the move going to Sydney, or Camden, or Liverpool. Her brother Edward Lomas too was very active, off to Bong Bong one day, Liverpool another, sometimes escorting his sister Betsy to see friends at Wollongong, or going down the Burragorang Valley with cattle.

Meanwhile Ellen and her mother and Betsy were kept busy washing, ironing, making jam, and hot cross buns, or butter to sell in Sydney. Bush fires were a real threat, and Ellen wrote one February, '*Father & old Tom had to go out all the afternoon to prevent the fire which was running through Catherine Fields from getting on Raby. Very hot day and high winds.*' Floods too made life difficult, as in August when '*Mr Hurst came after breakfast as he could not get over Camden Bridge, stayed & preached at night.*'

Sometimes the floods meant '*No preacher came on account of the river having risen*

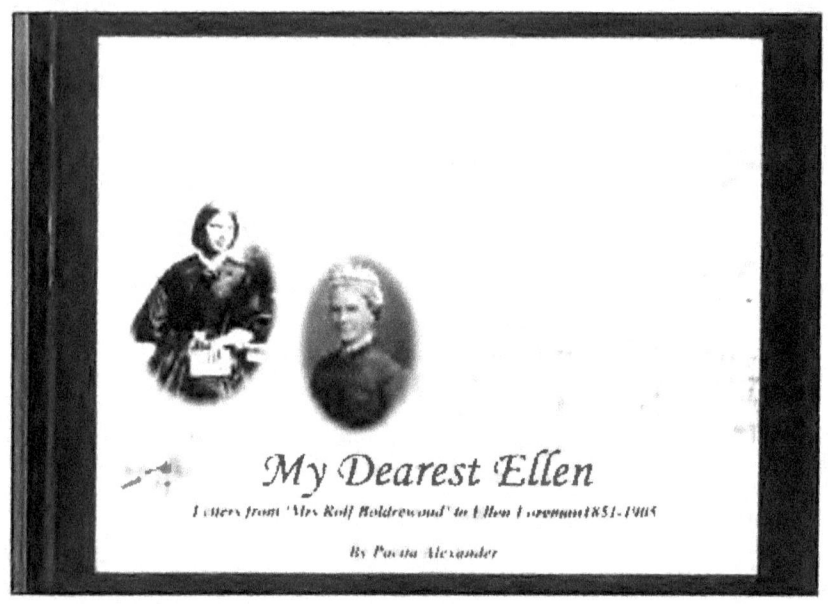

My Dearest Ellen
Letters from 'Mrs Rolf Boldrewood' to Ellen Foreman 1851-1905
By Pacita Alexander

so *high with the rain they could not pass.'* Ellen went to church regularly. This church was St Mary the Virgin, built on the original [Denham Court] property. It is now separated from Denham Court by a highway ... When Margaret was home from boarding school, one can image her sitting in church with the tribe of [her] Blomfield cousins, looking across the pews at the Moore family, especially her friend Ellen ...

The second extract from Pacita's book is the charming first letter that has survived, in the collection of about forty letters, from Margaret to Ellen, written on 4 March, 1851 from Denham Court. The affectionate thirteen-year-old girl Margaret started the letter to her thirty-two-year-old friend,

> How is my dear Ellen this morning? – quite well – and puzzling her head about the "Stone House"! That is right. I hope the work is progressing. I send you these few lines this morning to tell you Mr and Mrs Tyrell are still with us ... Oh & Ellen all the late peaches are ripe now. <u>Cartloads</u> rotting on the ground so if you wish for any to preserve you had better come <u>immediately</u> ... My good love to you hoping your Mother & all with you are well.
> With a <u>light</u> kiss, Believe me, Your ever affectionate child, Margaret M. Riley.

The author Pacita has aimed to give a glimpse into the lives of two pioneer women in nineteenth century Australia and the story of their unlikely association and friendship. This delightful book is available from the Wollondilly Heritage Centre at The Oaks ( ), the Camden Museum, and Sinclair's Newsagents for $20.

CAMDEN HISTORY

Journal of the Camden Historical Society Inc

September 2014, Volume 3, Number 8

CAMDEN HISTORY
Journal of the Camden Historical Society Inc.

ISSN 1445-1549

Editor: Dr Ian Willis

Management Committee

President: Bob Lester

Vice Presidents: Dr Ian Willis, Rene Rem

Secretary: Lee Stratton

Assistant Secretary: Julie Wrigley

Treasurer: Dawn Williams

Assistant Treasurer:

Immediate Past President: John Wrigley OAM

General Committee: Cathey Shepherd   Sharon Greene
                    Roslyn Tildsley   Julie Wrigley
                    Robert Wheeler   Stephanie Trenfield

Honorary Auditor:

Honorary Solicitors: Bowring, Macaulay and Barrett

Society contact:
P.O. Box 566, Camden, NSW 2570. Online <http://www.camdenhistory.org.au>

Meetings
Meetings are held at 7.30 p.m. on the second Wednesday of the month except in January. They are held in the Museum. Visitors are always welcome.

Museum
The Museum is located at 40 John Street, Camden, phone 4655 3400 or 46559210. It is open Thursday to Sunday 11 a.m. to 4 p.m., except at Christmas. Visits by schools and groups are encouraged. Please contact the Museum to make arrangements. Entry is free.

Camden History, Journal of the Camden Historical Society Inc
The Journal is published in March and September each year. The Editor would be pleased to receive articles broadly covering the history of the Camden district . Correspondence can be sent to the Society's postal address. The views expressed in the articles are solely those of the authors and not necessarily endorsed by the society.

Donations
Donations made to the Society are tax deductible. The accredited value of objects donated to the Society are eligible for tax deduction.

Cover: John Hawkey's Presentation Tea Service (C Shepherd)

CAMDEN HISTORY
Journal of the Camden Historical Society Inc.

September 2014 Volume 3 Number 8

Contents

President's Report 2013-2014 Bob Lester	275
Dick Inglis Death of a Fine Camden Citizen John Wrigley	280
John Martin Hawkey's Presentation Tea Service Cathey Shepherd	282
RAAF Central Flying School 1940	286
Book Launch, Author Address, Ministering Angels, the Camden District Red Cross, 1914-1915 Ian Willis	290
Red Cross Book Launch Julie Wrigley	293
Official Opening of Liz Kernohan Drive Lee and Brian Stratton	295
Museum Volunteers Rene Rem	297
The Paradox of Beauty from the Great War John Wrigley	299

President's Report 2013-2014

Bob Lester

It is with great pleasure that I present the president's report for the year. The past twelve months have been both enjoyable and busy as the Society undertook a number of major projects and initiatives for the benefit of members and the community. The Society's committee has continued to look at measures to improve the way we operate more effectively and how we can continue to present and promote the rich history of the Camden district.

The year saw the Society continue to play an important role within the local community, providing information, awareness, and opportunities for local residents and visitors to see and hear about the many stories associated with Camden's past. Through the continuing high numbers of Museum visitors, the wide range of requests for information, hits on our webpage, visits from local schools and community groups and increased attendance at its monthly meetings, the Society continues to maintain its focus and direction.

Library and Family History Partnership

A strong partnership with the Camden Library and the Camden Family History Society continues to be maintained. Committee members have attended regular meetings to coordinate activities during History Week and Heritage Month. Also the availability online of the Society's photographic collection occurs through the partnership with the Library resources enabling easy access and the capability of people to obtain good quality prints.

The value of this partnership was reinforced with the provision by Council of additional storage at Narellan for Museum items and materials and the use of the Galleria area for our book launches and functions.

Museum

The management of the Camden Museum remained a major focus of the Society during the year with a number of exciting exhibitions and events undertaken.

The Red Cross exhibition was the major attraction for visitors with the displays of colourful posters, badges and tablecloths showing the work of local volunteers of the era. Officially launched in August 2013 it will culminate in the launch of Ian Willis's book on the 30 August this year to mark 100 years of service by the Red Cross in Camden and Australia. A great deal of work behind the scenes on the exhibition led by curator Julie Wrigley has occurred by many Society members which is greatly appreciated. There is also an ongoing oral history project as part of the Camden Library partnership with interviews being conducted by Leonie Jackson.

The World War 1 exhibition complimented the Red Cross displays wonderfully with banners outlining the various chapters of the book written by Janice Johnson. Janice's book was successfully launched by the Federal Member for Macarthur Russell Matheson at a function held by the Society in April where local RSL members and guests joined in remembering the stories told in letters from soldiers and their families.

Both of these exhibitions and book publications were made possible through grants received by the Society from the Australian Federal Government. I wish to thank them for their support of such projects and we look for further opportunities over the coming years.

Visitor numbers for 2013-2014 have maintained their high level with 6,811 coming through the doors to view the displays, as part of a school or group visit or to attend a Society meeting or function. These numbers shows that the Museum is being well used and is an important tourist destination for Camden visitors. The Museum volunteers continued to play an essential role in making our visitors feel welcome, able to access the research files and leave with a bit more knowledge and understanding of Camden's past. Our Volunteer Coordinator Rene Rem continues to do a wonderful job ensuring the front desk has been staffed on all shifts, enticing more people to become volunteers and facilitating a volunteers training day during the year.

Society Meetings

Whilst our monthly meetings enable us to properly manage the society's affairs, they are more important as a means to maintain member and community interest, increases their knowledge, tell stories about our collective histories and bring new members and visitors to the Museum.

Guest speakers for the year were:

> Heritage Furniture Paul Gregson
>
> 100 years of Cricket in Camden Neville Clissold
>
> Preserving old Photographs Charles Cowell
>
> Red Cross in Camden Ian Willis
>
> The lost plane over Burragorang David Funnell
>
> Memories of Cobbitty Joy Thorn
>
> Camden Remembers Ray Herbert
>
> Flooding in Camden Janice Johnson and John Wrigley
>
> 100 years of Camden Boy Scouts Kent Palmer

Society members were also involved in two meetings showing their old family photos and telling their story of how they came to Camden, celebrating History week and Heritage Festival both participated in by the Society.

During the year Annette Macarthur-Onslow was conferred life membership of the Society to acknowledge her significant long term contribution to the Society. Janice Johnson was successfully nominated for a Local Historian Award for her work in researching information and stories for the World War 1 book. Congratulations are extended to Annette and Janice.

Communication

The Society's website has been maintained by our webmaster Steven Robinson with input by Ian Willis. The web is important to enable younger generations and the not so young to research our records and keep in touch. Regular newsletters have been developed by Ian Wills and printed by our Federal Member's office. Ian has also been the editor of the Society's much valued Journal which is well read by all concerned and reflects the variety of research undertaken by our members and other contributors. Ian's History Blog is a personal history project which has links on the society website.

Attendance at the Camden Show and Camden Antique Fair each year remains a valuable way of communicating with the public with our display of publications gaining a great deal of interest. Thank you to all who have volunteered to be part of these displays and to the people who have organised them. Society members again took part in NAIDOC Week celebrations including the Flag raising ceremony outside of Council and the promotion of our Museum Aboriginal display.

New publications have regularly hit our sales area with books on a variety of subjects and interests. They provide a source of income for the Society and a way of communicating stories on aspects of life in Camden. By reading these books and the weekly articles that appear in *Back Then* in the District Reporter no Camden resident should be unaware of Camden's rich local history. The larger TV installed in the Museum has improved the viewing of DVD's by visitors and presentations at Society meetings.

Collaboration

This year saw the opportunity for the Society to work collaboratively with The Oaks Heritage Society in a series of workshops on aspects of Museum management and recording of local history. Significance Assessment Workshops enabled members to produce significance statements on a range of Museum items which have increased the information available on each and the associated stories that can be told about them. A follow up workshop on photography provided members with skills and understanding of recording museum items. The Society thanks the Museums and Galleries NSW for providing the funding and Kylie Winkworth and other presenters for leading them.

A workshop was held with Lee Abrahams on writing articles for the Back Then page of The District Reporter. This was well attended and follow up workshops will be held to increase the number of people writing articles.

The Oxley Anchor project continued to be developed during the year led by Robert Wheeler. Following discussions with Council and the securing of support by the Macarthur Lions it is anticipated that the anchor will be moved to Curry Reserve where it can be more easily appreciated by the community. The financial support given by Mr Gordon is acknowledged and greatly appreciated.

Our committee

Like all community organisations nothing gets done without the efforts of people who dedicate a great deal of their time and energy in the many tasks that need to be performed to make things work effectively and meet the expectations of our members. I wish to thank all members of the committee for their efforts, knowhow and time in making the Society tick. Everyone had a role to play in our successes this year and I look forward to working with them again in the year ahead.

Dick Inglis

Death of a Fine Camden Citizen

John Wrigley

Local residents have been saddened to hear of the loss of one of the district's great characters with the death of Dick Inglis, at Cobbitty on June 13 2014, aged 93 years. Richard Reginald Inglis had been a much admired citizen for many decades and known through his many business and community activities.

Born into the well-known family of auctioneers he conducted the Camden Saleyard stock auctions in Edward Street for most of his long career. His distinctive gravelly voice was no doubt partly a result of those long years of conducting auctions in all weathers. His knowledge of stock and of cattle in particular was vast and his opinion was valued by many. In 1948 he married the beautiful Lorna McIntosh of 'Denbigh', Cobbitty.

His love for the Camden Show and his abilities led him to be the President of the Camden Show Society from 1963 to 1974 and Vice President for many years. During his presidency he promoted the establishment of the popular rodeo and upgraded the lighting of the main arena. A pet hobby of his was conducting the sheepdog competition of the show, where his skill with dogs was evident.

Another favourite was the Camden Show Ball, held for decades in the historic show hall. Here he was renowned for compering the famous 'Slide'. This test of skill involved a number of young bucks taking turns to run into the hall from Argyle Street and seeing who could slide the entire length of the hall while still standing upright. Often this resulted in the entrant sliding most of the way on his dinner suit or shirt!

He said of his many years of voluntary work for the show: 'I got a lot more out of the show than the show got from me'. Vic Boardman has said that Dick's contribution to the show was unprecedented and that his commonsense way of doing things managed to unite the committee behind him in many major decisions.

In his later years Dick was a popular and amusing guest speaker on the history of Cobbitty and the district. In his prime he was a great storyteller and very good company. His voice and laugh could be heard from quite a distance. His last years were difficult with health problems and in accordance with his wishes a private family funeral has been conducted.

Dick Inglis is survived by his loving wife Lorna and his children Reg, Jamie and Ros and their families. As the death notice said: We have lost a great Australian!

John Martin Hawkey's Presentation Tea Service

Cathey Shepherd

On display at the Camden Museum there is a silver tea service which dates from 1936 when it was a presentation to John Martin Hawkey. The silver-plated tea service consists of teapot, milk jug, sugar bowl and tray. The teapot is engraved *"Presented to Major John Martin Hawkey MC by the officers of the 21st Light Horse Regiment in appreciation of his Services as Adjutant."* The stainless steel tray is engraved "21st Light Horse Illawarra Light Horse - *Virtu in Ardus*", which refers to the virtue of courage in adversity.

John Martin Hawkey was born in Menangle on 12th October, 1877. He was the 12th child of Richard Hawkey (1836 -1901) and Mary Ann Burton (1837-1887). They arrived in Australia on 11th February, 1857, from Cornwall on the ship 'Plantagenet'. Richard was living on the Camden Park estate, when John was born. Richard was the farm manager of the Estate, as was his son William after him. Many of Richard and Mary Ann's other children worked as servants, gardeners, housekeepers and farmers for the Macarthur family. It was on the Camden Park Estate that while still a schoolboy, John learnt the farrier trade and took a great interest in matters of a military nature, before joining the army as a farrier for the Mounted Rifles.

John was to continue his distinguished military career, taking part in Queen Victoria's Diamond Jubilee celebrations in London (1897), the Boer War (1899), the First World War and in the Second World War, he worked as a 'man power officer at the Lancer Barracks, Parramatta'. His military career was as a member of the Mounted Rifles and the Light Horse contingents.

The first mention of John Martin Hawkey's services as an adjutant appears when he was appointed Adjutant to the 36th battalion, in World War One in France. Newspaper articles from the 1920s also mention he was a popular adjutant when he was a member of the 21st Light Horse regiment in the Illawarra. The definition of an adjutant, from the Latin *adjutans*, in the colonial forces, was usually a senior Captain, sometimes a Major, and a man of significant influence within his battalion. As the colonel's personal staff officer, he was also in charge of all the organisation, administration and discipline for a battalion or regiment and was the regimental operations officer.

The tea service was made by the Phoenix Manufacturing Company Pty Ltd of Victoria which was established in 1916. Their trademark, a phoenix, is found on sterling and electroplated silverware produced by the company. All designs were Australian, as were the machinery and dies used in the manufacture of Phoenix products. By 1920 the company designed plain heavy-gauge EPNS tea and coffee services for commercial use. In addition they patented an improved spout for their hardwearing tea and coffee pots. From the 1920s and 1930s Phoenix Plate was stamped 'Made in Australia'. In 1932 the Phoenix Manufacturing Company introduced their "Imperial" brand EPNS table wares. This "Imperial" EPNS, quality silverware was made in 18% nickel silver. The Phoenix catalogue included a range of domestic silverware and many items for military presentations, together with new and popular Art Deco styled goods. The Hawkey tea service is marked 'Made in Australia' and has the 1930s Art Deco appearance.

The tea service was a presentation to John Martin Hawkey for his services as an adjutant and was donated by his grandson, John Rothwell Hawkey. This grandson also inherited J.M. Hawkey's military medals and other items, such as a smoking tray, and believes he inherited the tea service because he and his wife collected silverware. Other military memorabilia of John M. Hawkey, such as uniforms and helmets, are in

the Lancer Barracks, Parramatta, being donated by Ken Hawkey (also a military man and the son of John M. Hawkey).

In the 1920s and 30s the military presentation of a tea service seemed in military circles to be the ultimate gift for a highly respected army officer. John Martin Hawkey was a prominent person in the unit and the gift shows the respect and affection of his men to John Hawkey. There are numerous newspaper articles on 'Trove' about his role as adjutant, his skills and efficiency in the role and his popularity in the position. John M. Hawkey had distinguished himself at Queen Victoria's Jubilee, The Boer War, World War One and his work in the military. He was awarded the Military Cross (MC) in World War One. At the time of the presentation of the tea service, John Martin Hawkey was a Major but he later became a Lieutenant-ColonelThe item has clear provenance, with three owners, all in the immediate family. The owners were John Martin Hawkey; his son Major K. Hawkey also a military man; and his grandson, John Rothwell Hawkey, who donated the items to the Camden Museum.

The tea service is an attractive item in the Art Deco style of the 1930s. It was made in Australia of silver plate made by the Phoenix Manufacturing Company Pty Ltd. In the 1920s the Phoenix Company was the largest manufacturers of electroplated and sterling silverware in Australia. This tea service is a good example of silverware manufactured from the finest silver of heavy gauge and finished by skilled craftsmen. The good condition of the tea service suggests it was used only for display and adds to its significance. The item's inscription is rare and the fact it was domestic table ware presented in appreciation of the soldier's work as an adjutant. J.M. Hawkey was presented with other memorabilia throughout his long military career, but they were of a military nature, for example medals and citations.

The tea service and inscription represents the Mounted Rifles' role in protecting both the colony and country of Australia, and shows the type of men who were required to lead and organise a military unit. These men protected Australia through war and peace. It also indicates the role of a Camden man, who was born and bred in Camden, who rose through the military ranks with distinguished service, both on and off the battlefield, and chose to protect the newly-founded country of Australia.

Camden Retrospective

'NERVE-CENTRE' OF R.A.A.F.
CENTRAL FLYING SCHOOL.

Instructors Trained.

By OUR AVIATION CORRESPONDENT.

The Central Flying Training School at Camden can be described as a 'nerve-centre" of the Empire Air Training Scheme in Australia, and of service flying for the defence of the Commonwealth. At this school, trainee flight Instructors and service pilots undergo courses in Air Force instruction, and "refresher" and conversion syllabuses.

The staff has been specially selected and consists of well-known service officers who were in the RAAF before the war, as well as former commercial airline pilots and private Instructors.

For instance, Captain H Purvis previously a Douglas commander with Australian National Airways and a Lockheed pilot with the Dutch air line, the KNILM, is now chief Lockheed Hudson instructor with the rank of Flight-Lieutenant.

Mr G S Coleman, before the war chief flying instructor of the Royal Aero Club and the Kingsford Smith Air Service Co. at Mascot Is a Squadron-Leader and chief flight Instructor.

The former flight superintendent of Australian National Airways, Mr K Frewen, is a flying-officer, and Mr C Higginson, who operated his own air taxi service and flying school at Archerfield Aerodrome, Brisbane, is also a flying officer.

Another well-known former private pilot stationed at Camden is Pilot-Officer B Monk, who was Instructor with the Royal Aero Club of NSW. These pilots joined the service at considerable financial loss, particularly Purvis, who is receiving about one-fourth the salary he was paid with the Dutch air line and Coleman.

The misconception that service and commercial pilots cannot get on together is disproved at Camden, where graduates from both branches of aviation are combining their most useful experience to supply an efficient flight nucleus for the Empire Air Scheme and Air Force stations throughout Australia.

CAMDEN STATION

The Macquarie Grove Aerodrome at Camden was originally planned and built by Mr E Macarthur Onslow and when war was declared he offered it to the Commonwealth Government as a complete flying training school. It had the advantage of a good surface, reasonable weather throughout the year and quiet rural surroundings. The offer was accepted by the late Minister for Air Mr JV Fairbairn.

Since the Department for Air took over the site the approaches to the landing field have been improved by shovelling away a hill and lopping trees. The longest runway has been lengthened to 1,000 yards. Huts for quarters for officers and airmen have been built, new hangars have been completed to house training aircraft, a control tower has been erected, the Macarthur Onslow home has been turned into the officers' mess, a hospital has been added, and a parade ground, roads, and lawns have been made.

Unlike some other Air Force stations the huts at Camden have been built of timber instead of galvanised iron, and are, therefore, cooler in summer. The timber was not properly seasoned before being used, and the cracks and gaps in the sides of the huts are popularly referred to as "a good example of jerry building." The Department of the Interior was responsible for the buildings.

Some of the officers who have joined up at financial sacrifice live in the town. They like the rural surroundings, but have a definite grouch against landlords, who have increased rents a little too obviously since the Macquarie Grove aerodrome became an Air Force station. They contrast the rising rents with the favourable treatment and co-operation they have received from tradespeople and others.

RANGE OF AIRCRAFT

The full complement of staff and trainees at the Central Flying Training School total about 500. Aircraft used for instruction range from the 90 horse-power De Havilland Moth Minor up to the Avro Anson. The intermediate gaps are filled by the Avro Trainer, Wirraway and Fairey Battle. Other types may soon become available to the school namely the Wackett Monoplane Trainer and the Lockheed Hudson.

Pilots being trained as instructors and attending "refresher" schools undergo both ground and flight instruction courses. Link trainers are kept busy up to nine o'clock at night.

A new system of aerodrome control has been devised which will probably be standardised throughout the RAAF. Aldus signalling lamps as used at Kingsford Smith airport, for instance, are not favoured.

It is interesting to note that use has been found for the 50 Moth Minor aircraft which were bought by the Commonwealth Government from England. They are being employed to give preliminary flight experience before instruction to men selected as instructor-trainees who have had about 50 to 60 hours private flying experience.

The Central Flying School prepares flight manuals for the operations of new types of aircraft in the RAAF such as the Fairey Battle. These instructions for efficient handling of aircraft are prepared after the types have been flown extensively.

In about a year, 300 instructors have "gone through" the Central Flying Training School which was shifted from Point Cook to Camden in May this year. In addition to its training activities the school is almost self-contained. The staff carries out most overhauls and all but major repair work.

Another useful work carried out by the officers of the Central Flying Training School Is the testing of all service pilots. This periodical testing checks any flying errors which individuals may develop, and is a valuable safety precaution in preventing injury and loss of equipment.

The Central Flying Training School is under the command of Wing-Commander E C Bates who served with the Royal Air Force. The efficient lay out of the huts, hangars, and other buildings is largely due to his use of available facilities and personnel. The bearing and spirit of officers and men at the station are highly creditable.

Source: The Sydney Morning Herald, Wednesday 6 November 1940, p.12.

Book Launch
Author Address

Ministering Angels, the Camden District Red Cross, 1914-1915

Ian Willis

Camden Historical Society Inc

Published August 2014
ISBN 9780980303964

The inspiration for this book was an interest in Camden wartime history many years ago and I am still working on it. The Red Cross was the subject of my MA thesis in the mid-1990s and I have since given a number of conference papers. The book is a combination of all these works.

I have taken the title 'Ministering Angels' from the 1940 cover of the Red Cross magazine – The Australian Red Cross Quarterly. But the term is not new. In 1918 the Hobart Mercury published an article called 'A Ministering Angel', and in 1919 The Register in Adelaide published another article under the headline 'The Ministering Angel, Tribute to Red Cross Work'. Both articles wrote about the founders and volunteers of the Red Cross movement.

Russell Matheson MP (Member for Macarthur) Ian Willis, Judy Wilson (Liaison Officer Camden Red Cross), Lola Beck (Past President Camden Red Cross) (M Willis)

In essence this book is the story of conservative country women doing their patriotic duty in an outpost of the British Empire. It tells the story of how from 1914 Camden district women joined local Red Cross branches and their affiliates in the towns and villages around the colonial estate of the Macarthur family at Camden Park. They sewed, knitted and cooked for God, King and Country throughout the First and Second World Wars, and the years in-between. They ran stalls and raffles, and received considerable community support through cash donations from individuals and community organisations.

I have used the themes of soldier and civilian welfare, patriotism, duty, sacrifice, motherhood, class and religion in the narrative to explain how the place-based nature of the Red Cross branch network provided an opportunity for the organisation to harness parochialism and localism for national patriotic purposes.

In the book I have delved into the story of how Camden's Edwardian women provided leadership at a local, state and national level and created ground-breaking opportunities that empowered women to exercise their agency by undertaking patriotic activities for the first time. The book details how Camden women were encouraged to immerse themselves in the Red Cross ministering angel mythology, and serve 'their boys' by volunteering at branch sewing circles and fundraisers or as voluntary aids at military, civilian and Red Cross hospitals.

I maintain that in their wake Camden women created the most important voluntary organisation in district history, a small part of the narrative of the Australian Red Cross, arguably the country's most important not-for-profit organisation. Their stories were the essence of place, and the success of the district branches meant that over time homefront volunteering became synonymous with the Red Cross.

Ministering Angels, I maintain, is a local Red Cross study of volunteering in war and peace that provides a small window into the national and transnational perspectives of one of the world's most important welfare organisations. Local studies like this book are not common and they tell the story of ordinary people doing extra-ordinary things in extra-ordinary times.

My wish would be that hopefully the book might encourage others to do similar studies in our district for there any many similar untold stories.

Red Cross Book Launch
Julie Wrigley

The Red Cross book launch of the book "*Ministering Angels - The Camden District Red Cross 1914-1945*" by Dr Ian Willis, held at the Camden Museum on Saturday 30 August was attended by 78 people, including Russell Matheson MHR, Chris Patterson MLA, and Councillor Eva Campbell. A number of apologies were received including the Mayor and Council General Manager.

Current members of the the Australian Red Cross, Camden Club, who attended the afternoon tea included Lola Beck, June Head, Pat Herd, Joan King, Joyce Thorn OAM, and Judy Wilson, the Liaison Officer of the Camden Red Cross Club, who launched the book.

Organising the afternoon was a team effort by Camden Historical Society members Joy Aitken, Jo Booth, Michael Booth, Rene Rem, Stephanie Trenfield, Cathey Shepherd, Lee Stratton, John Wrigley and Julie Wrigley. The Society was very happy with the community response and the help from the Camden Country Women's Association in providing the delicious afternoon tea.

Bruce Cunningham and Peter Mylrea (J Oliver)

John Wrigley presenting Jos & Ruth Ferguson with Service Certificate (L&B Stratton)

Official Opening of Liz Kernohan Drive 29 August 2014

Lee and Brian Stratton

Ten years after her death Camden Council honours Dr Liz Kernohan AM by officially opening the Liz Kernohan Drive at the intersection of the Camden Bypass, Elderslie.

The construction of this drive and its surrounds was a partnership involving the NSW Government's Planning and Infrastructure Department allocating $9 million and Camden Council contributing $4.4 million to the project.

The opening was carried out by the former Premier The Honorable Barry O'Farrell MP, Member for Ku-ring-gai, a long time parliamentary colleague of Ms Kernohan. Also speaking at the opening was Chris Patterson State MP and former Mayor of Camden together with the present Camden Mayor Lara Symkowiak. All three spoke highly of Liz the person and of her commitment to public service for over three decades.

Chris Patterson MP, Barry O'Farrell MP, Lara Symkowiak Mayor (L&B Stratton)

Following the speeches was the unveiling of the commemorative plaque on a large rock and concluded with a tree planting ceremony performed by the official party.

Also present on the occasion were Councillors Penny Fischer and Theresa Fedeli and representatives from Urban Growth NSW (formerly Landcom). The Camden Historical Society was represented by Secretary Lee Stratton and members Maggie Cole and Brian Stratton OAM. The museum displayed Liz's election poster and her number plates 'LIZ MP'.

This was a fitting occasion to celebrate the person who supported our Society over so many years and we are the proud custodians of much of her memorabilia.

Barry O'Farrell MP, Margaret Cole. (L&B Stratton)

Museum Volunteers

Rene Rem, Volunteer Co-ordinator

Throughout the history of Camden Historical Society volunteers have been the backbone and lifeblood of the Society. Without their efforts the Society would not exist today.

Volunteers are just as important today as they have been in the past. Over the past two years we have seen a great increase in the number of visitors attending the Museum. Part of the reason for this increase is the way in which our volunteers "meet and greet". The visitors are made to feel welcome and "at home".

Volunteering is not only about the meet and greet and there are many behind the scenes jobs which volunteers do. There are the regular display changes (we have seen quite a few of those in recent times) and there are also the care of our artefacts, both on display and in storage. I should also acknowledge the work done by volunteers who conduct the various tours for visiting service groups and schools. They lead groups through the Museum and also through the district, and bring our society to the attention of people throughout Sydney and the state.

The society has been improving the use of technology to make access to the museum a more enjoyable experience and new challenges have arisen for volunteers. We now have a new, larger television screen, which was installed with the assistance of volunteers. It is being maintained with the assistance of Warren Sims. Two of our volunteers are also working on updating and tidying our numerous files, and at the same time digitising them onto our computer; making it easier access for members, visitors and other researchers to obtain the information they require. This work is being ably carried out by new volunteers Stephanie Trenfield and Dianne Matterson.

I would like to take this opportunity to thank all our volunteers, past and present, for the wonderful job being done to make visiting The Camden Museum an extremely pleasant experience.

Rene Rem and Stephanie Trenfield volunteering at book launch (J Oliver)

The Paradox of Beauty from the Great War

John Wrigley

One of the most decorative items in the Camden Museum is paradoxically a reminder of the brutality of war.

The brass shell case was a souvenir from World War One. It is a 75mm diameter German-made shell manufactured for Turkish army use in the Middle East. The item has embossed Arabic patterns and applied silver and copper ornamentation with Arabic script around the base and the wording 'Damascus 1918' in English on a panel.

The item is a souvenir of the victory of the British and Australian forces led by General Edmund Allenby (later 1919 Field Marshall Lord Allenby) over the Turkish troops of the Ottoman Empire. The last battle in Palestine saw the city of Damascus fall on 1st October 1918 with the Australian Light Horsemen entering the city, having cut off the Turkish retreat. The classic film 'Lawrence of Arabia' dramatically portrayed the taking of Damascus at that time. The Great War in Europe ended on 11th November 1918, shortly after the battle of Damascus.

The shell case was donated by Miss Virginia West, granddaughter of Dr West, a well-loved and highly respected local doctor. He practised in Camden from his home 'Macaria', 37 John Street from 1901 until 1932. Dr West's sister Minnie West was a nursing sister in World War One, serving in Salonica, and she brought back several souvenirs, some as presents for her brother. This may have been one of them but it is not known how this souvenir came into the West family's ownership. Some of Sister West's souvenirs are on display in the Camden Museum.

During and after World War One, shell casings and other items from the war were made into souvenirs called trench art or shell-case art. Some trench art was made in the trenches, by soldiers during the war.

Other items were made by prisoners of war and interned civilians. When the war ended the mountains of millions of discarded shell casings and equipment were slowly recycled. Official war photographs show huge piles of these shell cases discarded on the battlefields. This

Decorative World War I shell case (photo by Nitsa Yioupros).

item may have been sold to some Allied soldier or nurse by an Arab craftsman trying to make a living after the country had been ravaged by war between the Ottoman and Allied troops.

The item is a hard brass cylindrical case on a turned steel base, with brass screwed charging plug, made about 1917 by Friedrich Krupp A G, of Essen. The Krupp family was a German dynasty of industrialists. Fried Krupp A G started the first major steel-works in Germany in 1811, and their enterprise expanded rapidly to become one of the world's largest companies and Germany's leading supplier of armaments. The case is made from the highest quality brass and steel. Before it came to the museum the case was polished and lacquered to prevent tarnish.

There were a number of 75mm Krupp field guns brought back to Australia as war trophies. At the Australian War Memorial in Canberra there is a 75mm Krupp field gun which would have used this sort of artillery shells.

This spent shell has been decorated as a souvenir from the end of World War One, marking the battle at Damascus, where the British and Australian Light Horsemen were victorious over the Turkish and German force in Palestine. It was made by a very skilled craftsman who has identified himself as 'Zachariah' in Arabic lettering. We have to thank two visitors to the Museum from Egypt for translating the Arabic text. The craftsman Zachariah decorated the shell case probably for sale to an Allied soldier or nurse in 1918. The high quality of the art work in the embossing of silver and copper on brass with intricate Arabic designs, the inscription 'Zachariah' in Arabic lettering, and 'Damascus' in English lettering all contribute to the significance of the shell case. This is an unusual and highly collectable item. There are many other examples of trench souvenirs but the art work is not of such a high quality as this item.

The object is relevant to Camden because it is a souvenir brought back by an unknown member of the West family, and was donated to the Camden museum by a granddaughter of the highly-respected Dr West who practised in the town from 1901 to 1932. It may have been brought back by Sister Minnie West, Dr West's sister, who served overseas. The shell case is in good condition and is an excellent example of its type of war memorabilia. The item is currently being used in the Camden Museum's display *World War I Camden Diggers*. It evokes images of the lives lost in war, from the Turkish side as well as the Allies. The word 'Damascus' is a reminder of the lives lost in battles on Arabic soil and the sacrifices made during war.

The item has recently been one of a number of museum treasures which have been having their significance reassessed. Camden Museum volunteers co-operated with those from the Wollondilly Heritage Centre at The Oaks to take part in a series of training workshops with museums consultant Kylie Winkworth. The Camden Museum volunteers appreciated that a conservation photographer, Ms Nitsa Yioupros from the Powerhouse Museum, was able to take this excellent photograph of the item for the use of the Museum and for this article.

CAMDEN HISTORY

Journal of the Camden Historical Society Inc

March 2015, Volume 3, Number 9

Special Issue

CAMDEN HISTORY

Journal of the Camden Historical Society Inc.

ISSN 1445-1549

Editor: Dr Ian Willis

Management Committee

President: Bob Lester

Vice Presidents: Dr Ian Willis, Rene Rem

Secretary: Lee Stratton

Assistant Secretary: Julie Wrigley

Treasurer: Dawn Williams

Assistant Treasurer:

Immediate Past President: John Wrigley OAM

General Committee: Cathey Shepherd   Sharon Greene
　　　　　　　　　　　　Roslyn Tildsley   Julie Wrigley
　　　　　　　　　　　　Robert Wheeler   Stephanie Trenfield

Honorary Auditor:

Honorary Solicitors: Bowring, Macaulay and Barrett

Society contact:
P.O. Box 566, Camden, NSW 2570. Online <http://www.camdenhistory.org.au>

Meetings
Meetings are held at 7.30 p.m. on the second Wednesday of the month except in January. They are held in the Museum. Visitors are always welcome.

Museum
The Museum is located at 40 John Street, Camden, phone 4655 3400 or 46559210. It is open Thursday to Sunday 11 a.m. to 4 p.m., except at Christmas. Visits by schools and groups are encouraged. Please contact the Museum to make arrangements. Entry is free.

Camden History, Journal of the Camden Historical Society Inc
The Journal is published in March and September each year. The Editor would be pleased to receive articles broadly covering the history of the Camden district . Correspondence can be sent to the Society's postal address. The views expressed in the articles are solely those of the authors and not necessarily endorsed by the society.

Donations
Donations made to the Society are tax deductible. The accredited value of objects donated to the Society are eligible for tax deduction.

Cover: Astley John Onslow Thompson

From the Old to New South Wales the life of Astley John Onslow Thompson

Annette Macarthur Onslow

CAMDEN HISTORY
Special Issue
Journal of the Camden Historical Society Inc.

March 2015 Volume 3 Number 9

FOREWORD

Camden News. 13th May, 1915

"When the news floated to Camden that Lieutenant Colonel Thompson had fallen in action at the Dardanelles, quite a shock was experienced in the district, and his death cast a shadow over the community. He was popular and greatly esteemed."

"It is not generally known that during his lifetime he did a good deal in his quiet way, not letting his left hand know what his right hand did in assisting his fellows."

"He was level headed and had a wonderful gift of being able to consider a question in all its bearings in a short space of time."

These attributes made him an exceptional manager of Camden Park Estate and its outstations, Richlands at Taralga and St. Clair in the Hunter Valley. He was a director of the Commercial Banking Co. of Sydney and of the Colonial Sugar Refinery, president of the Agricultural, Horticultural &Industrial Society, astute in finance, a skilled draughtsman, designer of buildings and a member of the Royal Society of New South Wales – above all, for our purposes, he was a soldier, and a leader.

In compiling his story I owe thanks to my great friend, the late Jeanine McMullen in Wales, and to the many people she enlisted to help me: Mr. John Bilsborough of Glyn Abbey, Mr. Hywel Davis, Mr Rusty MacLean, archivist of Rugby School, Mr. John Creasy of the Rural History Centre at the University of Reading, and to Thompson descendants, Pamela Palmer and Helen Robinson (nee Pickett) who provided many photographs.

My Australian research is from family papers, interviews, and official documents from the Australian War Memorial, State Archives and local newspapers.

I also owe special thanks to Mr. Charles Cowell for the fine copy of the Drill Hall plan held by Camden Historical Society; to the late Charles Inglis and The Oaks Heritage Centre for extra details of Thompson's life, and to Janice Johnson for her technical ability and help with this production.

From the Old to New South Wales

Astley John Onslow Thompson was born in South Wales in 1865. His English parents were creatures of their time, drawn to profit from the immense industrial development and, by the same token, to become its victims.

His father, Astley Thompson, was an Iron Master from Manchester, who had been sent to South Wales to straighten the affairs of the Melyn Griffiths Iron Works, by the Cardiff and West of England Bank.

His mother, Udea Onslow came from London. A collateral to the Peerage, she was a descendent of Arthur Onslow, Speaker of the House of Commons. Her brother Douglas, a J.P. was a director of the Burry Port Smelting Co. in Carmarthenshire. Both Thompsons and Onslows featured in that company and Astley Thompson was, for a short time, Chairman.

After their marriage in 1864, Astley and Udea settled first at the tiny Ynys Cottage in Pentyrch, Glamorgan, but after the birth of their first son, Astley at nearby Eglwysilan and with the prospect of a growing family, they moved in 1866 to Glyn Abbey, a large house on a handsome estate in Carmarthenshire.

Astley Thompson

Udea Thompson (nee Onslow)

The Thompson family at Glyn Abbey (from photograph sent by Helen Robinson)

Glyn Abbey had 503 acres of well timbered grasslands, screened from the SW winds, with fine views over land and sea. It had "Seven capital farms let to excellent tenants" and apart from its Home Farm buildings, stables, coach house, gardens and orchards, had underlying "valuable seams of fireclay, ironstone and coal". Astley Thompson borrowed heavily to buy it.

It was within easy reach of the Burry Port Smelting Company which had opened in 1865 to trade mainly in lead and silver. Together with brick-works and iron stone mines, the company owned New Lodge Colliery and other collieries in the Gwendraeth Valley. Hundreds of workers were employed and the houses built for them at "Silver Row" Burry Port I am told are still standing. They owned a ship, the "Udea" (87 tons) which transported their products to other parts of the country.

All went well for about eleven happy years. The large house full of servants was a centre of hospitality. The Thompsons were popular and well loved, caring for the poor, supporting national culture, particularly eisteddfords and other musical events, upholding the local spiritual needs by establishing a place of worship and in every way they were good community workers and exemplary leaders.

They had eleven children of whom two died in infancy. The eldest, Astley jr. was schooled at Rugby – England's most prestigious progressive school where he did well and it is thought may have learned the skill of draughtsmanship in the newly opened art department.

In 1871 Astley Thompson senior was appointed High Sheriff of Carmarthen, a rare honour for an Englishman. Then in 1877 disaster struck. The Company went bankrupt with liabilities of about £300,000, which today would be millions. The coalmines Astley had excavated on the property had proved worthless.

The Thompsons continued to live at Glyn Abbey only to be met by a second disaster in 1883 when Udea, the most "loving wife, devoted mother and good mistress" died of peritonitis at the age of 43.

At this point, Astley junior aged 18, having left school and having worked for the Lands Department, set out for Australia, in his own words "friendless and penniless" to take up a position with the "Harbours and Rivers" branch of the Public Service. His father, a broken man, tried in vain to sell Glyn Abbey, but ended moving with his children, (the youngest of whom was barely two years old) to Tenby to live next door to the John family where the children played with the young Augustus John.

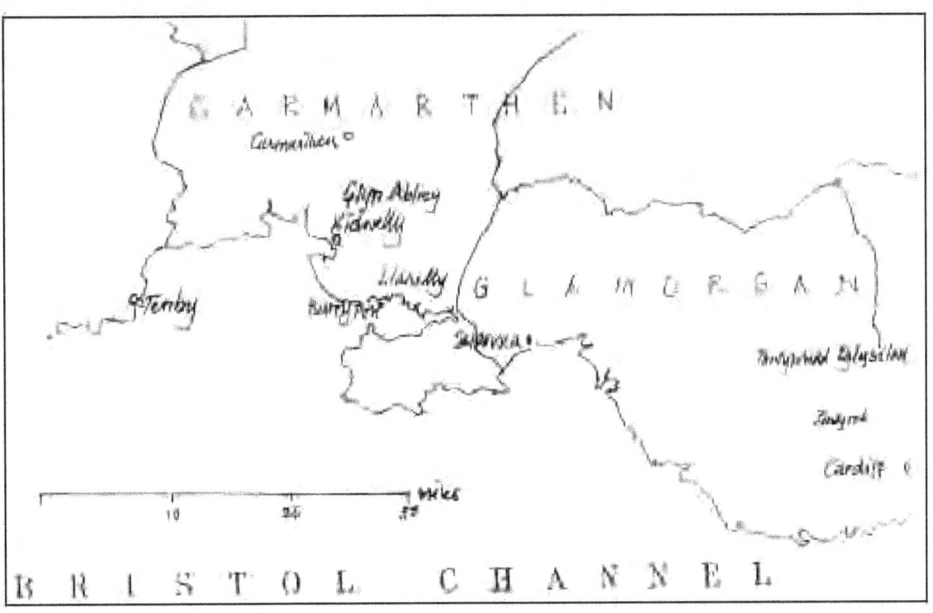

Astley Thompson senior died in 1887 and the many valuable contents of Glyn Abbey were put up for sale in 1890.

With little else to support them, the younger Thompson children were cared for by their uncle, Major George Manners Onslow at Sendhurst Grange, in Surrey.

Astley junior did what he could to help from a distance, but his term as protector always remained limited, even from the late 1880s when, under the wing of his Onslow cousins at Camden, New South Wales, he became manager of Camden Park.

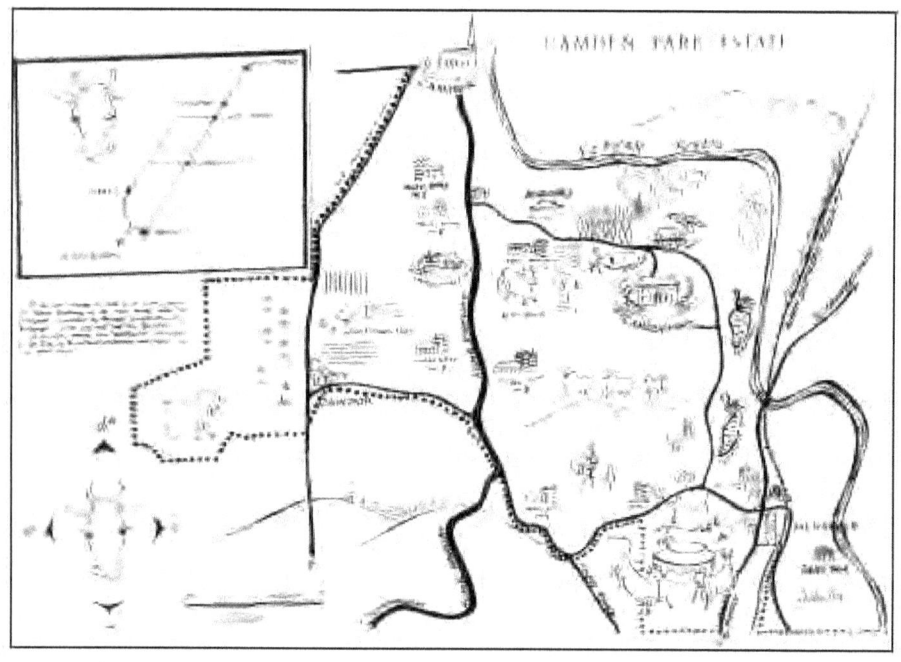

Camden Park Estate as it was drawn for the 1958 Estate booklet when the milk industry was at its peak. It shows both the model dairies and the Rotolactor 42 years after the death of Onslow Thompson. The original acreage has shrunk to 10,000 acres. I have included the Menangle Water Tank. (A Onslow)

2

Onslow, as he became known in Australia, was first cousin-once-removed to Captain Arthur Alexander Walton Onslow RN who had married Elizabeth, granddaughter of John Macarthur and sole heir to Camden Park.

In 1882 the huge load of this inheritance had fallen to Elizabeth with the death of her uncle, Sir William Macarthur. Her mother, her husband and her youngest child had also died in the space of two years. She had a young family to bring up and now a vast estate to run. The old overseer, Thomas Dawson, had given notice, so it was clear that a capable new manager was needed..

Her father, James Macarthur who, with his brother William, had developed and run the farm through periods of wool, wheat and wine, had died in 1867. The wool industry had gone up-country to better sheep pastures. Wheat had succumbed to the wheat rust of the sixties and vineyards which had produced Australia's first commercial wine were ruined by the world-wide spread of phylloxera. Dairying was now being considered the future industry of the property.

The Old Dairy

Engraving showing vista of farm and Camden village from the Cemetery Hill (Andrew Garran, Picturesque Atlas of Australasia, 1886)

For a short time James Chisholm, Elizabeth's cousin by marriage, helped with the management, but the greatest assistance was given by P.G. King MLA, grandson of Governor King and former manager of the Australian Agricultural Company. King was something of a father figure to Elizabeth, advising her on family matters, keeping records and guiding farm management.

It was King's suggestion that she should take her young family to England, to the home of her husband's people for their education, and that Onslow Thompson, who had resigned from "Harbours & Rivers" work, should join forces to study the dairying industry there with a view to becoming manager of Camden Park.

Worldwide changes were underway. Refrigeration had made transport of whole milk possible, so Camden Park's butter industry which had existed since the 1840s could now expand to include whole milk.

In Australia where propensity to drought and adverse conditions made pasture a risk, feeding dairy cattle remained a problem. In England, at the Aylesbury Dairy Co, in Sussex, ensilage, an age old method of storing fodder had been much improved by C.G. Johnson's stack method. This produced a sweeter product than that from the usual silo or pit.

Onslow Thompson returned to Australia in 1889 and set about re-arranging the farm and introducing new English methods. He quickly became accepted leader of a group of old farm hands who had been wont to disagree among themselves.

Farm buildings and cottages were renovated and many new ones built. The old dairy beside Belgenny Lagoon was closed and a new complex established at Menangle beside the railway line. Here the butter factory and the first of a group of creameries became the centre of a co-operative system.

The idea of the co-operative system had been pioneered in 1881 by the South Coast and West Camden Company and under the directorship of the Porter family, had already been in operation at Westbrook (Mount Hunter) with a number of Camden Park's tenant farmers.

That company had fallen on hard times, so Onslow would eventually buy and improve the creamery they had built and add two more depots – one at Cawdor and the more elaborate "Butter, Bacon and Refrigeration Works" in Camden.

Disagreement with Camden authorities resulted in closure of the latter and its replacement by the Home Farm Creamery set up in the old Coach House at the Farm.

Among the many other improvements to farming Onslow Thompson introduced piped water, constructed holding tanks and repaired old roads. The estate now populated with tenant farms, had up-to-date dairies, sheds and cow-yards paved with stone. Under his management the one-time wool, wheat and wine property gradually turned to dairying. Activities of the orchard and cut flower industry, sheep, pigs and poultry formulated patterns which were followed until recent years.

The very name Home Farm (now known as Belgenny) referring to home management as opposed to the tenant farms, can be plainly seen to date from Onslow Thompson's time.

3

All through the years of her childrens' schooling, Elizabeth Onslow divided her time between England and Australia, checking the progress of the farm and sending her instructions to Onslow Thompson.

Thanks to the invention of carbon paper, much of the late 19th century correspondence exists in copy book recordings. Onslow's letters to Elizabeth were often accompanied by plans for the buildings he had designed. To speed her replies he sometimes devised a code to be sent by the Overland Telegraph..

Onslow worked tirelessly to reform the estate and its outstations. He managed Elizabeth's finances, avoided the bank crashes of the 90s and helped her to inaugurate the family company, Camden Park Estate Limited in 1899, whereby the structure of management changed. Now each of Elizabeth's children would be Directors and Onslow Thompson, would be the first managing Director of the Company.

Former rights of the eldest child were now limited to a subdivided block surrounding Camden Park House. This property would remain in perpetuity for the family.

For a short time Onslow's younger brother, Iver joined him doing light farm work and keeping the books. Later, when the tenant farm co-operative dairy scheme was established, Iver Thompson, joined by an elderly cousin Foot Onslow, (descendent of Sir Thomas Foote, Lord Mayor of London) was given the job of running Channel's farm, south of Menangle. Foot Onslow's name is remembered there by a road sign at the local creek crossing.

Another Onslow who joined the clan was Harry Hamilton Onslow, a mining engineer who had lost the use of his right arm through an unfortunate accident and was given recuperation time at Camden Park. It is thanks to H.H. Onslow that we have the beautiful plans of the orchard and the old dairy complex, which he drafted with his left hand after much practice.

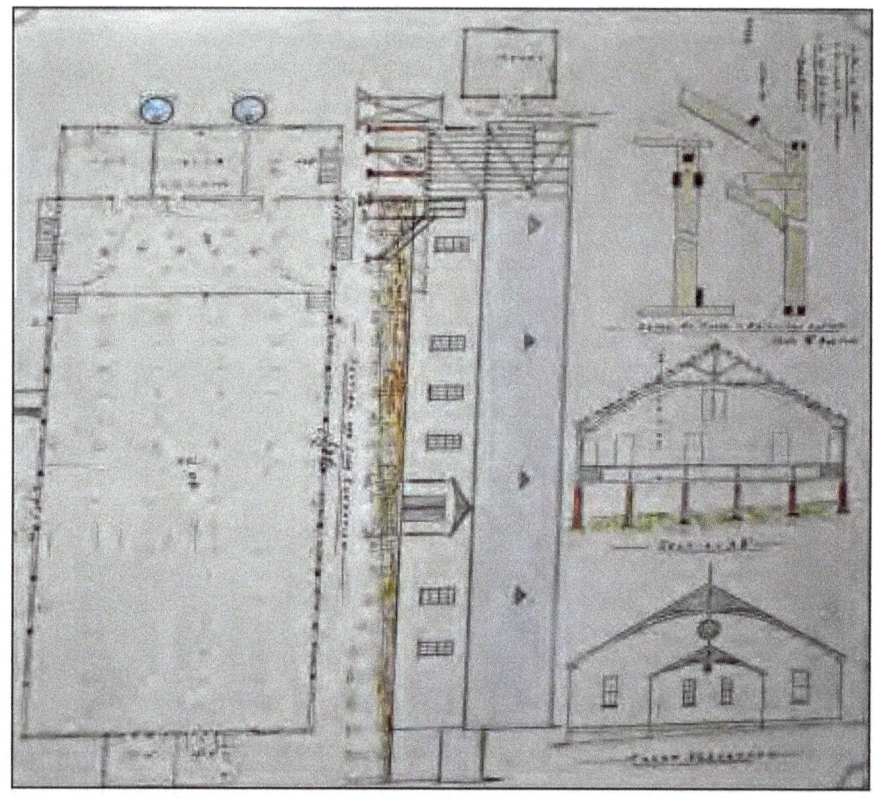

Plans for Drill Hall in Onslow Park, now the Camden Show Society's Agricultural Hall

In the matter of construction, Onslow Thompson had the devoted assistance of the resident builder, James Joseph English to carry out the work. All James Joseph's sons were involved in the Camden district building trade, but only the youngest, Herbert, remained life-long resident builder at the farm.

In 1957 I recorded Herb a year or so before he died. The old man spoke regretfully of the sad decline of the farm he had known. He added that he was the very last person of his generation still alive, to remember Onslow Thomson's years.

Not only had Herb known the "Old Major", as he called Onslow Thompson, but he had been taught how to draft plans and specifications by this admired master.

Onslow's living quarters and the Estate office were in the North Wing of Camden Park House. About twice a week, whenever he had time, Onslow would send for Herb to join him to practice drawing.

According to Herb, Onslow Thompson designed the Drill Hall for the Mounted Rifles. I have checked the plan for the Drill Hall which is held by the Camden Historical Society, and I can confirm that it is Thompson's work. It is mistakenly listed as the work of Sir John Sulman.

Onslow Thomson played a decisive role in the raising of the Camden Squadron of NSW mounted rifles. Starting at the rank of Lieutenant in 1892, he was promoted to Captain in 1895, enlisting recruits from the estate – Elizabeth's sons, Jack and Arthur and from the workforce, young Herb English, Bill Hawkey, John Veness and Alf Dowle.

Members of the Camden unit in camp at Rookwood in 1899. L to R. Back row: Alf Sharp, Alf Dowle, JB Huthnance, R Ferris, W Nethery, C New, H English, ? Stanton, J Gillespie, W Gunn.

"It finished up that all the regiment was employed by the Estate and our masters was our commanders" said Herb.

Every Tuesday night they met at the showground and learned to drill, to box and to fight with fists as well as with rifles. They were given wooden rifles with collapsible bayonets, some of which were rediscovered during Camden's more recent building operations.

Herb described himself as a "big useful fellow who could ride well". Military officers came from Sydney to put the men through their paces and with rigorous training they became the unbeatable A Company – " the best riders and the largest and heaviest men."

Herb described the opening night of the Drill Hall – an occasion of elaborate feasting and carousing which lasted for three days. The Drill Hall has since become the Camden Show Society's Agricultural Hall.

When World War 1 began and Onslow Thompson was requisitioned to fight overseas, he gave final instructions to Herb, and left him a parting present of his board and all his drawing implements.

At the time of our interview, Herb still had all these treasures. Deeply moved by the whole thing, he said that none of the boys really knew what was there, only he, Herbert realised the great value of the gift he had been given.

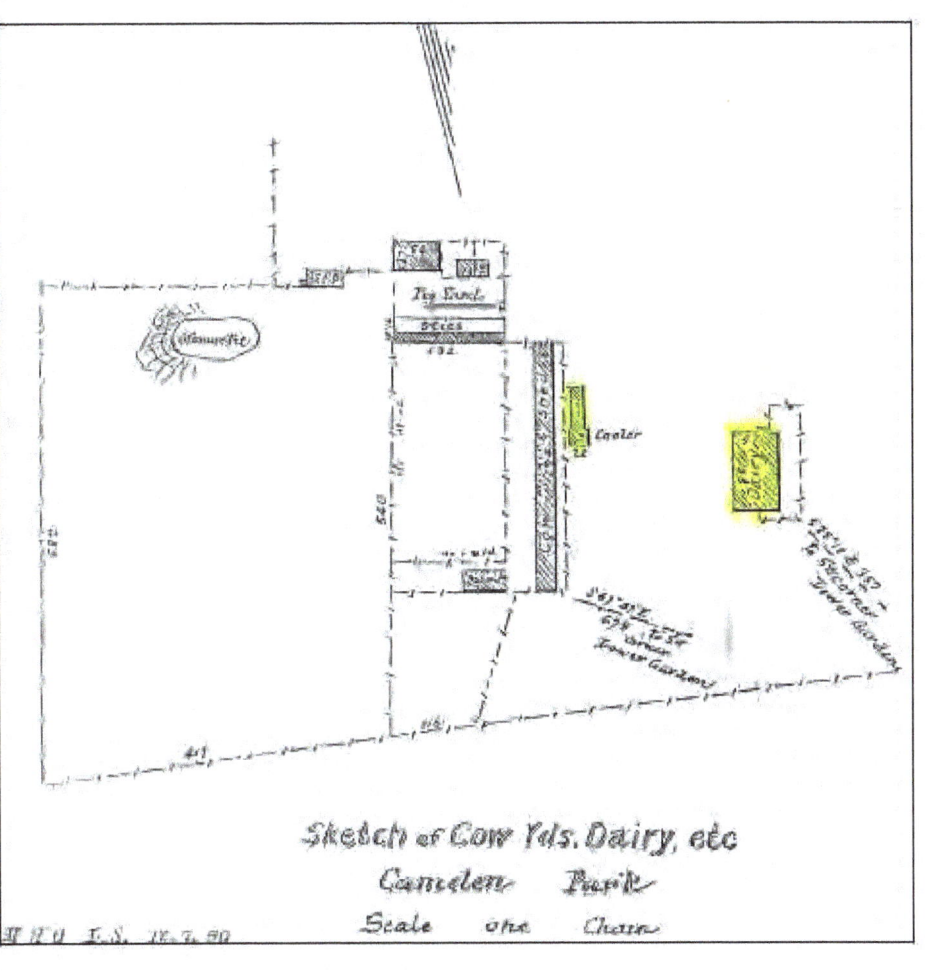

Plan of the Old Dairy Complex drawn by Harry Hamilton Onslow (see p. 314)

4

There was an undeniable grace about Onslow Thompson. He held a respectedly high position in farming, business circles. He was on the Board of CSR and the Commercial Banking Co. of Sydney. He was chairman of the Camden AH&I Society and, as a lay preacher he officiated at local church services. Seeking nothing for himself, every spare penny of his wages went to help his sisters in England. While there, he had helped to tutor Elizabeth's younger children, particularly in Latin.

Of his surviving brothers, the elder, Sedgeley died at sea in 1904, while the forementioned Iver managed Camden Park's outstations, Richlands and later St. Clair. Iver married and eventually retired to his own property – Maryvale in the Hunter Valley.

As a Captain of the mounted rifles, Onslow was acting Adjutant to Colonel Lasseter and part of the select detachment which travelled to England in 1897 to take part in the Queen's Jubilee Celebrations.

Colonel Lasseter gave the following description to the British press:

> "I command men who are probably as well disciplined as any in the British Army, and they can ride and shoot to perfection. Their selection is as a result of a keen competition at home. We bring our own horses, which are

bay and brown thoroughbreds, and lighter than the mounts in England. Our expedition is to cost £5,000 of which £4,500 has been subscribed by the regiment itself and £500 given by our government. The men have sacrificed their employments for the magnificent wage of 1s 9d per day, so that this is to be no feather-bed business with them. They are a good average lot. The tallest man is 6ft 3.5in. high. All are as hard as nails, and carry not an ounce of superfluous flesh; and I am confident that they will give a good account of themselves, no matter what difficulties they encounter."

While in England Onslow spent time training with the Scots Greys. He remained Adjutant to Col. Lasseter for some years after   return to Australia but he did not go to the Boer War (1899 – 1902) as did Elizabeth's sons.

He had his own war to fight with the mitigation of the worst drought to ever affect eastern Australia (1902 – 03) a drought which brought the district to its knees and Sydney's water supply at Prospect Reservoir to a trickle.

Generating Station, Menangle

So great was the problem that the government took drastic action, tapping into the Nepean River at Menangle, and building a large pumping station to direct water to the Main Canal, some distance away, from thence to flow by gravity the sixty four kilometres to Prospect.

It was to be a temporary measure until the dams were built. It must be remembered that the rest of Sydney's water supply – the Upper Nepean dams – were still on the drawing board. Cataract, the first of the four dams was not complete until 1907.

All the Plant for the Menangle pumping station was imported at great expense from Britain, and housed in a large brick building.

The canal itself had been in operation since the 1880s and a large volume of water had been impounded at Menangle where the Dept. of Public Works had constructed a weir near the railway bridge.

The first instance of falling water levels had been in 1901 when Onslow Thompson learned from the Railway Commissioners that the holding tanks, which also provided water for Camden Park's butter factory, were to be removed.

With his usual diplomacy he persuaded them to allow him extra time to replace this supply.

Elizabeth Onslow's eldest son, James William, had been pumping water for his newly built family home, Gilbulla from a famously deep area of the river known as Black Hole.

Gilbulla was built on land owned by Camden Park Estate, so, foreseeing the capabilities of a joint effort, Onslow purchased Gilbulla's boiler and pump and set about designing and building an overhead 8,000 gallon tank on high ground near the river.

Gilbulla

Menangle Water Tank (drawing by Annette)

With the combined skill of several workmen and master builder James English, he had the project completed within weeks, delivering water by gravity through pipes and channels to both the butter factory and Gilbulla.

This amazing structure is still there today beside the M5 motorway. It raises a lot of questions from passing motorists curious about the roofed structure on stilts. It is, I think, a splendid memorial to the early days of Menangle and the part it played in the local water supply.

By comparison the elaborate and expensive Government pumping station, built to supply Sydney water, started operating in 1903 just as rain began to fall. The project was abandoned and machinery was taken for use elsewhere.

Never letting an opportunity go by, Onslow Thompson purchased the building for £35 and made good use of the bricks and roofing-iron on other parts of the estate.

5

The green allure of the Cowpastures which had brought the early cattle and settlers to the area had dominated Onslow's first decade. It was deceptive. The turn of the century showed another face and the welcome rain of 1903 gave little relief from the spectre of drought which hovered over the new century.

The abundant rain of the nineties was now replaced by short, sharp showers and long dry periods – periods of extreme heat and cold.

In July there was even "a little snow" in Camden. Then frost delayed the spring and in September came three very hot days when everything dried up. There were thunderstorms, but no prolonged rain to fill the waterholes.

Added to this were areas of bushland where fires had broken out. A section of the Razorback range, known as Maher's Bush, was being cleared for firewood. A well which had been opened there to provide water, turned salty, and two

Timber cut from Maher's Bush and stacked at Menangle

newly dug dams waited in vain for rain.

Drinking water was carted daily from Menangle for the twenty men and their horses working there. 200 tons of wood a week was being brought to Menangle.

By late 1902 the river had almost ceased running. Notices were posted in Camden, Campbelltown and Liverpool that water might have to be cut off. Gravel for garden paths could now be collected from the dry Menangle creek-beds, while roads around just ground to dust which blew away.

In April 1902, Onslow was hand feeding young cattle mainly on straw and molasses. Feeding stalls had been built at the Farm and in the Racecourse paddock. He found this method less wasteful and the cattle did so much better.

Racecourse Feeding Shed 1902

There was not a blade of grass on the place.

The Racecourse dam was the last to hold out. Every other dam on the place had dried up, bar Long Pond and Spectacle which were reserved for the garden.

The Long Range Forecaster, Mr. Russell, had a 19 year cycle theory. Onslow cited the drought of 1862 when there was some rain in January and not another drop until the end of December. The total for the year was 15 inches, but this had followed a year of heavy flooding and was itself followed by 18 good years with the exception of 1865.

Now in 1902 cattle continued to die, particularly the older and younger animals. Onslow's feed bill was enormous. By August he reckoned £7,000 worth of fodder comprising Hay, Chaff, pollard, oil cake, molasses and rye had been bought, his object being to save the herd at all costs.

There were other problems. Rats, whose fleas were the vectors of the Bubonic Plague then raging in Sydney, infested the homestead cellars where the fortified wine was stored. Much had to be cleared and rebuilt.

The old winery itself in the vineyard to the south of the Big House, was in a parlous state. Onslow feared that if not carefully dismantled, it would fall, breaking all the precious timber. "The roof" he wrote "has slipped over two feet, and all the floor is unsafe, a good deal of it having fallen into the vaults below Taking down the roof would not interfere with the lower portion and it could be rebuilt again." He added: "A strong westerly might blow the whole thing over."

Two aspects of Camden Park Winery

It wasn't rebuilt. Wine making had long ceased and the vineyard turned to table grapes where the remains of the vaults are still evident.

The market was turning to fruit production. Camden Park orchard had won the state prize in the 1890s. At the request of the Central Cumberland Fruit growers, Camden Park and the Farmers' Co-op opened a fruit selling branch in 1902. This at least was a positive step, but everything else in those years was a struggle.

One senses that the grim path to World War One was being paved by disasters.

Milk and butter were still being produced but thanks to the drought, even the Mounted Rifles statewide gave up attending encampments.

With no relief in sight, Onslow finished the Company Report for 1907 with the following words:

> I regret to have to state that the prospects as far as the immediate future is concerned, could hardly look less bright. The whole district is in a deplorable state, almost denuded of livestock, with no grass and no water.
>
> For miles around the country resembles a desert. It will take a succession of favourable years to restore the district to the condition it was in seven years ago – before the 1902-3 drought.
>
> The river is dry from Menangle Bridge to some miles below Camden, with the exception of a few small isolated holes, but fortunately there is still a fair supply both at the Farm and Orchard pumps.

Onslow faced all these trials with equanimity. He had a practical answer to most things, but one wonders if the eventual outbreak of war might have stirred action in a spirit which felt it had little else to live for.

6

Onslow Thompson never married. He remained a servant to the family and, in his correspondence, he always addressed Elizabeth as "Mrs. Onslow".

I have no doubt that she preferred to keep it that way, even to the point that Thompson's military rank should not exceed that of her eldest son, James William.

She was proud of her sons and their peace-keeping abilities as young officers. That any of them might perish in war seemed out of the question, but then she was not to experience the distress of World War 1. While on a visit to London in 1911, she died of heart failure and was buried at Sendgrove cemetery, her grave marked by a tall Celtic Cross.

Rumour has it that Onslow might have married Sibella. They were certainly fond of each other and Onslow's gift of a beautiful Retriever Spaniel named "Link" for the sake of family togetherness, was very close to Sib's heart.

Sibella with dogs, Laddie, Link and Pansi

Sib meanwhile worked tirelessly for women's rights. For some years she had been writing, editing and preparing the family history, work she had inherited from her grandfather, James Macarthur and her mother Elizabeth, which would now be published as war began.

Onslow discussed the careers of all Elizabeth's sons. Jack, he thought should definitely be a farmer, while his elder brother James William would of course be the family "figure head", having little time or taste for farm work. George, who had more public concerns would become Mayor of Camden, a good soldier and farm manager. William adopted a military role, and joined the British Army, while Arthur, whose Boer War experience made him detest army life, settled for farm management and business, and he too became Mayor of Camden.

In 1903 Onslow Thompson was promoted to Major in command of the 2nd Australian Light Horse. Noted for his conviviality and preference for dining with the men rather than partaking of the lavish feasts of his fellow officers, Onslow's popularity was recalled in a letter from the Warrant Officer of his regiment at the time of his resignation in August 1913: "We feel that in your leaving us a tremendous gap has been made in the Corps. It has been our privilege to serve under an able soldier and gentleman."

When World War I broke out, Onslow Thompson aged 49, enlisted and given the rank of Lieut. Colonel, was placed in command of the 4th Infantry Battalion. This must have seemed a come-down for a cavalryman, but Onslow's answer to his troops rings famously:
"If is is good enough for me to walk, let it be good enough for you."

Horses would not be needed where they were going.

So they set out with the first Expeditionary Force on 28 October 1914, embarking at Sydney on His Majesty's Australian Troopship "Euripides," joining the rest of the Force at Albany and after some training and conditioning time in Egypt- they crossed to the Dardanelles in April 1915 arriving amidst the chaos on the Gallipoli Peninsula.

One may wonder if coming from Australia in a ship named after Greece's great tragic playright "Euripides" might have boded disaster. Rumour has it that a wicked trick resulted in the slaughter of many gallant men.

Our heroes took their place in the scheme of things and on 26 April 1915, when a message was passed down the line for the battalion to attack and capture the guns in front, they proceeded to a dangerous position close to the Turkish lines.

They were on the ridges of the 400 Plateau at Lone Pine, where trenches had been dug. General Bridges who had found the trenches too shallow ordered the lines to be straightened and dug in, but his orders were vague. Battalions under the illusion that an advance was being made, moved forward and, as they did so, the Turks opened fire.

It was in the midst of this mess that Onslow, leading his men was shot. I leave the closing lines to Lieutenant R.J.A. Massie who was with Onslow when he died.

> *"It was a great shock when he was killed. He and a few more of us got out in front and when the remainder were driven back by shrapnel we became isolated. It was when we were withdrawing from this position that he was shot in the head and died instantaneously. I was with him and he never moved again after he went down..*
>
> *He behaved in the most gallant manner during the attack, personally leading us with rifle and bayonet. He was the last to withdraw and it was probably this which cost him his life. His death was a great grief to us all. He was loved and respected by all and there was no man in the regiment who would not have done anything at all for him.*

For two weeks his body lay exposed there, it being too dangerous to collect it for burial which finally took place on 11 May.

> *"He was buried at night amid gun fire. The service was conducted by the Padre and the funeral was attended by all the officers who could be spared from the trenches."*

7

Postscript

Onslow Thompson is commemorated by a plaque in St. Illtud's Church, Pembury in his home country, Wales. His name is on the Roll of Honour in St. John's, Camden, but in this district there is little to mark the passing of a great man who did so much for the place.

There is however a silent tribute in the many old farms and barns still around with rusting roofs – there are the orchard cottages and at Menangle particularly the mighty roofed tank on stilts which still attracts attention. There is the Camden Agricultural Hall, and the noble Corn and Implement shed (now called the Granary) at Belgenny. And until recently, the re-designed and re-built Creamery at Mt. Hunter.

One might say, as was said more famously in another place – "If you seek a monument, look around."

Astley John Onslow Thompson

CAMDEN HISTORY

Journal of the Camden Historical Society Inc

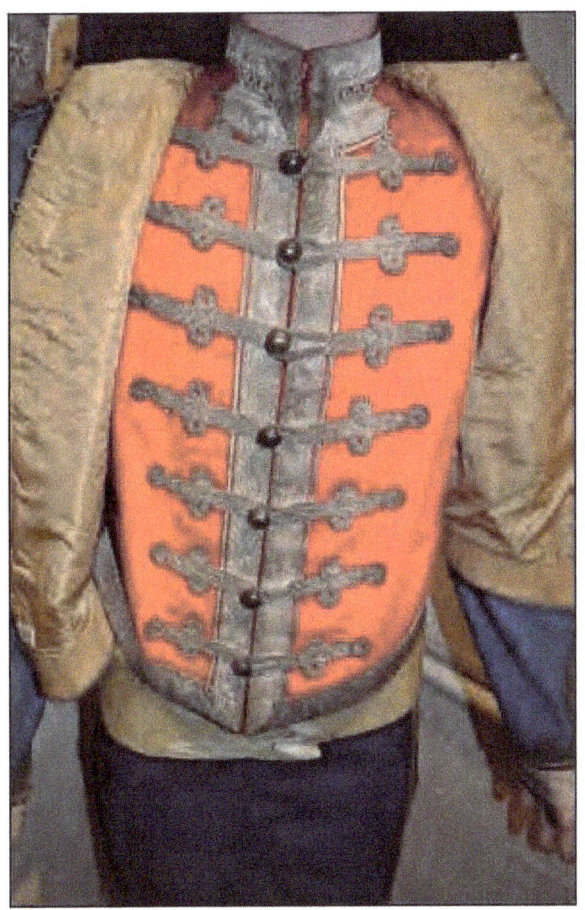

September 2015 Volume 3 Number 10

CAMDEN HISTORY
Journal of the Camden Historical Society Inc.
ISSN 1445-1549
Editor: Dr Ian Willis

Management Committee
President: Bob Lester
Vice Presidents: Ian Willis, Rene Rem
Secretary: Lee Stratton
Treasurer: Dawn Williams
Immediate Past President: John Wrigley OAM
General Committee: Sharon Greene   Stephanie Trenfield
                     Roslyn Tildsley   Rene Rem
                     Cathey Shepherd   Robert Wheeler

Honorary Auditor:
Honorary Solicitors: Bowring, Macaulay and Barrett

Society contact:
P.O. Box 566, Camden, NSW 2570. Online <http://www.camdenhistory.org.au>

Meetings
Meetings are held at 7.30 p.m. on the second Wednesday of the month except in January. They are held in the museum. Visitors are always welcome.

Museum
The museum is located at 40 John Street, Camden, phone 4655 3400 or 46559210. It is open Thursday to Sunday 11 a.m. to 4 p.m., except at Christmas. Visits by schools and groups are encouraged. Please contact the museum to make arrangements. Entry is free.

Camden History, Journal of the Camden Historical Society Inc
The journal is published in March and September each year. The editor would be pleased to receive articles broadly covering the history of the Camden district . Correspondence can be sent to the society's postal address. The views expressed in the articles are solely those of the authors and not necessarily endorsed by the society.

Donations
Donations made to the society are tax deductible. The accredited value of objects donated to the society are eligible for tax deduction.

Cover   Waistcoat for Madras Cavalry Uniform

CAMDEN HISTORY
Journal of the Camden Historical Society Inc.

September 2015 Volume 3 Number 10

Contents

Romani convicts and Camden connections Christine Yeats	333
The Faces In The Street Donald Howard	338
An Admiral's Wife In Camden Peter McCall	351
The Telephone Exchange – Werombi Dawn Williams	358
2nd Madras Cavalry Uniform Assessment of Significance Collection Item No. 1970.264 Janice Johnson, Margaret Wheeler and Julie Wrigley	361
President's Report 2014 – 2015 Bob Lester	366

Romani convicts and Camden connections

Christine Yeats

"Why there are no Gipsies in Australia", John Plummer's 1881 article, argued that:

> "...Australia is not a country wither they care to emigrate. To them it offers no inducements superior to those possessed by European climes; moreover they would become severed, as it were, from the main body of the gipsy nation, a contingency which they dread as the harbinger of their general disappearance from the face of the earth."[1]

Plummer was ignoring the Romani men and women from the UK transported to the Australian colonies as convicts.[2] No doubt this group was largely forgotten in the post transportation era, with its concerns about the stain of convictism. Contrary to Plummer's expectations, Romani did come to Australia and today the population could be as much as 25,000, spread across villages, towns and cities.[3] Long time residents of The Oaks and Camden for example, remember the Romani families living there in the 1940s and into the 1960s.[4]

There are no exact figures on the number of Romani convicts. English Romani scholar Dr Ian Hancock makes reference to the transportation of Romani to the colonies in *The Pariah Syndrome*. He states that the Romani word for magistrate is 'the transporter', suggesting that transportation was well known and affected more than just a few individuals or families in England.[5] Given the long history of persecution of the Romani in England, beginning with the 1530 'Egyptians Act', it is likely that word was in use for many centuries. The purpose of that legislation was to expel 'Gypsies' and ban their immigration. 'Gypsies' were accused of robbery and deception (principally through fortune telling) and given sixteen days to leave the country, their goods and properties being confiscated in the process. The reference to 'Egyptians', and its derivative 'gypsies', stemmed from the mistaken belief that they came from Egypt. In fact their origins can be traced back to India.

Cheryl Brandner discusses the English Romani convicts she identified in her 1997 MA thesis *A History of Romanis (Gypsies) in Australia*. Brandner highlighted the challenges in identifying convicts with Romani ancestry. She makes the point that while annotations such as 'gipsy' or 'gypsy' in the convict records offer some indication of Romani ancestry; they may simply reflect an official's assessment or prejudice.[6] Nevertheless, such annotations are important and, when considered in conjunction with reference to tradi-

Brownlow Hill homestead in the 1870s built on Alexander Macleay's grant of 1827. Additions to the house in 1834 are attributed to colonial architect John Verge. The property was leased by Downes family in 1859.

tional Romani occupations and names, provide strong evidence supporting Romani ancestry.

To date, the number of Romani convicts transported to NSW from England who have been identified using official sources, newspapers and family histories, is currently 100. As 80,000 convicts were transported to NSW between 1788 and 1842 this represents only 0.125%. It is likely that appreciably more English Romani convicts were transported to NSW over the period. In most cases however, their Romani ancestry is not noted in the records. Despite this, references to Romani ancestry can sometimes be found in other records and newspapers, which are now accessible as a result of large scale digitisation projects in Australia and the UK.

Despite the small number trends are emerging. Only a handful of Romani women were transported. There are several examples of brothers transported together. Septimus and Obadiah Davis, with their links to Camden, are one such example. The first clue to their Romani origin is their occupation of 'basketmaker', a traditional Romani trade, which was recorded on their Convict Indents. The newspaper account of their trial provides the next clue. The case was heard on 9 January 1827 at the Wiltshire (Devizes) Quarter Sessions. Described as gypsies, they were charged on seven different indictments with stealing seven asses, the property of seven different individuals in various counties. Despite the seven charges they were only tried on two indictments. They were found guilty of both offences and received separate sentences of seven years and one month.[7] Their 18 year old companion William Townsend, also described as a gypsy, received the same sentence but instead of NSW, he was transported to Bermuda in 1828.[8]

The Davis brothers were transported on the *Marquis of Hastings*, which arrived in Sydney on 31 July 1827. The Convict Indents record where they were assigned — the 21 year old Septimus to Alexander McLeay and his 20 year old brother Obadiah to David Maziere. By 1828 Septimus was working for George McLeay at Camden, probably at the Brownlow Hill estate, owned by George's father the Colonial Secretary Alexander McLeay. Obadiah was part of George Wyndham's household at Dalwood, Luskintyre.

From 1828 the brothers' history took very different paths. Septimus remained in the Camden area until his death in 1875 aged 67. He received a Ticket of Leave in 1832. Two years later he received his Certificate of Freedom, which confirmed that he had served his sentence. He received permission to marry the 18 year old convict Catherine Kilmurry in 1836. Despite receiving the necessary permission, the wedding did not go ahead. Catherine received permission to marry on five separate occasions before marrying John Barrett in 1837. Septimus eventually married Ann Newton in 1851.

On 7 February 1833 Obadiah Davis was arraigned in the Supreme Court before Justice Dowling on a charge of burglary to which he pleaded guilty. According to the *Sydney Herald* of 11 February 1833

> "although cautioned by the learned Judge, [he] persisted in the plea. When judgment of death was recorded against him, the Attorney General informed the Court that he had received an excellent character from his late master, Captain Anley. His Honor observed, that such being the case, he should make as strong a recommendation to the proper quarter as the circumstances of the case would admit."

Obadiah's death sentence was commuted and he was sentenced to be transported to Norfolk Island for 10 years. Returned from Norfolk Island on 27 May 1840 he was charged with larceny and absconding from No. 3 Stockade in the Hunter. Then on 22 July he was apprehended after absconding from the Australian Agricultural Company.[9] He was brought to Sydney, placed in Hyde Park Barracks and, after time on an Iron Gang, he was moved to the Maitland Stockade.[10]

Despite these setbacks Obadiah received a Certificate of Freedom in 1842. Dated 16 January 1842, it bears the annotation "Was transported to Norfolk Island 7 February 1833 by the Supreme Court Sydney for a burglary". Obadiah eventually settled at Camden and married assisted immigrant Mary Langridge at Cobbitty in 1844. Mary and her family were living at Camden. According to Davis family history Obadiah and Mary remained in Camden for some years before moving to Young, where Obadiah died in 1867.

William Davis, older brother to Obadiah and Septimus, was transported to NSW on the *Recovery*. Arriving on 25 February 1836 he had a life sentence, having been convicted of horse stealing at the Wiltshire Assizes held at Devizes. Interestingly, there were six other Romani convicts under life sentences on the same ship, including the Lee and Boss brothers. The Convict Indent notes William's relationship to Septimus and Obadiah and that he was married with five children, two males and three females. His occupation is shown as 'tinman and basket maker'. 'Tinman' is another occupation closely identified with the Romani. William received a Ticket of leave in 1844, allowing him to remain in the Camden district. This was altered to Paterson in 1848 and in 1849 he received a Conditional pardon. Whether his wife and family joined him in NSW is yet to be determined.

The history of the three Davis Romani convicts did not differ markedly from others transported to NSW, despite Obadiah's recidivism. Following his marriage he appeared to settle into family life and stay out of trouble. Septimus was apparently a model convict. William's life after receiving his Conditional pardon has proven more difficult to trace but his absence from the records suggests he did not reoffend. While Romani convicts may have been largely forgotten, stories of 'gypsies' offering to tell the fortunes of travellers stopped on the Razorback Mountain, is an enduring twentieth century anecdote, harking back to the sixteenth century 'Egyptians Act'. Convicts or fortune tellers, Australia's Romani are a fascinating part of our shared history.

Christine Yeats
Senior Vice President
Royal Australian Historical Society

Footnotes

[1] John Plummer, "Why there are no Gipsies in Australia", *Victorian Review*, 1 April 1881, 728-34 at 734.
[2] The word 'Romani' or 'Rom' comes from the Sanskrit *'domb'a*, meaning 'a man from a...group who were musicians'.
[3] Estimates vary between 5,000 and 25,000.
[4] Elva McDonald and Kevin, Wintle "Gypsies at the Oaks", *The Oaks Histori-*

cal Society Newsletter, September 2013

[5] Ian Hancock, *The Pariah Syndrome* (Ann Arbor, Karoma Publishers Inc, 1987), 95-96.

[6] Cheryl Brandner, *A History of Romanies (Gypsies) in Australia*, MA Thesis, La Trobe, 1997 p. 46

[7] *Devizes and Wiltshire Gazette* of 18 January 1827.

[8] Convict Prison Hulks: *Registers and Letter Books*; Class: HO9; Piece: 8 (Between 1824 and 1863, the British Government shipped over 9,000 convicts to Bermuda to build the Dockyard.)

[9] *NSW Government Gazette*, 1840.

[10] Newcastle *Gaol Description and Entrance Books, 1840.*

The Faces In The Street

Donald Howard

A picture of local identities against the background of Camden's "CBD"[1] in the early 40's

In 1940's Camden it was neither the best of times nor the worst of times – but "the times they were a-changing". Time itself, for the town was set in stone: Pansy left punctually at 5 past 7 (or was it 5 to?) and twice daily a cavalcade of trucks, utilities and spring carts converged on the milk depot at the end of Argyle Street fixing a timetable which remained constant through months, seasons and years.

Tuesday Sale Day, and Friday night and Saturday morning shopping were the only events that packed our town. The kerb was then lined with cars and a sulky or two, the three cafes roared with business and even those who had no need to shop were happy meeting family and friends.

Camden had clawed its way out of depression; war casualties had so far been light; everyone knew his or her place. As a young Methodist I paid my first visit to St. John's Rectory to deliver a monthly account from Whiteman's store. An august figure opened the door, I smiled and asked, "Mr. Paul?" The terse reply (without any smile) was, "*Rector* Paul!" I thought, "How strange these Anglicans and their ways!"

Years later the words of ex-premier John Fahey brought the era to mind. Unable to become an articled clerk in Camden because he was a Roman Catholic, he said: "It was a WASP town and the church on the hill declared this for all to see."

His observation brought back how one foggy morning I stopped my bike on top of the Macquarie Grove hill to view a scene beyond one's imagination: dense fog blotting out the valley with one visible landmark– St. John's steeple and roof.

Descending the Grove hill at breakneck speed each morning we made first contact with our pleasant little town[2] (pop. 3000) -- the sound not of the anvil chorus but an anvil solo emanating from the local "smithy". This was set deeply back on the northern side of Elizabeth Street towards Exeter Street. We clearly picked up the sound from Mr. Thomas Burford's striking as we panted up the sharp rise from the Grove Bridge.[3]

Today's blacksmith's shop – where one exists – is comparatively clinical: a hand-turned forge boosts the heat, the muffled roar of the mighty bellows is stilled, horseshoeing is usually the task of the farrier: a virtually soundless and prosaic performance claims little attention.

As our equivalent of the village blacksmith plied his trade, several horses would be tethered as they waited in the shade of a few giant eucalypts awaiting their turn, their owners puffing a pipe or two. They passed the time away with some gossip, while watching a master of his craft.

Longfellow described it faithfully in *The Village Blacksmith*...

I learned the rudiments of blacksmithing at Hawkesbury Agricultural College and later worked in the blacksmith's shop on the farm where my mother was born, on properties large and small around Australia. No matter where it was, one felt immediately at home in each place with its bellows, forge and anvil. Today a photo of the Cobbitty smithy is hanging in the Heber Chapel and is typical of a once familiar and enchanting sight.

Elizabeth Street in those days presented a contrast with today's built up area. While the southern side until a few years ago was much the same as in the 40's, little development had occurred on the opposite side. There was quite a bit of bush as far as the railway station, except for Laurie Taplin's busy mechanical workshop and retreading business.[4]

Mass destruction of surplus railway property when the line was closed in the 60's was a great loss. Camden's station was a reminder of a past closely woven into the town's fabric; preservation of Elderslie and Kirkham stops, each with a sign about as large as the platform, would be of historic interest today.

Narellan Station, complete with the ubiquitous Avery platform scales (where I weighed myself each Monday while en route to school), stood at the end of a tree-lined lane, resembling something out of a Hornby train catalogue.

Traffic lining the short length of Station Street at Camden was busier with vehicles (horse and motor) than it is today. Parcel traffic was reasonably heavy and rail service efficient. Jack Blattman of the well-known local family was junior porter until he enlisted in the RAAF.

A ramp led to the platform which, as was the custom in those days, was covered with a neat fine pale gravel surface, carefully raked by Jack between trains. Another Jack, Jack Hurst of Colin Clark's pharmacy, and I would generally ride down together to collect any parcels that had arrived mid-morning.

St John's Church at the top of John Street in the 1920s. The church dominated the town from the top of the hill, just like an English style village that poets and journalists wrote about when they visited the town.

"FCW CMDN" was all the identification I needed for Whiteman's goods which could generally be placed on the handlebars of my bike. On some days the firm's spring cart was needed, while Jack's bike had a basket as he also delivered household orders.

Jack and I would race to the station, speed up the ramp to finish with a "wheely" (in today's terms) on the gravel, drawing the ire of the junior porter. At least, that was the plan.

For some reason on one day I did not ride down. The next morning as I swept Whiteman's path, what appeared to be a young Negro was emulating my efforts at the pharmacy. When he turned and waved, closer examination revealed Jack! The day before he had torn up the ramp as usual, mis-timing with the brake to hurtle off the platform and smash his face on the coarse gravel between the tracks. The only pleasing factor was that no train pulled in.

He picked himself up, then his bike, scrambled onto the platform and rode up Argyle Street to arrive at the pharmacy with his face literally a bloodied pulp. Colin Clark magnanimously gave him the day off and he rode home. No ambulance; no X-ray: (neither facility existed); no needles, no doctor. It was "Home Jack! And don't spare the cycle!" Today a minor facial scar is Jack's sole memento of a solid scab from crown to chin, with two ears thrown in for good measure.

An aside: station and post masters were two of the leading figures in any country town until at least the end of the 50's. I remember the biography of a leading British political figure, daughter of the station master in a small English town, his uniform richly braided to show his rank. She recalled how her father was treated with utmost respect by the citizenry irrespective of social status. (It also so happened that as a keen Whig he appealed to the prevailing sentiment of his fellow townsfolk.)

From the corner of Station Street, there was only minor development towards Argyle Street in what was to all effects a large grassy paddock. Mr. and Mrs. Catt, English migrants who I think had a family connection with those of similar name in Burragorang Valley, conducted a steam laundry. I have no recollection of "Crick's Corner".

Leading to the depot was an old cottage used by one of the two undertakers, Mr. Peters. The house is still used for the same purpose. The large railway property which held the goods shed, coal loading facilities and the necessary track network lay behind and fronted Edward Street.

The second undertaker, Mr. Percy Butler and his son Gordon, used the rear of their home in Broughton Street to make their coffins. When a funeral was held, all traffic was held up while the undertaker led his cortege clenching the brim of his top hat before him – and all this in what was then the Hume highway!

When a funeral service took place in St. John's, the sexton, Mr. Prosser, who walked with the aid of a crutch, would climb up John Street to the church and toll the bell for the number of years which the dead person had lived. When in the street I would, as most others did, count the chimes. It was sobering at times when only a few were sounded.

While the scene so far has on the whole been quite placid, Argyle Street held the stage with a vigorous and never-changing performance. Morning by morning and again each afternoon a long and lively cavalcade streamed in two directions to the life-centre of town, the MILK DEPOT! Here the Dairy Farmers' Co-operative was a busy enterprise as cans clanged, steam hissed, milk was poured and measured, with voices at full pitch if they wanted to be heard. The smooth but hectic task proceeded smoothly to its conclusion after a continuous 3-hour performance.

Trucks, utilities and a few horse-drawn spring carts queued across the railway line which crossed the street slowly but surely edging towards their goal. Many, such as the drivers from the Holz Brothers, Moffatt and McIntosh properties from Cobbitty, later took their lists, parking outside FCW and Sons in order to collect their orders, dropping them with the empty cans on their way home.

There was Angus Gunn from Denbigh (not the full five feet but still the "full quid"), Albert Hore, Jack Moffitt and others. Frank Thorn, father of Keith who with his wife Joy later conducted Cobbitty P.O.) was built along the lines of a heavyweight wrestler. I greeted each by name – "Mister" plus the surname – no undue familiarity in those days.

They would collect bread, meat, hardware and grocery items, sometimes popping into the railway parcels office or goods shed, leaving the orders when they dropped the empty cans on their way home.

Last call in hot weather was the depot once again. Here activity had slackened or come to a halt as they collected the ice. This was covered with empty cornbags to lessen melting from the hot sun.

 Bread was ready in heaps at Stuckey Brothers as they went up the lane (no longer existing) at the side. Groceries came mainly from Whiteman's or Clifton Brothers, but there were often orders from Furner Brothers hardware store with its much bigger range. This even included hand-made circular rain tanks from the yard where many now park their cars.

Shopping for hardware at Furner's was vastly different from popping into Mitre 10. Should one want five bolts of a certain type and seven of another, one bought five or seven bolts, not a plastic bag (still waiting to be invented). And instead of grabbing a bag which contained the needed items, the salesman (often Mr. Percy Furner himself) would put down his pipe, leave his desk and attend to one's needs.

There would be no rush: first, an exchange of greetings, followed by a query on the health and welfare of one's family, the obligatory mention of the weather, a discussion about the size of the required items, frequently causing Mr. Furner to move the ladder (FCW's and most other shops also had them), place it against the shelves and climb slowly up knowing exactly where to look.

Descending, he would then place them on the counter for inspection, fill in the docket, take the money and place it in the till, hand over the change, then wrap the item. In what is now the parking area behind the present Bloom's

Pharmacy, a Mr. Rowley Gordon, a skilled English tradesman, made circular corrugated iron tanks from flat sheets of galvanized iron. He fed these through a giant hand-operated "mangle" which gave the curve and corrugations. One of the many trades which have passed into oblivion.

Mr. Furner was one of Camden's fixtures. Reminiscing with his daughter Audrey before her death a few years ago, she recalled how nervous she and her mother would be after closing time for five nights a week (and late on Fridays) as they knew the head of the house would be carrying the day's takings home in his cashbox. Who knew whether or not one of Camden's brigands might not accost him on the shaded paths of John Street or Menangle Road! Audrey said they didn't relax until he put the key in the lock.

This might be the place to comment on the dominance of Camden Methodism: Whitemans and Cliftons, plus Haffenden and Henderson at the southern end with a specialist grocery shop, were all Methodists; Stuckeys the bakers and Boardmans the butchers were the same, plus Mr. Sidman who owned the *Camden News* and Colin Clark the leading pharmacist. We had the "joint sewn up". It was, in effect, a "God-fearing town". An open air meeting at the intersection of Argyle and John Street with at least 20 voices would perform a quality program between several speakers of acceptable standard. *Abide With Me* was always the final hymn.

Turning right into Argyle Street from Elizabeth Street, the two Pinkerton brothers ran a tailoring business. When they returned from the war, they established a successful electrical appliance business. One of them at least reached fame as a lawn bowler. Then came Mr. Rupert Rofe's hairdressing salon where I received a haircut for sixpence. Tobacco sales were the mainstay in the barbering business in those days.

Moving south, the next place of note was Tait's Newsagency and Milk Bar. Mrs.Tait's son, Colin, a fine-looking man, was awaiting call-up for the RAAF Reserve. Sadly he was shot down over Europe. I cannot recall any of the other business houses before the Plough and Harrow Inn. The implements on the upstairs verandah are presumably the same ones displayed today.

A tailor established himself next door towards the close of the war. His name was Airds, but he came after I had left the town.

Alongside the tailor, Frank Whiteman, a cousin of Keith and Charlie and the "Sons" in F.C. Whiteman's General Store, had a stationery shop and a subagency for newspapers. His son Peter followed his father's footsteps as an organist. His father swept (an apt term) the music along at the Methodist

Argyle Street Camden looking in an easterly direction towards Sydney. The Anderson drinking fountain was moved to Macarthur Park and the Bank of New South Wales building was finished in 1938.

Church, the singing led by a proficient and enthusiastic choir. Some years after the death of his first wife, Frank married his assistant, Ida Smart, a highly successful exhibitor of jams and preserves in Camden Show.

Next came Britton's Pharmacy conducted by Mr. and Mrs. Ernie Britton, both qualified pharmacists. The contrast between the town's two pharmacists could not have been greater: on the opposite side was Colin Clark, the essence of conservatism, while "racy" well-described his counterpart. Customers in the Clark Pharmacy were dealt with in the customary manner like most chemist's shops; the Britten business was much noisier and bustling.

When I returned over 20 years ago, Mrs. Britten, who had survived her husband, asked me when I was acting rector, to bury her at St. John's. This was when she was moving to the central west where one or both of her twin sons lived. We discussed the days of 60 years ago and she lent towards me and asked quite frankly, "You knew that Ernie was a 'bit of a rogue,' didn't you?" I agreed. Although his reputation for so-called roguery was really due more to his manner and appearance (somewhat dashing and with a dark pencil-stripe moustache which seemed quite in keeping with his lively style), he was a mover and shaker of Camden's commercial life.

Next along was the Capitol Café conducted by two highly respected Greeks, the Cassimatis Brothers. Had not a fire destroyed the interior some years ago, we would today boast a classic "art deco" soda fountain – beautifully appointed and of classic design. Now it has become *Cafe Creme Della Crème*.

Both the Capitol Lane (now the Capitol Arcade) and the lane (were there two?) beside the Camden Inn have disappeared, but the façade of the hotel is virtually unchanged. My main recollection of the inn is when traffic came to a standstill late one afternoon as a large crowd (well, large for Camden any way) converged to see the first "Jeep" to hit "the ol' burg" – parked and placed under the eagle eye of a "Yankee doughboy".[5] Within a few weeks, jeeps and large US Army trucks rarely raised an eyebrow as they thundered through our quiet backwater.

This might be a convenient time to comment upon the attractive appearance of our main street in those days. A centre garden divided the two sides which had room for two lanes only: one for traffic and one for parking. The town gardener, Mr.Charlie Smart, worked consistently and (like the painters on the Harbour Bridge) realised that by the time he had finished it was time to start again at the beginning. Charlie maintained neat lawns and colourful flower beds the year round. As the Hume Highway still used the town, the time came to reduce the "nature strip" to its present width.

Now, you might (possibly!) recall that we have been moving down the western side of Argyle Street. For a long time Fuller Brothers ran a busy "fruit barrow" from a lane on the John Street side of the hotel. Then came the Rural and Wales banks, with the landmark of the Commercial Banking Company (now NAB) on the opposite corner.

Many an early Australian film will show the CBC, often with a line of sulkies and carts trotting up John Street. The last one was "Dad Rudd MP. *Gledswood* was the scene for quite a few, including the debut of "Chips" Rafferty.

Between the bank and the post office, where St. George Bank now has its premises, was D and M (or "DM"?) Maloney' Drapery. Owned by Miss Maloney it was managed by a Mr. Evans. A successful business, mainly because of strong Roman Catholic support, it always had a warm and friendly "feel" when one entered.

Camden Post Office was free of all the items which clutter the space today. Behind the polished timber counter was the "administrative department", with the Postmaster (Mr. McLeod) seated at his large desk. Mr. McLeod used to swim the year round at Little Sandy, along with Mr. Bensley (another Methodist!) who operated a large market garden at the foot of Chellaston

Street on the left hand side.

After the PO came the office of *The Camden News* where Mr. Michael Watts has his optometry practice. The newspaper was the quintessential example of an ultra-conservative country news sheet. I cannot recall a double column introduction or a large type headline. But it did provide a detailed account of local doings. Every prizewinner in the local show from the champion draught horse to the person entering the best pickles was there. My name and that of Reg Smart appeared as messenger boys when the Air Raid Precautions came into force early in 1942. Not a birth or death escaped notice.

When a Mr. Gibson started *The Camden Advertiser* in opposition, we saw what a real newspaper looked like. It was bright and breezy with a freshness in local news items quite foreign to the older publication. The owner established a wartime fund to supply every serviceman and woman from Camden with a regular supply of Christmas cake and other items. As a free paper, it enjoyed a wide circulation, but battled against a strong conservative opposition. Whiteman's store, for example, never advertised in it. The editor journeyed by train to Parramatta each week where it was printed, returning with several bundles of the edition that afternoon.

There might have been a shop or two between the paper and the Olympic Theatre (site of Treasures on Argyle). The theatre went out of operation a few years before the war and was let for the occasional private function.

Tildsley's Butchery did a brisk trade on the lower corner of Oxley Street which was largely residential. Today's butchery might be the only business operating on the same site with the same name apart from the hotels and the Commonwealth Bank.

Kelloway's Café, the third in the town, operated where Camden Photo Centre is established today. Mr. Kelloway was mayor for some years. Mrs. Kelloway was an accomplished musician and had her own band. My family told me how she played a piano on the back of a truck leading a large and appreciative crowd in Argyle Street singing patriotic songs on the night the war ended. Their son, I faintly remember, was a trumpeter and returned safely after being in a Japanese POW camp.

From then on, several private dwellings took over until the Crown Hotel. One served as a dental surgery for some time.

At the corner of Murray Street and the Cawdor Road stood Poole's blacksmithing and wheelwright business, undergoing several changes of ownership over the years.

There was only one enterprise conducted in Murray Street on the northern side. This was Matron Heise's maternity hospital, in a converted home. Turning the Argyle Street corner, quite a few former homes were altered to various businesses seeking space.

About the first was Alfie Ahrendfeldt's dry cleaning which he opened upon discharge from the army. He married Helen, daughter of Mr. and Mrs. Tom Holz, of Cobbitty, at about the same time. The steam press was on the old front verandah and I think the main part of the house was given over to the relatively recent real estate agency conducted by Mr. Keith Smart with the assistance of his father, Hiram.

Other businesses run from a house included a boot repair shop of a member of the Driscoll or Clissold family and a green grocery owned by Mr. Fred Betts. The latter sold produce in Cobbitty and other areas near town.

Clifton Brothers' grocery opposite the Post Office opened in modern premises shortly before the war. Mr. Wesley Clifton took it over after his brother, the other partner, died. It was more modern than the grocery department of Whitemans' store and functioned until the store took on its identity of Sinclairs.

The first corner with John Street was home to the Commonwealth Bank. It was a small building, possibly a brick house when it was built. The staff consisted of the manager, Mr. de Saxe, an accountant and a teller. At lunchtime (when I usually banked my weekly pay), one of the above two generally handled the transaction.

Crossing John Street stood Boardman's Butchery. Then under the control of the founder, under his son, Alan, and up to the time of the recent disposal of the business, by Noel with his enterprising prizewinning meat recipes. When a young man, Alan rode a side car with a large box of meat orders. The meat was not refrigerated but the rider almost was on frosty mornings.

Then came two shops, the first occupied by Mrs. Wilmington with one of those haberdasheries where ladies who like sewing, knitters and home dressmakers could usually find their needs met. The proprietress, renowned for her pleasant voice, often sang at church services and on social occasions.

Next door, travelling north, Jack Roberts ran a small grocery shop. His major clientele lived in the valley, so each week he loaded up his tourer and presumably stayed with one of his customers overnight. Later he closed the

Argyle Street with a northerly aspect and Elizabeth Street to the east c.1920. The businesses from the left of the image are the Plough and Harrow Hotel, Lewis McMinn Newsagency, Rupert Rofe Barber, James Pinkerton Tailer, chemist, Roy Holsworth's Star Garage and Royal Hotel on corner. (R Nixon)

shop and worked for Clifton Brothers.

Then came Stuckey Brothers and Whitemans, with Colin Clark's pharmacy next door. This was a somewhat multi-faceted business, two cupboard doors opening to reveal the charts and apparatus for spectacles. The proprietor was also an optometrist! After a lane was the FCW produce store. [6]

The Whiteman family owned all the property to Hill Street. First there was a butchery, then Charlie Butler's bicycle shop with Mr. Henning's jewellery business on the corner. "RAC" Adams, a former Australian champion pole-vaulter, had his solicitor's office upstairs. He was a large-than-life swash-buckling sort of character – best described as "Hail Fellow – Well Met!"

Unfortunately I cannot recall what was on the opposite corner of Hill Street, but the large building now occupied by a store selling women's clothing was Dunk's Motor Spare Parts Shop for about 40 years. Until it closed in the last decade, it always looked like a collection of junk, but the proprietor knew his stock and could unfailingly lay his hands on any part he needed for a sale.

The only building of substance I recall was the 2-storey gentleman's residence still standing and now occupied mainly by a Thai Restaurant. One day, the owner Mr. Charlie Boardman complained to the milkman about short measure. (All milk was delivered in bulk by horse-drawn cart with two tanks containing the milk. A hand-held measure was filled from the tap, carried into the home and poured into the customer's billy.)

When Charlie complained, the milkman advised him to keep an eye open after he left. Charlie did so and saw a well-nourished red-bellied black snake emerge from a ventilator in the foundation, gently lift the lid and drink to his heart's content. Next morning's drink was his last.

Along the street from the View Street corner was Redden's large garage. "Service Station" was not yet a familiar term, despite service being provided to every driver stopping at the bowser: tank filled, oil, water and air checked, windscreen cleaned – all free. Redden's business was followed by an engineering workshop with market gardens leading to the bridge over the Nepean River.

Chinese worked the gardens on the northern side leading to the bridge, while in later years at least, a local family worked the opposite property. Dick Nixon described how the head of the family made a coup from a suspect trotting bet, presumably at Menangle Park.

Apparently he put the takings in a tin, burying it in the garden. Unfortunately he died and left his treasure hidden "in the field" as in one of Jesus' parables. From the vantage point of an upstairs window at the milk depot, Dick watched for some time as each afternoon one or two of the family would systematically probe the soil with a sharp stake. When I asked whether they ever found it, he replied, "Well, one will never know."

And that was Camden, peopled with faces on the street which were all familiar to each of its citizens in the 1940's.

Donald Howard
Camden Historical Society
12 November 2014

References

1 As far as I am aware, the term "CBD" was then unknown, at least in Australia.
2 Houses and business premises had not yet been numbered. After all, most of us knew where everyone lived and where to shop for our needs
3 This took us past the "sewerage depot", the evidence of its function easily identified by the atmosphere. In winter we felt as if we were inhaling noxious gas on the

steep sprint; in summer the reaction was similar. It was largely a matter of indifference in the afternoon as we "powered" down the hill in contrast with "ploughing" up on the way to work.

4 This, as far as I can remember, might have been in Edward Street.

5 US soldiers were known as "Doughboys". Jack Davey, famous wireless announcer and comedian, composed and wrote a song of that name: *Mr.Doughboy. doncha know boy...* which became the signature tune for a radio quiz which he conducted for both Australian and US troops. The words varied with thenation and the arm of the service being featured, ie., Army, Navy, Air Force.

6 See the author's *The Hub of Camden*, published by the Historical Society and on sale in the museum. The book describes the store and the bakery.

An Admiral's Wife In Camden

Peter McCall

Tucked amongst the many thick volumes in the library at Camden Park House is a thin paper covered book. It is about the campaigns of the British Eighth Army in North Africa between 1941 and 1943.[1] The poor quality paper on which it is printed indicates the shortage of paper brought about by the war. Inside I found a letter. It was addressed to W. Macarthur-Onslow and dated 1st November 1944.

I knew W. Macarthur Onslow was the owner of Camden Park at that time, but nothing about the writer, Eva Keyes, who was writing from "Ginahgulla," Bellevue Road, Sydney. In the letter I was surprised to find that she had flown back from Bega on the afternoon of 30 October. It seemed unusual that it was possible to fly from Bega to Sydney during the war. Eva Keyes must have been a woman of some importance, especially as she thanks Mr Macarthur Onslow for taking her suitcase to Government House.

Further investigation revealed who Eva Keyes was. She was the wife of Roger, 1st Lord Keyes of Zeebrugge and Dover. He was famous as Admiral Roger Keyes who led the British attack on the German submarine base at Zeebrugge in Belgium in 1918. Fame of course is fleeting and his name is not well known today, but he would have been well known to people whose memory stretched back to World War One. He had also had a fairly high profile in the early years of World War Two as Director of Combined Operations (June 1940 to October 1941), where he was in charge of commando operations.

However, this did not explain Eva's link with Camden Park. It became necessary to follow the career of her husband after his resignation from Combined Operations. Keyes had been a "gung-ho" Director who had ruffled the feathers of the armed services heads with his plans for commando operations that ran roughshod over their plans and ideas. Churchill had supported him, but eventually let him go by reducing his position from Director to Advisor, a position that Keyes would not accept.

Speaking in the House of Commons on November 25th 1941 (quoted in *Combined Operations Command United We Conquer: Roger John Brownlow Keyes*). Keyes criticised the "brass hats of Whitehall" for "frustrating every worthwhile offensive action I have ever tried to make."[2] He continued to promote an aggressive approach to the war, not realising the political issues involved. He was put in charge of War Weapons Week, perhaps a suitable

post for a retired admiral (Keyes was approaching seventy), but that was not how he saw it. He wrote, "You cannot realise what I have been through in the last year- completely out of the war, my only value, apparently, being to induce people to invest in war savings." [3]

In January 1943 he was raised to the peerage as a Baron and continued his critical surveillance of the war effort from the House of Lords.
In July 1944 Lord and Lady Keyes left on a goodwill trip to New Zealand and Australia. They travelled via the USA and Canada. The trip was proposed by Brendan Bracken, British Minister of Information. [4]

By September they had reached Australia, arriving in Sydney on the 22nd. They were in Canberra from the 27th September and travelled back to Sydney on the 4th October. Here they separated; Lord Keyes travelled to Brisbane and then moved on to New Guinea, where he had been invited by the US General Douglas MacArthur to observe the preparations for the invasion of the Philippines. [5] Up to this point, Lady Keyes had acted as her husband's secretary. [6]

However, now she remained in Sydney, presumably as travelling in New Guinea in war time was seen as too dangerous for a woman of Lady Keyes' age (62) and position. She stayed at Government House.

During her time in Sydney she was involved in a number of activities, many of which were reported in the press. So on the 6th October she accompanied the NSW Governor and his wife (Lord and Lady Wakehurst) to observe a Victory Loan March through the streets of Sydney and commented on the fine marching of the W.A.A.A.F. (Women's Auxiliary Australian Air Force).[7] On the 13th October she was with the gubernatorial couple when they visited an Allied hospital.[8] In fact her part in the tour seems to have been specifically directed at supporting women's role in the war effort. This is reinforced by her later Country Women's Association tour. Most of the references to her in the papers are of meetings with women, except when she is accompanying her husband.

She planned to rejoin her husband in Brisbane when he returned from New Guinea after a few days. However, on the 9th October she received a telegram informing her that her husband would not be returning to Brisbane until after November 3rd.[9] This left her without a program or place to stay for more than three weeks.

However, if you are a baroness and the wife of an Admiral of the Fleet, there are plenty of people willing to "put you up" in an emergency like this. The immediate answer was supplied by Mrs Enid Macarthur Onslow, wife of the W. Macarthur Onslow who was the recipient of the letter mentioned earlier. Lord and Lady Keyes regularly wrote to each other when they were apart, and her letter of 10th October 1944 from Government House, Sydney, explains what happened:

> *A nice Mrs McArthur-Onslow* (sic) *came and spoke to me and left her husband's cards, and said if we had any time to spare, they would love to have us stay in their country place. So when I got your letters today I got Colonel Wynn to ring them up and have arranged to go there on Saturday 14th when I have to leave here as Mrs W-E returns.*[10]

Colonel Wynne was aide de camp to the Governor. Mrs W-E was Mrs Walter Elliot, Lady Wakehurst's sister.

From the vice-regal section of the *Sydney Morning Herald* on Monday 16th October we learn that Lady Keyes had left Government House. As the paper was not published on Sunday this must refer to Saturday 14th October, as Lady Keyes had foreshadowed that she would have to leave Government House by that date.

We know that she was at Camden Park on the 14th October. The *Camden News* of Thursday, 19th October reports that Lady Keyes opened the Annual Garden Fete in St John's Rectory Gardens on Saturday 14th October. Mrs Enid Macarthur-Onslow, who was to have opened the fete, "owing to sickness, was unable to be present."[11] The article continues that Lady Keyes was accompanied by Mrs Rothe, who was Mrs Macarthur Onslow's daughter.

There is really no other information about Lady Keyes' stay at Camden Park, except for a few scraps from the letter of 1st November she had written to James W. Macarthur Onslow. She thanks him for returning a bag to Government House. Perhaps this bag was left behind as she was leaving on a trip around NSW for the Country Women's Association and it was inconvenient to have too much luggage.

Furthermore, the bag is returned to Government House, as this was where Lady Keyes had come from before Camden Park; she was actually staying elsewhere in Sydney by then. Obviously James Macarthur Onslow didn't know where she was going when she returned from her CWA trip, and it seems likely Lady Keyes was also uncertain. In fact, as mentioned above, she was at "Ginahgulla" in Bellevue Hill, staying with Miss Fairfax. Miss Fairfax had taken her to lunch at the Queen's Club in Sydney where she was waited upon by the maid who had been at Camden Park.

From her she learnt that the "General [William Macarthur Onslow] had his new appliance and that it is a success." The nature of the appliance is unknown. She also sends him the book on the Eighth Army mentioned above. This would imply that there had been conversation concerning Lord and Lady Keyes' eldest son's death in North Africa in 1941 and the subsequent award of the Victoria Cross. He had been involved in an unsuccessful commando raid to kill or capture Rommel. On the inside cover of the book she specifically mentions the pages with the relevant section referring to the death of Geoffrey Keyes. She also thanks James for "my very pleasant visit to your hospitable house."

Lady Keyes did not sign the Visitors' Book at Camden Park (there are virtually no entries for October 1944). It is not clear when she left the Macarthur-Onslow residence. On Monday 23rd October she sent a telegram to Lord Keyes. She was staying at Manar via Tarago and told her husband that she had been "sent on a tour by the CWA and have been staying at different places each night."[12] The *Braidwood Review and District Advocate* reported that she had been "entertained" at "Hazeldell" in Manar, no doubt the place she was writing from on the 23rd October. It also states that she had been at

"Khama Lea," Braidwood where she had been the guest of Mr and Mrs AW Hill.[13]

On the same day the *Goulburn Evening Post* reported that Lady Keyes had been in Goulburn and district over the weekend (which would have included Tarago). She would return on the next day to have an informal meeting with Goulburn women at the CWA Rest Rooms about the homefront in England with an emphasis on the role of women.[14] An article in the same newspaper of the 25th October reports the meeting and said that she continued on by train to Cooma on the 24th.[15] A summary of Lady Keyes' speech was given in the paper as well.[16]

Lady Keyes returned to Sydney from Bega on Monday 30th October. This was presumably the end of her CWA tour. My initial interest in Lady Keyes was wondering how it was possible to fly from Bega to Sydney during wartime. However, further research showed that Butler Air Transport had a regular service between Bega and Sydney in 1944.[17] On the 2nd November Lady Keyes flew to Brisbane where she was reunited with her husband and the goodwill visit continued. Lady Keyes did not return to Camden.

Lord Keyes had had an eventful time in New Guinea and further north. Once he reached New Guinea, the US Navy invited him to observe the American landings in Leyte Gulf in the Philippines. Keyes was eager; after all this was the type of maritime event he had been advocating during his time in control of commando operations and after. He was on board the *USS Appalachian* during the Battle of the Philippine Sea (21 October) and was badly affected by smoke inhalation from a smoke screen. Although he made a reasonable recovery, this was one of the causes of his death in December 1945.

Whilst recuperating he observed that *HMAS Australia*, damaged in the battle, would have to go to the American dockyard at Espiritu Santo (in Vanuatu) for repairs, as they worked there to a 24 hour schedule, whereas the Sydney dockyard only worked 8 hours a day. He felt sympathy for the sailors on *Australia* who were thereby denied the chance for shore leave in their home country. When he reached Brisbane he made a speech on 2nd November critical of Australian dockworkers for not giving their all as members of the armed forces were.[18] No doubt he was aware of the amount of industrial action occurring at this time in Australia and felt that Australian workers were not doing their bit.

The speech attracted much negative attention in Australia, including from the Minister for the Navy[19] and of course the dockworkers themselves. Keyes met with some of the trade union leaders at Trades Hall in Sydney on 9th November and the issue was put down to "misunderstanding",[20] although on the

14th he denied strongly that he had retreated from his opinions.[21] Keyes was probably wrong in his statement, as the main reason for the working hours at Garden Island was lack of labour as many workers were already in the armed forces and serving elsewhere. But the admiral's forthright approach was typical of his complete commitment to the war effort. The resentment at Lord Keyes' statements about Australian workers is also a reminder of how the unity of British and Australian interests was beginning to break down. Lord Keyes could be seen as representing a Tory England unconcerned with Australia; we were no longer going to be chastised by the "mother country".

Historically, the letter Lady Keyes wrote to James Macarthur-Onslow in November 1944 is of little importance. But investigating the background reveals some interesting themes that arise in Camden and Australian history. From the Camden perspective there is the role of the Macarthur-Onslow family as social leaders and the role of Camden Park House as a place for "celebrities" (admittedly an anachronistic term for the Keyes in World War 2) to have a rest from busy schedules and coincidentally add to the social status of the Macarthur Onslows.

In terms of the wider Australia context, it gives us a view of our closeness to Britain and perhaps the beginning of the end of that closeness, the proximity of the memory of the "Great War" to people in World War 2, the dangers to which the war exposed people, the specificity of gender roles at the time and also the liveliness of industrial relations at the time. It is a little reminder of a time when life was changing.

With thanks to John and Edwina Macarthur-Stanham for access to the library at Camden Park, and also to the British Library for access to the Keyes Papers. Newspapers were accessed through the National Library's Trove website.

References
1 His Majesty's Stationery Office, *The Eighth Army September 1941 to January 1943*, London, 1944.
2 Quoted in *Combined Operations Command United We Conquer: Roger John Brownlow Keyes* http://www.combinedops.com/Roger%20Keyes.htm Accessed 2.2.15.
3 C. Oglander-Aspinall, *Roger Keyes: Being the Biography of Admiral of the Fleet Lord Keyes of Zeebrugge and Dover G.C.B., K.C.V.O, C.M.G., D.S.O.* London, 1951. p426
4 Oglander-Aspinall, p433
5 Oglander-Aspinall, p437
6 See for instance *Perth Mirror* 21 October 1944, p19
7 *Sydney Morning Herald* 7 October 1944, p5

8 *Sydney Morning Herald* 14 October 1944, p2
9 British Library- Keyes Papers. MS 82567 9 October 1944
10 British Library- Keyes Papers MS82396 10 October 1944 p198
11 *Camden News,* 19 October, 1944, p2
12 British Library- Keyes Papers MS 82396 23 October 1944 p208. Lady Keyes spells Manar "Manor"
13 *Braidwood Review And District Advocate,* 24 October, 1944, p3
14 *Goulburn Evening Post 23* October 1944, p3
15 *Goulburn Evening Post* 26 October 1944, p6
16 *Goulburn Evening Post* 25 October 1944, p3-4
17 *Frog's Hollow Flyers- Frog's .... From The beginning* http://www.frogshollowflyers.com.au/#!frogs-from-the-beginning--/c22eh. Accessed 2.2.15.
18 *The Courier-Mail*, 3 November,1944, p1
19 *Sydney Morning Herald,* 6 November, 1944, p4
20 *Sydney MorningHerald,* 10 November, 1944, p3
21 *Sydney Morning Herald,* 15 November, 1944 p4

The Telephone Exchange – Werombi

Dawn Williams

Mrs Phyllis Stuart of Werombi ran the post office and telephone exchange from her home near the junction of Silverdale Road and Werombi Road. From 1951 until 1970 for the phone exchange and 1971 for the post office when new technology took over.

Phyllis was born in Adelaide in 1915 and recently celebrated her 100th birthday on the 21st June, she was the first grandchild on both sides. The family lived in a block of flats, and like a small community helped each other out when things were tough. Work was scarce and so were supplies. It became known that a farm in NSW was looking for labourers at a place called Ariah Park (near West Wyalong), so the family packed up and made the move, Phyllis was about seven years old. She started school in the new area and was only there for about six months when she was sent back to Adelaide to visit with her Grandparents where she remained for the next eight months. When she returned to NSW her parents had moved to a farm of their own, they later left this property due to drought and weather conditions and moved back to town.

The family lived in Buddigower (also near West Wyalong), where her mother took on the running of the P.O. and telephone exchange. Phyllis started school again, and then developed measles, and later conjunctivitis (called Sandy Blight in those days) and was isolated for a time so she was about 9 years old when she officially started school on a permanent basis. Phyllis and one of her siblings walked two and a half miles to and from school daily. Later when she left school she also lived at Thulloo and West Wyalong. She had 4 sisters and 1 brother, she still has three sisters living, two of which are in their 90's and the youngest will be 87 in October. While in West Wyalong as a married woman with a young family they lived in the station masters house as the station master lived in the family home close by, but when a new station master was appointed the house was required for that family and so they had to move.

Mrs Stuart's mother by this time was living in Burragorang but had to relocate when the dam went in, so she moved to Werombi. Due to the housing shortage after the war Mrs Stuart and her family came down to stay with her mother, this was in 1951.

Her husband acquired work on Warragamba Dam and the property where she lives now became available on the market as a working P.O. This arrangement suited her as she had experience of a working P.O. and telephone

exchange through her Mother, and it suited her to be able to work at home with her young children. She purchased it in her own name (very adamant about this point) and paid for it with her earnings. The salary that was paid was calculated on the previous year's takings.

The property consisted of 90 acres (she later sold off 40 acres) and three small buildings. The house was in two sections with a breezeway between them. The P.O. was housed in one section on the end of the verandah, and the exchange was in the older part in the dining room, and it would have cost as much, if not more to restore than to rebuild because the building was constructed of just logs on the ground with floor boards nailed over and with tin covering any holes. The front portion housing the exchange was taken down to allow for a house to be built and the exchange was relocated and permission given so the P.O. and the exchange could operate side by side. The lot was eventually demolished and the current house she lives in was built in 1966 (Contracts signed 14/2).

The P.O. sold stamps and postal notes, sent and received parcels, and the exchange switchboard was a plug in plug out system with a wind up handle to ring the various extensions on the line. There was only one trunk line for out of area calls which was timed. She says this was no trouble to her as everyone around were farmers like her and would not use it unless it was an emergency, she knew their routines and timing and did her own farm chores to fit in.

To get a call to Wallacia or Warragamba, first you had to ring Camden exchange and tell them who you wanted to speak to, and they put you through to Sydney then through to Penrith and then to the person you required. At first the hours were 9-12 and 1-6pm, then it changed to 8-12 they always closed down for the "dinner hour" between 12 and 1 o'clock, then 1-10pm until eventually continuous service 24 hours a day. She remembers blackberry time very well – she would be watching the clock for 12.00 and she would run out and pick blackberries during the "dinner hour" to make jam, she says she could pick 6lbs during that time on a good day.

The ever discreet Mrs Stuart still will not tell any tales which were overheard or interrupted, due to other people wanting to use the line, but she does have a chuckle and a smile regarding "learnt of love affairs" when she had to interrupt and was only greeted by a sigh on both ends. She knew everyone's voices but didn't know what most of them looked like. She is a very private and independent person and enjoyed the contact with people without having to face them. She didn't have to go out to work so it was easier for her, the children and the family.

She still remembers some of the extension numbers: 1-Barney Duck; 2-Allan Varlow; 3-Badger; 4-Wadsworth; 5- orris; 6-Charlie Duck; 7-Jimmy Duck; 8-Weir; 9-Unknown; 10-Mother; 11-Eric Rudd; 12-Harry Cuthell; 13-Unknown; 14-School; 15 & 16-Unknown; 17-Angilleys; 18-Martins; 19-Public Phone which was on the verandah outside the P.O. and 24-Colin Dunbar and somewhere the Smalls.

Phyllis' daughter could also recite them off one after the other.

I have learnt since her 100th Birthday that her real claim to fame was a very exciting 'Joyflight' with Sir Charles Kingsford-Smith. I wonder how many other people could tick that off their TO DO list.

Phyllis is a wonderful lady, still very reserved and very private but she has so many interesting stories to tell. When I asked what her secret to a long life is, she says simple living and the best therapy is her gardening. Phyllis has three children, nine grandchildren, 22 great grandchildren and five great great grandchildren. That in itself is five generations, she has also known her own parents, grandparents and great grandmother, and she is the only person I know who has had contact with eight generations of her family.

Madras Cavalry Uniform, 1882
Assessment of Significance
Collection Item No. 1970.264

Janice Johnson, Margaret Wheeler and Julie Wrigley

Description
Officer's mess uniform consisting of five items:

1. Officer's blue mess jacket with silver lacing, braiding and 5 plaited decorative frogs, pale buff cuffs and collar.
2. A scarlet mess waistcoat with silver lacing, braiding and buttons.
3. Navy blue trousers with silver lace stripes.
4. Scarlet and silver forage cap.
5. Beige cummerbund with silver olivets.

History and Provenance
The uniform belonged to and was worn by Francis Montgomery Onslow of the Second Madras Cavalry. Francis Montgomery Onslow was born 9 November 1843 in Tiruchchirappalli, (known as Trichinopoly in English), Tamil Nadu, India and died 30 January 1932 in Larchfield House, Farnham, Surrey, England. He served with the British army in the

> Abyssinian war in 1867-68 with the Land Transport Train and received a medal for this action. This was a rescue mission and punitive expedition carried out in 1868 by the armed forces of the British Empire against the Ethiopian Empire.

> Second Anglo-Afghan War between the British forces and the Afghan forces, and fought in the Battle of Ali Masjid at the western end of the Khyber Pass on the border between Afghanistan and India on 21st November 1878 under Lieutenant-General Sir Samuel James Browne.

The Onslow family tree held at Camden Park shows:

Colonel Francis Montgomery Onslow (born 1843) married 1 June 1881 Westminster, London, Mary Charlotte (nee Girardot), widow of Lt. Gen. Frederick William Jebb (1835-1880) of the 67th Foot who also served in Madras. Francis was the younger brother of Arthur Alexander Walton Onslow and Alexander Campbell Onslow. It was Captain Arthur Onslow who married the Macarthur family heiress, Miss Elizabeth Macarthur, from whom all the Macarthur-Onslows are descended.

The uniform is believed to have passed from the Onslow family in Send, Surrey, England to the Stanham family. Brigadier (Richard) Quentin Macarthur-Stanham donated the uniform to the Museum in June 1970 when the Museum first opened.

Owners, donors and community recollections

The donor, Quentin Macarthur-Stanham, was born and raised in England. When his mother, Lady Stanham, born Helen Macarthur-Onslow unexpectedly inherited Camden Park in 1947, his parents decided to move to Australia with Quentin to live in Camden Park. They took on the role of being the heads of the Camden family and continued in those roles until their deaths. Quentin was always very community-minded and supported the Camden Museum at various times and made several donations to the collection.

Francis Montgomery Onslow, on the recommendation of his father, was nominated by Ross Donnelly Mangles as a cadet for the Madras Cavalry. Francis' father, Arthur Pooley Onslow, had recently retired from the Madras Civil Service[1]. His mother, Rosa Roberta (nee Macleay) had died at Ganjam, India in 1852. Francis was passed by the Examiners on 5th June 1860 and was appointed Second Lieutenant 9 September 1860, Lieutenant 25 December 1861[2], Captain 5 August 1870[3], Major and Squadron Commander of the 2nd Madras Cavalry 4 September 1880, and Lieutenant Colonel 7th May 1886. He retired on 7th May 1886, but was also listed as having retired 7 October 1890. Following his death in 1932 his widow was awarded a pension of £196.1.8 per annum during her widowhood.[4.]

Miss Annette Macarthur-Onslow recalled that a Camden News article on Wednesday June 24, 1970 showed a photo of her looking at the uniform with the caption:

Miss Annette Macarthur-Onslow inspects the colourful uniform of the Madras Cavalry displayed at the Camden Historical Society's museum which was opened last Saturday by her uncle, Sir Denzil Macarthur-Onslow. The uniform, once the property of the Onslow family of Camden Park, was donated to the museum by the Macarthur-Stanham family, the present owners of Camden Park..

Context

During the Nineteenth Century the British military objective was to impose advice and a military presence on Afghanistan in order to keep the Russians far from India. The 2nd Madras Cavalry went on to participate in the Third Anglo-Burmese War 7 – 25 November 1885 but Francis Onslow may not have been involved.

The Onslow uniform was worn by Francis Montgomery Onslow in the Madras Light Cavalry as part of the British Army. The Jacket does not conform to the 1883 dress regulations which stipulate the jacket should be Cavalry Grey. However the 1883 General Orders state – *"Those officers who have already supplied themselves with any articles of dress not in conformity with these regulations, are permitted to wear them till they require renewing."*

Francis Onslow was promoted Major and Squadron Commander of the 2nd Madras Cavalry on 4 September 1880. At the time of the 3 April 1881 census Francis Onslow was living with his father at Send Grove. He was married on 1 June 1881 at St. John the Evangelist, Westminster, London. He was promoted Lieutenant Colonel 7th May 1886 and retired from the same date.

Related Places and Collections

There is an Afghan War Medal and Ribbon 1878-1880 in the collection at Camden Park House. The medal is as follows: Afghanistan Medal 1878-79-80 with a bar 'Ali Musjid'. Engraved on the edge is: CAPT. FRA. MONTGOMERY ONSLOW 2nd MAD. CAV. [Madras Cavalry]

The medal itself is silver depicting Queen Victoria (head in profile, designed by Joseph Boehm) on one side and an elephant carrying a gun accompanied by cavalry on the reverse (designed by children's book illustrator, Randolph Caldecott). It was engraved by Leonard Wyon at the Royal Mint. The ribbon is green with a crimson panel down each side. An early idea was that battle clasps would merely be added to the 'Frontier Medal', but Roberts, for one, championed the idea of a unique medal for those engaged. A proof of the medal was first displayed in August 1881 at the Dockyard Gates, Portsmouth, and was considered 'of great artistic excellence'.

Criteria
Historical Significance:
The Onslow uniform dates from 1882 and belonged to an officer who served in the Second Anglo-Afghan War between the British forces and the Afghan

forces.

Aesthetic Significance:
The Onslow uniform is unusual and colourful, and a good example of the Madras Light Cavalry uniform.

Provenance Affecting Significance:
The Onslow uniform came from a prominent local donor, Quentin Macarthur-Stanham, who is a family descendant of the wearer of the uniform.

Rarity or Representativeness Affecting Significance:
The Onslow uniform has unusual qualities which distinguish it from other items in this category as the uniforms changed from time to time and were worn for different occasions.

Condition Affecting Significance:
It is in good condition for its age but there are some moth holes and tarnishing.

Interpretive Significance:
The item represents colonial history and the military history of the Onslow, Macarthur and Stanham families.

Summary Statement of Significance

The Onslow uniform dates from 1882 and belonged to Francis Montgomery Onslow, a British Army officer who served in the Second Anglo-Afghan War between the British forces and the Afghan forces. The uniform was donated by the Macarthur-Stanham family to the Camden museum in 1970 when the museum opened. When the uniform was moved from the plaster model, on which it had been displayed for 45 years, it was found that all items of the uniform except the cummerbund had labels which confirmed it was made by the military tailors "J.B. Johnstone, London and Dublin" in 1882. The labels state "Major F.M. Onslow, 3 Madras Cav. [Cavalry]" although Major Francis Montgomery Onslow was appointed as Major of the 2nd Madras Cavalry in 1880.

The Onslow uniform is unusual and colourful, and a good example of the Madras Light Cavalry uniform. This may be the only version of this type of uniform to have survived, and therefore is internationally significant, in terms of the history of uniforms worn by the Madras armies. The Onslow uniform has unusual qualities which distinguish it from other items in this category as the uniforms changed from time to time and were worn for different occasions.

It is in good condition for its age but there are some moth holes and tarnishing. The material in the trousers is rather brittle and the seam at the back of the jacket was under stress until the uniform was moved to a wire mannequin in 2015.

The Onslow uniform came from a prominent local donor, Quentin Macarthur-Stanham, who is a family descendant of the wearer of the uniform. It is rare to have the provenance of a uniform from the 19th century. The uniform is part of the connection between the Onslow, Macarthur and Stanham families and their long historical military tradition.

References

[1] The University of California Digital Library, "Record of Service of the Honourable East India Company" by Charles Campbell Prinsep, published 1885, page 108. Arthur Pooley Onslow's career, in the section Madras Presidency 1741-1858 (archive.org/stream).

[2] Edinburgh Gazette 9/8/1864 – General List of Cavalry Officers

[3] London Gazette 22/8/1871 – General List of Cavalry Officers

[4] Regimental and Service Records Madras. It should be noted that the dates given in the Gazettes differ from the official service records.

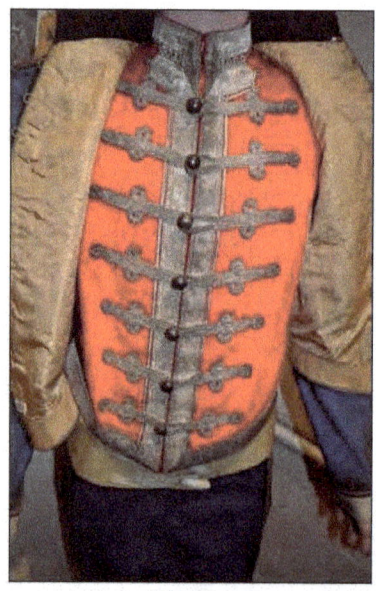
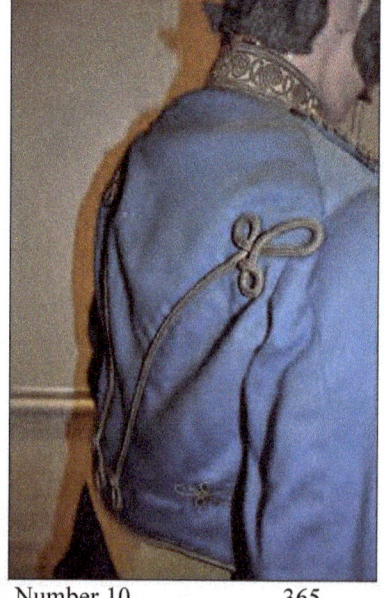

President's Report 2014-2015

Bob Lester

I hereby present the President's Report for the year 2014 to 2015 being my third report for my term as president of the society. Through the reading of this report I hope you gain an understanding of the Society's activities, the operation of the Camden Museum over the past twelve months and the involvement of the society's committee members and volunteers who really make things happen.

The society has continued to play an important role within the local community, keeping our history alive and relevant to an ever growing and diverse population within the Camden local government area and its surrounds.

Within The Community
The society has been active within the wider community through attendance at community events including:
Camden Show
Camden Antique Fair
NAIDOC Week
RSL Memorabilia Weekend
ANZAC commemorations
Australia Day Parade
Kelvin Park Open Day
Chamber of Commerce Tourism meeting

These events are an opportunity to provide people with information, showcase publications available for purchase and display photographs and information from our museum collection. Over 550 people visited the museum on Australia Day and 200 visited during ANZAC Day.

In response to Camden Council's proposals to redevelop the central area of Camden the society, after consulting its members, made a submission outlining its views on the proposed works. Committee members subsequently attended meetings with senior council staff and the mayor voicing our disapproval of the paving and street furniture selections. Individual members have been active in the community action against council's proposals, attending the various meetings held by council and the community.

The society supported the viewpoint of the need for further consultation between council and the community to achieve a better outcome that reflects the rich heritage of the Camden township. This is an issue that the society will remain an active participant in over the coming months.

Society Meetings
Whilst the purpose of the monthly meetings are to conduct the affairs of the society they are also important in providing its members and the general public with information and knowledge on local history. Over the past twelve months various guest speakers have made presentations at our meetings:
Ian Wills - Camden and the Great War
Brian Stewart – Life's Little Stresses
Donald Howard – Memories of Camden in the 1940's
Milton Ray's - Home Movies on Camden
Brendan and Rachel Powell, Peter Hayward and John Wrigley – Camelot Then and Now
John Hockney – Unlocking Our Family Memories
Bob Gosling – The Great War WWI
Nick Sherwood - Lt Col. A J Onslow Thompson
Vince Taranto and Denis Gojak – The Old Hume Highway
Chris Flatherty – Uniforms of Our Past

To assist speakers and discussions during meetings a portable PA system has been purchased which will add to the enjoyment of our members and the many visitors that come to our meetings.

This year Brian Burnett was made a life member of the society for his many years of involvement in compiling and publishing local history and as a volunteer at the museum. He joins a number of past and present members who have been given this honour for their contribution to the society and the community, which has been recorded in a booklet compiled by Julie and John Wrigley. Unfortunately we also saw the passing of our life member Vic Boardman who was much loved by all who knew him.

Volunteers
Our volunteers remain the backbone of both the society and the museum without whom we would not be able to operate at the level we currently do. Work on our photographic collection, improving our research files, operation of the website, exhibition formation and collection conservation are some of the many roles volunteers undertake behind the scenes. Coupled with the work on the committee and at the front desk of the Museum there is much to keep people interested and involved.

Volunteers have been supported through a training day, a visit to the Liverpool Regional Museum for a workshop on museum curators and an afternoon tea, which enabled people to meet and learn about what is happening at the museum. After many years of trying council agreed to install air conditioning in the museum. This became fully operational in time for winter much to the delight of our volunteers. We greatly appreciate this support of the museum by council.

I would like to thank volunteer co-ordinator, Rene Rem, for all the extra yards he took on to keeping the museum operating and the added tasks he always was happy to do. He was able to gain additional volunteers for our museum roster and fill in on many occasions, often at the last moment.

Museum operations
The Camden Museum remains an important port of call for many people visiting Camden. We continue to attract a healthy level of visitors from the local area, the wider Sydney region, interstate and from overseas. Many are first time visitors out for a day in Camden while many are return visitors looking for more information on their family or to view the number of exhibitions held throughout the year.

Schools continue to visit the museum as part of their learning curriculum along with organised tour groups on a bus trip around the area. All told over 6,000 visitors came into the museum over the past twelve months.

Exhibitions presented over the past twelve months have focused on the remembrance of World War One with the conclusion of the Red Cross Display, the ongoing display of uniforms in the Research Room and the exhibition of a private collection of WWI memorabilia from a society member. Following research and conservation the Madras Uniform, after 45 years in the Museum, has been properly mounted on a wire frame and displayed behind a glass cabinet, which has increased its prominence within the collection. I thank Margaret Wheeler and other members for their interest in this particular item on our collection.

Photographic displays have been made on John Oxley, Camelot and the changing faces of Argyle Street that have been of interest to many visitors. We continue to gather more photographs from local residents with many included in our online collection in partnership with Camden Library. Many new items have been included in our growing collection with members undertaking Assessment of Significance statements to provide in-depth information of some items.

Ian Willis's *Ministering Angels, The Camden District Red Cross 1914-1945* was successfully launched at a function in August 2014 in the Galleria of the Library, attended by many former Red Cross ladies and society members. It was the 100th anniversary of the foundation of the Red Cross branch in Camden and the book has played a significant role in telling its story. The publication was funded through a grant received through the Commonwealth government who we thank.

New chairs were purchased for the research room that attracts many people each month to use our records, look up photographs and the maps we have in our collection. We have also upgraded the laptop used by our secretary and simplified access to the photocopier for the benefit of our volunteers. It is due to be replaced in the near future as it is nearly a museum item itself.

Partnership with Council
Our formal partnership with council continues to sustain an important link between the two organisations where we can share knowledge and resources for the benefit of the community. We participated with council and the Camden Family History Society in activities around Heritage Festival in April/May and History Week in September. The photographic collection online is a joint project between Camden Library and the society.

The society has made comments on a number of Development Applications before Camden Council dealing with places of heritage eg Orielton subdivision, Catherine Park house. It also submitted recommendations for street names and parks that reflect the names of past residents and historical events.

Council continues to support the Society through a yearly subsidy that includes our insurance, the provision of storage units and the maintenance of the museum itself.

Communication
The society has continued to provide a number of ways it communicates with its members and the community both in written form and electronically. Two journals were published through the efforts of its editor Ian Willis including a special one on Lt Col. Onslow Thompson. Ian also produces a number of newsletters for members and has allowed the society to include his history blog as a link to our website.

A new initiative has been the development of a Facebook page for the museum supported by Brett Atkins a highly regarded local photographer. This is seen as another means to let people know about the museum and what people can see when they pay a visit. It is already gaining an interest and hopefully younger people will see it as a means of learning about their local history.

Society members continue to contribute stories to the well read Back Then page of *The District Reporter*. Its editor Lee Abrahams was able to run a workshop on how to develop a story for publication. The society thanks Lee for her ongoing support of local history.

Financial Assistance
Two new grants were obtained by the society to enable members to undertake work on stories relating to Camden's history. Through the Royal Australian Historical Society/State Government a grant of $2,000 was received to enable Sharon Greene and others to write and publish a book titled the *Nepean River County Council – People and Power*.

Through a Community Grant of $5,000 from Camden Council the society in collaboration with Council's Cultural Officer, and also filmmaker Wen Denaro, will produce a DVD on the Chinese marker gardeners who lived and worked along the Nepean River and elsewhere in Camden.

Work has commenced on a Camden publications by Kingsclear Books which have produced a number of photograph publications on local area history. It will feature many of the photos in our collection to complement stories of our past written by Ian Willis. Due out in 2016.

The society continues to receive financial support for its overall operations through donations from local residents and visitors to the museum. This support, membership fees and sales of our various publications enables the Society to cover its operational cost each year. The society remains in a very healthy financial situation and I thank our treasurer Dawn Williams for the work she does maintaining our financial records and meeting our legal obligations and secretary Lee Stratton for all her hard work.

On conclusion I wish to thank everyone on the committee and all society members for their support over the three years that I have been president. I have been honoured to be able serve in this position in what is a highly regarded community organisation. I wish the incoming committee all the best for the coming year and encourage all members to continue to play an active role in the society whether as volunteers or attending our monthly meetings.

Robert Lester
August 2015

SENSATIONAL NEW FEATURES
on roomier, more beautiful models

THE COMPLETELY NEW CHEVROLET

This beautiful new Chevrolet is completely new. New arresting beauty of style; new riding comfort and seating; new features .. and altogether new performance — for its engine has been redesigned with bore and stroke nearly equal to give maximum output at lower engine revolutions, resulting in a remarkable new degree of economy.

Chevrolet's new interiors are more spacious and more comfortable, with wider and lower tunnel-free floors. There is more head room and ample stretch-at-ease room for six passengers .. on seats made wider, and so much more comfortable with the figure conforming restfulness of the new Relax-o-form seating .. Correct and comfortable driving positions are provided for drivers of different heights by the multi-adjusting driving seat. Ventilation in all seasons is ideal for No Draught ventilation is fitted on every model.

It costs little to own and run this New Chevrolet. Call in, accept our offer to drive it. You'll find it the finest car ever priced so low.

Unisteel "Turret" Top Bodies by Holden

A striking new body graces this thrilling car, longer, much lower, and rivalling costlier cars in grace and beauty. This new Unisteel Body by Holden is a masterpiece of engineering—a rigid, rattlefree and silent unit of seamless steel insulated by newer methods to make it noise-free; cool in summer; dust-sealed and draughtsealed; and strong and rigid enough to withstand weaving and road strains with unimpaired durability.

CHEVROLET'S BIG FEATURES
- Hydraulic Brakes.
- Safety Glass Windscreen.
- Synchro-Mesh Gears.
- Box Girder Frame.
- Hypoid Gear Drive.

Low Prices on all Models
from **£290**

All prices include Safety Glass Windscreen. All plus Sales Tax.

Model	Price
Commercial Roadster	£290
Sports Roadster	£305
Tourer	£312
Business Coupe	£325
Sports Coupe	£335
Sedan	£345
Master Prices from	£329

E. C. DUNK   PHONES: 52 (Day)   141 (Night)   **CAMDEN**

Camden Advertiser 14 April 1938

A CONTRIBUTION TO CAMDEN'S PROGRESS

STUCKEY'S NEW BUSINESS PREMISES IN ARGYLE STREET

The unvarying high quality of Stuckey Bros.' bread, cakes and pastry — backed by a friendly service — has won for the firm the goodwill of a thousand families scattered throughout the wide Camden district. 28 years ago—on January 8, 1914—the Stuckey Bros. (H. H. and L. C.) purchased the old-established bakery business from J. Fleming. Since then the trade has increased eightfold, and in January, 1940, the above new premises, fitted with every modern device, were opened.

•

YOU CAN DEPEND UPON

STUCKEY BROS.
FOR THE BEST BREAD, CAKES AND PASTRY

"PROCERA" BREAD A SPECIALITY

ARGYLE STREET, CAMDEN   Tel. Camden 35

Camden News 24 April 1941

www.ingramcontent.com/pod-product-compliance
Lightning Source LLC
Chambersburg PA
CBHW051534010526
44107CB00064B/2719